LEAVE
the OFFICE
EARLIER

Front cover ripped 9/28/08

LEAVE the OFFICE EARLIER

The Productivity Pro®

Shows You How to Do More in Less Time

. . . and Feel Great About It

LAURA STACK

BROADWAY BOOKS   NEW YORK

LEAVE THE OFFICE EARLIER. Copyright © 2004 by Laura Stack. All rights reserved. No part of this book may be reproduced or transmitted in any form or by any means, electronic or mechanical, including photocopying, recording, or by any information storage and retrieval system, without written permission from the publisher. For information, address Broadway Books, a division of Random House, Inc.

PRINTED IN THE UNITED STATES OF AMERICA

BROADWAY BOOKS and its logo, a letter B bisected on the diagonal, are trademarks of Random House, Inc.

Visit our website at www.broadwaybooks.com

First edition published 2004

Book design by Lisa Sloane

Library of Congress Cataloging-in-Publication Data
Stack, Laura.
Leave the office earlier : the productivity pro® shows you how to do more in less time—and feel great about it / Laura Stack.
    p.   cm.
1. Time management. 2. Self-management (Psychology)
3. Goal (Psychology) 4. Success. I. Title.

HD69.T54S728 2004
650.1'1—dc22
2003065597

ISBN 0-7679-1626-3

10 9 8 7 6 5 4

CONTENTS

FOREWORD

NOT MANY YEARS AGO, a professional services firm was ruled—and I choose that word deliberately—by a CEO who measured employee commitment by two standards: the time employees showed up at the office and the time they left.

Even the indifferent and untalented knew that a primary way to get ahead was to come early and stay late. One's presence was the critical factor, not actual results. The CEO's executive assistant routinely distributed his travel schedule to close friends, so they would know when to come in late and leave early. It was a wonderful system for the unmotivated and uncommitted but the pits for everybody else.

Too often leaders focus on input rather than output. There are times when arriving early and staying late are necessary, but the real test of an employee's abilities and commitment is accomplishment. The proof is in the results, not the recorded hours.

Recently I read an article by some confused consultant about the importance of being available 24/7 while on vacation. Load up with wireless technology, he suggested, so the office can reach you anyplace at anytime.

I feel sorry for him.

If the office can reach you, you aren't really on vacation. And if you don't have a team that can handle challenges and even crises in your absence, you can't call yourself a leader.

Today, good employees refuse to sacrifice their family and personal lives on the altar of antiquated employer expectations. If you are a leader, face the facts: you are renting talent, not buying the hearts and souls of workers. You will either focus more on results and contribution and less on desk time or end up with a team of posers. If you are a valued employee, find somewhere to work where your contributions are recognized.

I fear for you if

1. you're afraid that by getting more done in less time you still won't be able to leave the office earlier (i.e., on time) because Cro-Magnon boss will heap still more work upon you, or
2. you are a Cro-Magnon boss.

This book will help you and your peak performers if you embrace its message. Why not learn how to work reasonable, rational hours and still get spectacular results? If you apply the principles in this book, organizations will

- make strides toward being an employer of choice,
- reduce turnover among staff, and
- help employees get a real life that includes fulfillment on and off the job.

As an individual, you will

- achieve a better balance between work and family life,
- do your job more effectively,
- get more done in less time, and
- create more time to pursue activities that really matter to you.

So here's my message to leaders: let your people go home to their lives, and you do the same. My message to everyone else: get your work done and go home on time. There's no reason why, thanks to Laura Stack, you can't.

It was B. C. Forbes, a rabid capitalist if there ever was one, who sagely noted, "Let us never forget that the business of life is not business—it's living."

Now, *unless it's after hours,*get to work!

Mark Sanborn
President, Sanborn & Associates, Inc.
An idea studio for leadership development

ACKNOWLEDGMENTS

I DEDICATE THIS BOOK TO MY FAMILY. John, you are my knight in shining armor, my strength, my right-hand business partner, and my hero. Thank you for putting up with the incredibly long hours it took to bring this book to life and letting me leave for days at a time to write. Meagan, Johnny, and James, I love you. You are the inspiration for this book—I can't think of a better reason to leave the office earlier. Thank you for being so forgiving with a mommy who tries to practice what she preaches but doesn't always succeed.

To my mother-in-law, Eileen Stack, who gives so unselfishly of her time to support our family. Thank you for always being there when I need you and for your unfailing love.

To my parents, Kenneth Wenker and Paula Joy, for instilling the values and behaviors that have served me well. I love you.

To my gifted literary agent, Robert Shepard, who always said he needed this book, though I can't imagine why. It's rare to find such a thorough, responsive, and organized person who is kind and genuine as well. You are a blessing in my life. Thank you for believing in me.

To my wonderful editor, Tricia Medved of Broadway Books, for your excitement about this project and support every step of the way.

To the National Speakers Association (www.nsaspeaker.org)

for holding the Writing Lab in May 2002, which opened my eyes to publishing.

To my fellow authors Mary Marcdante, C. Leslie Charles, Susan RoAne, and Mary LoVerde for encouraging me to go to the Maui Writers Conference and guiding me throughout the process. Thank you for giving so freely of your time and knowledge in navigating the publishing world.

Thank you to Toni Boyle, who helped me create the proposal for this book. My appreciation also goes to Tim Polk, who reduced the book by one-third when it was much too long. My gratitude goes to editor Barbara McNichol, whose keen eye found every little mistake I made. I wouldn't have felt comfortable letting this book go to press until she gave it her seal of approval.

My gratitude goes to Kay Baker, my friend and colleague, for letting me use her house for my writing retreats when I had to be alone for a few days to crank out the work.

To my best friend, Melissa Hamilton, who helped me laugh and served as my cheerleader throughout the project.

Finally, greatest thanks of all go to my Lord and Savior Jesus Christ, for blessing me with the gifts of writing and speaking. I pray this book helps people work less and spend more time with their families in service of Him.

INTRODUCTION

REMEMBER THE SCENE from the Disney movie *Hercules* where Hercules battled the Hydra? Every time Hercules cut off one Hydra head, three appeared in its place. He fought faster and harder, but the monster soon overpowered him. Panicked, his trainer, Phil, shouted, "Will you forget the head-slicing thing?" It's not working!

Do you ever feel that way at work? You delete one email, and three more appear. Within moments, torrents of emails are gushing from your screen. Or you do an outstanding job on a new project, so you're given three more, each with successively tighter deadlines. Unable to keep up, you let the emails and projects spill over into your evenings and weekends, and your personal life begins to suffer. You work faster and harder, but your work soon overpowers you. "Will you forget the head-slicing thing?" It's not working!

Throwing more time at your work isn't going to save you. Working faster and harder is a battle you will never win, because you will always have more things to do than time to do it. You could work all day, every day, and still never finish your work. Therefore, the problem isn't time *shortage*; it's time *usage*. It doesn't matter how *long* you work; it's *how* you work. Indeed, a twelve-hour day can be more unproductive than a six-hour day.

In the past, when asked, "How are you doing?" most professionals would reply, "Fine." Today, the answer of choice is, "Busy." When's the last time someone replied, "Oh, I have so much free time on my hands, I just don't know what to do with myself!" *Everyone's* busy. "Busy" today has a totally different meaning: "Normal." If *everyone* is busy, by definition *no one* is busy, because it no longer means the same thing. Hey, even bees are busy. The important question is, What are you busy *at*?

Welcome to the world of work—post-recession, post-scandal, postwar, post-"new"-economy style. The Internet. Email. Downsizing. Fewer people doing more work. Fear of more layoffs. Juggling work and child care. Dazzling technological advances. No time with family. Deadlines. Weekend work. High stress levels. Longer hours and fewer vacation days than ever before.

Today's workplace demands high performance, reduced costs, and global competition. With an ever-present fear of more layoffs, employees are churning out work at warp speed. A scared employee is a productive employee, so people who survived the layoffs and recession with their jobs intact are working harder than ever. Indeed, in 2002, productivity in the United States turned in its best performance since the 1950s—4.7 percent. In the third quarter of 2003, the U.S. Labor Department reported productivity in the business sector was improving at a blazing 7.4 percent rate. That statistic—a measure of how much an employee generates per hour and a key ingredient in the economy's long-term vitality—should make businesses mighty happy. Because when productivity is high, organizations don't need to hire as many people. In the long run, it will make employees happy too, because companies will be able to pay *them* more money without raising prices, which ultimately is good for our economy.

But as an employee, it's hard to be happy about the potential of future earnings when your life gets thrown in the Dumpster.

No matter how hard you work, you're never caught up. In my estimation, most professionals have a backlog of two hundred or more hours of uncompleted work.

In the short run, the current balance of input versus output benefits neither the employee nor the organization. While organizations are focused on topping their sales quotas, doubling production, and streamlining efforts, employees are suffering, and not always silently. Employees are demanding more, and a rebellion is building. Professionals are experiencing a stronger personal need to do things differently. They want to balance the urgent demands of work and personal life without sacrificing either. They enjoy work, but they want it to have meaning in the overall context of their lives. They're stressed and want something different but are terrified to let go of a good job in a tough environment—not exactly a motivated workforce.

According to a 2003 workplace survey by CIGNA Behavioral Health called "Worried at Work: Mood and Mindset in the American Workplace," workers are stressed in epidemic proportions. It noted that 44 percent of employees surveyed said their jobs were more stressful today than a year ago. As a result, 45 percent said they've either considered leaving their jobs in the last year, have left a job, or plan to do so soon. Employers should be pretty darned concerned about the employee stress levels these statistics reflect. Why? When the pendulum swings back to favor the worker (and it will), the retention of key employees will become a big issue as people leave organizations in search of a better life. Leaders, when your organization no longer holds all the cards, will you be able to keep your key people? Employees, when the pendulum does swing, will you be in a position to take advantage of the job market with better productivity skills?

In my opinion, one side doesn't need to hold all the cards.

Productivity should be a mutual contract between employer and employee. The contract should look like this:

1. An organization identifies key employees, whose level of production and results are superior.
2. The employee learns to be more productive and creates those same results in less time.
3. The employee keeps the time gains and leaves the office earlier (goes home and gets a life).
4. The employer sees morale, job satisfaction, motivation, and retention increase.

Both sides benefit from a win-win productivity proposition: Employers still receive the results they need without pushing employees over the edge, and employees get their work done more efficiently so they can go home and live their lives. Employees will continue to perform at the high level the organization has come to expect and achieve those results in fewer hours. Employers won't simply cram more work into the time created.

Organizations that provide work/life programs regard them as a key competitive advantage that allows them to recruit the best talent. In turn, loyal employees give their best every day and would never dream of working anywhere else. Hundreds of my clients have embraced this philosophy and provided my productivity training to their employees, resulting in thousands of happy, productive employees around the globe. If your employer hasn't taken such steps, you can take on this program and discuss your efforts with your supervisor.

This book is for you, an employed professional who works ten or more hours a day. By picking up this book, you've taken the first step toward learning to be more productive, so you can get your work done in less time and leave the office earlier.

Leave the Office Earlier explores ten key factors that improve output, lower stress, and save time in today's workplace—and even at home. Some advice is appropriate to a traditional office place, and some advice is just for home. However, steps taken in one area often spill over into the other, increasing productivity but more importantly, a sense of well-being. As you become more productive at work, for example, you won't experience the panic you normally would wrapping the birthday present in the car on the way to the party. Improved productivity affects all areas of life, and good organizational skills can go a long way in diminishing chaos in your life in general. Life can get complicated when trying to focus on a job while making doctor's appointments for the kids and following up on unpaid insurance claims. The point is to find time to do the things that matter to you and to reorient the ways you spent time to support self-stated goals.

Each chapter covers one of the factors affecting personal productivity in the workplace. To make it memorable, the first letters of each factor can be put together to spell the word "productive":

P—reparation—planning and scheduling

R—eduction—time leaks and speed bumps

O—rder—organization and systems

D—iscipline—persistence and behavior

U—nease—overload and stress

C—oncentration—focus and attentiveness

T—ime mastery—activity- and self-management

I—nformation control—technology and tools

V—itality—physiology and self-care·

E—quilibrium—balance and boundaries

You don't have to read this book cover to cover. Start by taking the Productivity Quotient (PQ)™ assessment on the following pages. You will quickly see which areas need improvement first. Start with the chapter with the lowest score, and begin working on the item that gave you the most trouble. So if you're an organized person, great—you can skip Chapter 3. Perhaps concentration gives you the most trouble, so start with Chapter 6. After you complete each chapter assessment, you will be able to determine your PQ,™ a cumulative score out of five hundred possible points.

After taking the assessment, you can create a customized action plan. Because the assessment provides positive affirmation of what you're doing correctly and allows you to quantify increases in progress and productivity, you can use it in your performance measurements.

Practice the skills until you've comfortably integrated them into your work habits and your score has improved. Don't let the book overwhelm you; work on one thing at a time. Once you've developed a new habit in that skill area, you can start on another. You will see some overlap; often an approach that helps you in one area may work to strengthen another factor. So you can work on several items simultaneously, but don't overload yourself. Strive to constantly improve your PQ, without focusing on perfection.

"Will you forget the head-slicing thing?" It's not working! Here's to leaving the office earlier! Make it a productive day!

Laura Stack, MBA, CSP
President, The Productivity Pro®

**PLEASE CONTACT ME WITH YOUR IDEAS ON
IMPROVING PERSONAL PRODUCTIVITY.**

9948 S. Cottoncreek Drive
Highlands Ranch, CO 80130
303–471–7401
Laura@TheProductivityPro.com
www.TheProductivityPro.com

The Productivity Quotient (PQ)

	PREPARATION					
	To what extent do I . . .	to no extent	to a little extent	to some extent	to a considerable extent	to a great extent
1.	Abide by a personal mission statement for my life.	1	2	3	4	5
2.	Track my long-term goals and aspirations.	1	2	3	4	5
3.	Create high-quality performance objectives.	1	2	3	4	5
4.	Define my specific job responsibilities and related tasks.	1	2	3	4	5
5.	Maintain a list of projects to accomplish and break the larger ones down into concrete steps.	1	2	3	4	5
6.	Conduct weekly, monthly, and yearly reviews of my plans.	1	2	3	4	5
7.	Track my tasks, projects, and appointments effectively.	1	2	3	4	5
8.	Create and prioritize my to-do list each day.	1	2	3	4	5
9.	Schedule my day realistically, manage it successfully, and consistently complete what I've planned.	1	2	3	4	5
10.	Determine the best channel of communication to convey my message prior to sending it.	1	2	3	4	5
	COLUMN TOTALS					
	SUBTOTAL PREPARATION					

REDUCTION

To what extent do I . . .	to no extent	to a little extent	to some extent	to a considerable extent	to a great extent
11. Eliminate the cause of most problems and avoid crises.	1	2	3	4	5
12. Control and prevent interruptions.	1	2	3	4	5
13. Handle drop-in visitors and coworkers effectively.	1	2	3	4	5
14. Refuse requests I don't have time for.	1	2	3	4	5
15. Recognize and eliminate personal shortcomings that lead to decreased departmental and organizational productivity.	1	2	3	4	5
16. Avoid spending time in irrelevant, unnecessary meetings.	1	2	3	4	5
17. Eliminate all unnecessary responsibilities or tasks that belong to someone else.	1	2	3	4	5
18. Get rid of everything I don't need or use and live simply.	1	2	3	4	5
19. Delegate properly; I rarely do tasks that others are capable of doing.	1	2	3	4	5
20. Keep socializing during work hours to an appropriate level.	1	2	3	4	5

COLUMN TOTALS _____

SUBTOTAL REDUCTION _____

ORDER

To what extent do I . . .

	to no extent	to a little extent	to some extent	to a considerable extent	to a great extent
21. Realize that some people aren't "born" more organized than others.	1	2	3	4	5
22. Keep a clutter-free work surface.	1	2	3	4	5
23. Know how to organize "pending" items or papers requiring future action.	1	2	3	4	5
24. Maintain orderly and organized files; I can find essential information when I need it.	1	2	3	4	5
25. Sort, process, and store information quickly and easily.	1	2	3	4	5
26. Discard information quickly and easily.	1	2	3	4	5
27. Touch paper only once; I'm very decisive.	1	2	3	4	5
28. Avoid using sticky notes or scraps of paper to record phone messages or tasks.	1	2	3	4	5
29. Know the contents of every cabinet, drawer, and storage space in my home and office.	1	2	3	4	5
30. Have a systematic plan to stay organized.	1	2	3	4	5

COLUMN TOTALS _____

SUBTOTAL ORDER _____

DISCIPLINE

To what extent do I . . .	to no extent	to a little extent	to some extent	to a considerable extent	to a great extent
31. Know my natural energy cycle and work effectively during peak times.	1	2	3	4	5
32. Control perfectionism, realizing that some things are "good enough."	1	2	3	4	5
33. Avoid putting things off or waiting until the last minute.	1	2	3	4	5
34. Force myself to slow down when necessary; I know speed can be counterproductive.	1	2	3	4	5
35. Determine what I will accomplish each day, rather than allowing other people to dictate my schedule.	1	2	3	4	5
36. Work productively from my home office and avoid distractions.	1	2	3	4	5
37. Handle common, routine tasks on a daily basis so things don't pile up.	1	2	3	4	5
38. Arrive at appointments and meetings on time; in fact, I'm typically early.	1	2	3	4	5
39. Avoid workaholism; I rarely work more than forty hours per week. I don't take work home with me, on vacation, or to bed.	1	2	3	4	5
40. Work hard and put "my nose to the grindstone" every day.	1	2	3	4	5

COLUMN TOTALS _____

SUBTOTAL DISCIPLINE _____

UNEASE

To what extent do I ...	to no extent	to a little extent	to some extent	to a considerable extent	to a great extent
41. Determine the sources of my stress and work to eliminate things that drain my energy.	1	2	3	4	5
42. Take personal responsibility for my own stress levels.	1	2	3	4	5
43. Control my stress and emotions by monitoring my self-talk.	1	2	3	4	5
44. Think positively and maintain a great attitude.	1	2	3	4	5
45. Manage my stress well; stress doesn't affect my productivity at work.	1	2	3	4	5
46. Feel calm, cool, and collected, rather than hurried, rushed, or tense.	1	2	3	4	5
47. Maintain a good sense of humor and take things lightly.	1	2	3	4	5
48. Refuse to let stressful situations or people bother me.	1	2	3	4	5
49. Control my temper at work and don't demonstrate anger.	1	2	3	4	5
50. Flourish in the face of constant changes in my life and not get anxious.	1	2	3	4	5

COLUMN TOTALS _____

SUBTOTAL UNEASE _____

CONCENTRATION

To what extent do I . . .

	to no extent	to a little extent	to some extent	to a considerable extent	to a great extent
51. Have my office set up for maximum productivity and minimum distractions.	1	2	3	4	5
52. Avoid wasting time by daydreaming.	1	2	3	4	5
53. Remember things easily; I'm rarely absent-minded or forget where I put things.	1	2	3	4	5
54. Focus on a priority project without getting distracted.	1	2	3	4	5
55. Focus on one thing at a time; I don't multi-task or attempt to do too many things at once.	1	2	3	4	5
56. Make lists and record everything I need to do.	1	2	3	4	5
57. Read quickly and maintain concentration; I rarely reread sentences.	1	2	3	4	5
58. Recognize signs of brain overload and know how to get my mind focused again.	1	2	3	4	5
59. Get absorbed in a task and achieve a state of "flow" or "momentum" where time seems to fly.	1	2	3	4	5
60. Concentrate on a task that bores me or doesn't really interest me.	1	2	3	4	5

COLUMN TOTALS _____

SUBTOTAL CONCENTRATION _____

TIME MASTERY

To what extent do I . . .

	to no extent	to a little extent	to some extent	to a considerable extent	to a great extent
61. Manage my reading pile so it doesn't "mushroom."	1	2	3	4	5
62. Create systems for repetitive tasks.	1	2	3	4	5
63. Know and avoid my biggest time wasters.	1	2	3	4	5
64. Eliminate bottlenecks in my work caused by people or processes.	1	2	3	4	5
65. Recognize that different personalities relate to time differently; I understand how to work effectively with each style.	1	2	3	4	5
66. Know how much my time is worth and eliminate those things that are a waste of my time.	1	2	3	4	5
67. Save time in bits and pieces; I know that little things add up.	1	2	3	4	5
68. Make effective use of downtime.	1	2	3	4	5
69. Avoid time wasters within my department or organization.	1	2	3	4	5
70. Make decisions quickly once I have the appropriate information.	1	2	3	4	5

COLUMN TOTALS _____

SUBTOTAL TIME MASTERY _____

INFORMATION MANAGEMENT

To what extent do I . . .	to no extent	to a little extent	to some extent	to a considerable extent	to a great extent
71. Understand I can have too much information and try to reduce "information overload."	1	2	3	4	5
72. Use proper email protocol and don't waste the time of others with its use.	1	2	3	4	5
73. Leave effective voicemail messages.	1	2	3	4	5
74. Use my phone as an effective productivity tool.	1	2	3	4	5
75. Find electronic files quickly; my computer files are well organized.	1	2	3	4	5
76. Know the available productivity features of my email program.	1	2	3	4	5
77. Run regular maintenance routines on my computer to ensure high performance and protect my data.	1	2	3	4	5
78. Understand the features and purposes of electronic and paper systems and when to use each.	1	2	3	4	5
79. Eliminate email "spam."	1	2	3	4	5
80. Control my technology; it doesn't control me.	1	2	3	4	5

COLUMN TOTALS _____

SUBTOTAL
INFORMATION MANAGEMENT _____

VITALITY

To what extent do I . . .	to no extent	to a little extent	to some extent	to a considerable extent	to a great extent
81. Get adequate sleep each night; I'm not sleepy during the day.	1	2	3	4	5
82. Get sufficient exercise.	1	2	3	4	5
83. Use all my allotted vacation time each year.	1	2	3	4	5
84. Pamper myself on a regular basis.	1	2	3	4	5
85. Maintain a noise level in my office that is conducive to productivity.	1	2	3	4	5
86. Ensure my workspace is comfortable and ergonomically correct.	1	2	3	4	5
87. Practice healthy eating habits.	1	2	3	4	5
88. Take a lunch break every day.	1	2	3	4	5
89. Drink the proper amount of water each day.	1	2	3	4	5
90. Control my environment and rid myself of things that bring me down.	1	2	3	4	5

COLUMN TOTALS   _____

SUBTOTAL VITALITY   _____

EQUILIBRIUM

To what extent do I . . .	to no extent	to a little extent	to some extent	to a considerable extent	to a great extent
91. Allocate my time according to my values and the top priorities in my life.	1	2	3	4	5
92. Achieve my ideal life balance; I don't accept "close enough."	1	2	3	4	5
93. Set appropriate boundaries and stick to my guns.	1	2	3	4	5
94. Stop thinking about work at the end of the day and enjoy my personal time.	1	2	3	4	5
95. Ask for help when I need it.	1	2	3	4	5
96. Create rituals with my family to reconnect during stressful times and to create fond memories.	1	2	3	4	5
97. Spend appropriate amounts of time watching television, playing video games, or surfing the Internet.	1	2	3	4	5
98. Turn off the technology when I'm with my family or on personal time.	1	2	3	4	5
99. Take advantage of the wellness and family balance programs offered by my company to the fullest extent.	1	2	3	4	5
100. Consistently leave work on time.	1	2	3	4	5
COLUMN TOTALS					
SUBTOTAL EQUILIBRIUM					

TOTALS

CHAPTER	SUBTOTAL
1. PREPARATION	
2. REDUCTION	
3. ORDER	
4. DISCIPLINE	
5. UNEASE	
6. CONCENTRATION	
7. TIME MASTERY	
8. INFORMATION MANAGEMENT	
9. VITALITY	
10. EQUILIBRIUM	
GRAND TOTAL = PRODUCTIVITY QUOTIENT	

SCORING

To make your score meaningful, please visit my website at www.TheProductivityPro.com and look for the "PQ assessment" button on the homepage. We are gathering thousands of PQ scores from people all over the world, so we can statistically validate the data and assessment. Once we have sufficient baseline data, we can say with certainty that you're performing at x percent of all test takers. You'll also be able to compare your scores to others within your peer group and industry.

Not having quantified the statistical data on the PQ yet, I can use my own anecdotal evidence until empirical evidence is available. In my experience, I'd estimate that score in the following ranges:

421–500: YOU'RE A PRODUCTIVITY PRO! Spread the good word and teach others! Keep fine-tuning where needed.

341–420: IMPROVEMENTS NEEDED. Overall, this is still pretty good. Make adjustments where you scored low. Give yourself credit where you do well and acknowledge where you need to improve.

261–340: AVERAGE. "Middle of the road." You're not the most productive employee, but you're not the worst. Ouch! Who wants to be average? Really work on kicking it up a notch!

181–260: **MAJOR OVERHAUL REQUIRED.** Select one item every two weeks and work on systematically improving your productivity.

100–180: **RED FLAG!** You require emergency measures; your health and your job depend upon it. Start reading now!

CHAPTER ONE

Mastering the "P" in Productive

PREPARATION

PREPARATION RELATES TO HOW WELL you've planned and laid the foundation for your daily activities. Most people don't have well-articulated goals. Perhaps you don't know how to set them. Perhaps writing goals down seems like too much effort, or you simply haven't taken the time to write them. Perhaps your goals seem out of reach. It's worth the work to create goals, because the goals you set will provide *direction* for your life and *focus* your activities.

An established direction, outlined with purposeful thought, ensures your life won't be governed by whim. In *Alice's Adventures in Wonderland,* Alice stops at the crossroads to ask the Cheshire Cat which road to take. He asks her where she wants to go. When she tells him she doesn't "much care where," he replies, "Then it doesn't much matter which way you walk." And so Alice wanders somewhat aimlessly. In contrast, productive people devote a great deal of thought and time to planning their life goals.

The toughest part of setting goals is translating the lofty, long-term goals into actionable tasks you can work on *today*. The process itself looks like this:

VISION (personal mission statement) ➤
LONG-TERM GOALS (dreams with a deadline) ➤
SHORT-TERM GOALS and objectives (projects) ➤
MONTHLY PLANS (action steps) ➤
DAILY TASK LIST (specific activities)

When you start with your personal mission statement in front of you as a guide, create personal and professional long-term goals, break them down into short-term objectives, create monthly plans, and then daily activities, you have direction and focus. Bottom line, you achieve your long-term objectives by focusing on today. This section will help you define these things for yourself.

PREPARATION quiz item #1:

1. I abide by a personal mission statement for my life.

What Do You Value?

Much like a corporate mission statement, your personal mission statement defines who you are, what you're all about, and why you're on this earth. Why do you need such a statement?

- It helps you make difficult decisions when faced with the choices life presents.

- It helps you realize how very little time you truly have to accomplish the important things in your life.
- It helps you recognize when you're off course and steers you back in the right direction.

Life is precious, and time is short. The best engineer cannot create more time, and the best scientist cannot invent more time. You cannot accumulate time or borrow tomorrow's time. We all have the same amount of time—24 hours a day, 168 hours every week, 86,400 seconds every day. Since it feels like we have plenty of time left, we can take for granted our 86,400 seconds every day.

Discovering your true priorities

The main objective of a personal mission statement is to define what's important to you. Many people say "this is important" and "that is important," but how do you narrow it down to what's truly important in your life? I like to use the following visualization:

SCENARIO A: Picture a thick banded-steel cable about two feet in circumference and one hundred feet long, stretched out across the floor. You are standing at one end, and I'm on the other. I call out to you, "I'll give you $100 if you can step onto the cable and walk across it to me without falling off." Would you try it? Sure! Most people would. Why? Basically, it involves a fairly low risk with a relatively high payoff for the effort required. It could be fun and a little challenging.

SCENARIO B: Now we're going to suspend the cable just a bit. Have you ever been to the Royal Gorge Bridge in Canon City, Colorado? It's the highest suspension bridge in the world, with a cable like ours spanning a chasm with a rushing river below. A tram with a clear glass bottom hangs from the cable and carries passengers across the chasm. Except you don't get to ride the tram. You are standing on one side of the chasm, and I'm on the other side. The cable is suspended between us. I yell out, *"Hey!* If you can walk across the cable without falling off into the river below, I'll give you $100!" There is no way anyone in his or her right mind would attempt that. The risk is too high for the reward involved. But let's up the ante. Would you cross it for $250,000? No? How about $1 million? How much would I have to offer you? What if I let you crawl across on your belly? For some of you, the reward would never be high enough to risk your life.

SCENARIO C: Let's add a little wind (a slight 40 mph breeze) and a tad of rain to make the cable slick. I'm on one side of the chasm, and you're on the other. In my arms, I hold your child hostage. I yell, "If you don't cross the chasm in two minutes, I'm throwing your child in the river." Would you come now? Of course you would! Despite the incredibly high risk to your own life, the child is so priceless to you that you'd risk your own life to save that child.

Perhaps if you don't have children, it could be your parents, your significant other, or your friend. Clearly, that person is a core value in your life. What other things like that exist in your life? Probably not very many. What principles, values, or character traits are most important to you, such that if I were to rip them out of your life and throw them into the chasm, you would be willing to cross the bridge to save them? What things are so integral to who you are that you cannot imagine existing without them?

Determining your core values

1. Holding that visualization in your mind, read through the following list of values below. They may be important to you; they may not be. Circle any of the values you'd cross

the bridge for. Add any others important to you but not listed at the bottom.

Peace	Integrity	Power
Wealth	Joy	Influence
Happiness	Love	Justice
Success	Recognition	Spirituality
Friendship	Family	Career
Fame	Truth	Status
Authenticity	Wisdom	Acceptance
Health	_____	_____

2. Next, go back through the items you've circled and narrow the list down to only six. Which items are more important to you than the others? Place a star next to your top six values.

3. Now picture this: you've got those six items lined up with you on the side of the chasm. I have the ability to make you choose between them. You've got to throw three away. Which ones would go? If all you had left in your life were three values, what would they be? Cross out three of the six so that your top three values remain.

4. Last, rank your top three values. Which one would go first? Label it #3. Which one would go second? Label it #2. Label the remaining item #1.

You have just listed the top three most important values in your life. There are, of course, no "correct" answers, just the correct answers for *you*. Everyone's values are different. My values are spirituality, family, and health, in that order. Yours are probably different, but even if they are exactly the same, in the same order, we probably place different meaning on each of the words.

Defining your core values

Rewrite your top three values in order on the blanks below. Then for each value, write a definition, a statement of what it means to you to be successful in that area. At the end of your life, looking back, how will you know if you've been successful in that area? If "Family" is one of your values, how will you know if you've been successful as a family man or woman? If you put "Happiness," what does that look like to you?

1. Value: _____
"Success to me means . . ."_____
_____
_____

2. Value: _____
"Success to me means . . ."_____
_____
_____

3. Value: _____
"Success to me means . . ."_____
_____

Sit in front of a computer or with pen and paper and merge the three paragraphs together into one statement. It could be several sentences or several paragraphs. You've just created a personal mission statement for your life.

Your mission statement will reflect who *you* are and what's important to you. Think of your personal mission statement as your

constitution. It will become your benchmark. Your stan[...]
excellence. It will get your behavior in line with your val[...]
measure yourself against it and continuously ask yourself if an activity is moving toward your mission in life. For example, if taking care of my health is important to me, and I eat eight slices of
pizza and watch five straight hours of television, my actions are
not supporting my mission.

When you're making changes in your life and setting goals,
refer to your statement of purpose. I promise this activity will
have an impact on your productivity. It's been said that "true
character is the ability to carry out a goal long after the mood in
which it was created has passed." That's when the real challenge
begins.

PREPARATION quiz item #2:

> 2. I track my long-term goals and aspirations.

The Dream Machine

Do you remember the first thing you ever wanted to be when you
grew up? I wanted to be a singer. When I was five years old, I used
to tape record myself singing "You Are My Sunshine," "The Rain-
bow Connection," and "Wendy." My mother would play the
tapes in the car as she drove. My first public debut was playing
Ngana in *South Pacific* at the age of eight at the Air Force Academy.
I sang, danced, and acted my way through school. But then my
ballet teacher told me my legs weren't long enough to ever make
it into a company. My voice coach told me I had a nice voice, but
nothing I'd ever make any money with. My acting coach told me
I wasn't cut out for the big screen. Then I saw Zig Ziglar present

at a motivational rally when I was fourteen years old, and I was hooked. I wanted to *be* Zig Ziglar. I said to myself, "Hey, a little song and dance, a lot of acting, and I get to be in front of an audience. Perfect!"

No matter what my ballet teacher or acting coach told me, I was blessed to have parents who told me I could do anything I dreamed of if I worked hard at it. It's not enough to set your mind to something; you must also plan your time around those goals. So I set my sights on being a professional speaker. When I set that goal, it acted like a magnet, pulling me toward it. I interviewed professional speakers and discovered most of them owned their own businesses. Perfect! I'd owned lawn mowing and babysitting businesses in junior high school. So I based my high school and college curriculum around fully understanding how to run a business. I took speech, drama, marketing, instructional design, communication, and organizational management classes—all skills I knew I would require as a speaker. I skipped my last year of high school and received both undergraduate and master's degrees in business by the time I was twenty-one. Then I looked for my first job as a corporate trainer to start gaining "real" experience. The realization of my dream required some goals and action.

You need goals to:

- clarify your objectives in life,
- help guide you in the right direction,
- enable you to decide what's most important in your life,
- help you monitor yourself as you advance toward a desired outcome, and
- use your abilities more effectively.

Complete the following matrix, describing what you'd like to accomplish within each category and time frame.

CATEGORY	1–5 YEARS	5–25 YEARS
CAREER—title, job functions, industry, responsibilities		
INCOME—a specific dollar amount		
INTIMATE RELATIONSHIPS—significant others		
HOBBIES—classes to attend, things to learn, books to read		
FRIENDS—social relationships, changes, mentors		
FAMILY—extended members, children		
RESIDENCE—location and type of house		
TRANSPORTATION—what will you drive? Color? Model?		
TRAVEL—where would you like to visit?		
MATERIAL POSSESSIONS—things to purchase		
RECREATION—regular fun things in life		

CATEGORY	1–5 YEARS	5–25 YEARS
HEALTH—what activities? Doctors to visit? Aspirations?		
SPIRITUAL—your higher purpose or higher power		
EDUCATION— go back to school? Gain new skills?		
PERSONALITY— who are you becoming? What characteristics?		

You may want to photocopy the chart and carry it with you for the next couple of weeks, so you have sufficient time to brainstorm. Keep it somewhere accessible, so you can update it as necessary. With your future goals in mind, you can start logically preparing, instead of letting things "take care of themselves." Goals will give you a sense of purpose.

PREPARATION quiz item #3:

> 3. I create high-quality performance objectives.

Is This a Good Objective?

If the greatest enemy of action is the lack of a plan, the greatest enemy of a plan is the lack of action. Goals become merely wishful thinking unless you further define them as *objectives* with specific measurements and act upon them.

Let's use the example of a vacation to illustrate the difference between a goal and an objective. Say I wanted to take a one-week vacation in Hawaii. Would I take this trip without knowing when and how I'll get there? Of course not! Unless I lay out the steps I need to achieve that result, that beautiful week in Hawaii won't happen. Think of a goal as the destination of a trip (Hawaii), and the objectives are how you're going to get from here to there (when will we leave, which airline will we use, where will we stay, how much money can we spend, what we'll wear, what will we do once there, etc.). Each objective may have several action steps associated with it as well. By identifying and taking action on specific objectives, I can achieve the goal.

How to set a "good" objective

"Lose weight" is a goal, but it isn't a good objective, because it provides no direction or measurement. How much? By when? How? "Read the 100 greatest books ever written" is a goal, but it isn't a good objective. How many books per year? How many pages a day?

A good objective answers several necessary questions. I use the term "spaghetti" to describe the nine components of a good objective:

S—PECIFIC. Measure your progress in numbers, percentages, milestones, dates, etc. "Learn software program" isn't specific, but "Spend five hours a week learning software program" is. "Lose weight" isn't specific, but "Lose thirty pounds at one pound a week" can be measured by simply stepping on the scale. "Make more calls" isn't specific, but "Make five new outbound prospecting calls a day" is.

P—OTENTIAL PROBLEMS. What obstacles might you encounter when working on your objective? What may come up that would prevent you from obtaining it? Consider early in the process what could go wrong. Take action to put contingency plans into place and resolve problems before they occur.

A—CCEPTABLE. The objective should be *yours*. It's all right to accept advice and suggestions from others, but you will be more motivated to do something if it's something you really want to do. Be cautious about defining success in terms of what a spouse, parent, or mentor sees as success for you.

G—IFT. We stay motivated to work toward our objectives when we know the rewards. What will be your reward once you've accomplished the objective? Major accomplishments deserve a special treat. Give yourself something exciting to shoot for! What is self-motivating enough to make you want to strive for it? A vacation? A night out? A massage? Rewards can also be intrinsic, such as increased self-esteem, more confidence, the pleasure of a job well done, etc. Remember, if the "why" is strong enough, the "how" becomes easier.

H—ARD ENOUGH. Objectives should challenge you, but they shouldn't be a fantasy or daydream. Make them realistic so you don't set yourself up to fail, but make them hard enough that you will have to stretch a bit. When you experience success at reaching stretch objectives, you gain more confidence to set harder ones next time.

E—VALUATE. Milestones along the way help you evaluate your progress. Review your objectives periodically to ensure that they continue to be realistic, timely, and relevant. For example, measure your weight each week, summarize your sales calls every day, or determine how many pages you wrote each day.

T—ANGIBLE. Objectives must be written down, or else you will tend to edit in your head as you go along. Many people daydream about what they want to accomplish, but far fewer actually write this down. Once written, the objective becomes tangible and concrete. Written objectives are also a reminder and a historical record.

T—IME BOUND. Good objectives have target dates. Set time limits, define start and stop dates. Often you will have multiple action steps, each with a target date.

I—NSPIRATIONAL. The objective should be uplifting and positively phrased. Have confidence in yourself! We tend to rise to the level of our own self-esteem. Picture yourself reaching your objective. Picture the moment when you achieve your objective and how you will feel. Use positive self-talk and hear what others will say when the objective is achieved. When you're having a slow day, you can visualize that picture and get an immediate energy boost!

Let's take the weak objective, "Lose weight," and apply the SPAGHETTI model to create an effective objective:

S—pecific: Lose thirty pounds at one pound a week for thirty weeks

P—otential problems: Nothing healthy to eat, cookies always around

A—ccepted: This matches my vision of a healthier me

G—ift: Buy new suit

H—ard enough: It's realistic, but I'll have to work at it

E—valuate: I can measure my progress by stepping on the scale every Saturday

T—angible: Write down the objective several times and post it where I can see it

T—ime bound: Starting now, ending thirty weeks from now

I—nspirational: *I can do it!* I will feel so good!

Now set some objectives of your own:

S—pecific: _____

P—otential problems: _____

A—ccepted: _____

G—ift: _____

H—ard enough: _____

E—valuate: _____

T—angible: _____

T—ime bound: _____

I—nspirational: _____

After you apply the SPAGHETTI model, write out your goal in paragraph form. For example: "I will (verb) (measurement) by (date) because (motivation). I will evaluate my progress by (___). I will reward myself through (___)."

Poor objective: "Read 100 greatest books ever written"

Better: "I will read one book each month, so that I may read twelve each year and complete the set in ten years, ending 2014. I will be able to discuss these great works intelligently and use them as examples in my speeches. When complete, I will travel to the best place I read about in the series."

Write it out: _____

_____

_____

_____

If you are off target, ask yourself, "Do I have all necessary resources?" "Are there obstacles in my way and how can I eliminate them?" "Is this a truly obtainable goal, or am I pressuring myself unrealistically?" "Is there someone else who could assist me in completing one or more steps?" "Am I simply procrastinating?" Post your goals within sight, so you can evaluate your progress as you go and maintain your enthusiasm.

PREPARATION quiz item #4:

4. I define my specific job responsibilities and related tasks.

Would Anyone Notice If I Stopped Doing This?

If you sat down with your boss and asked her or him to list the ten most important responsibilities in your job, and you created the same list, would those two lists match? In order to create effective work objectives, you need to know where you are expected to invest your time, energy, talents, and company resources. If you are to be evaluated on your successful accomplishment of work objectives, do those performance objectives *really* match what you do during the day? The things you want to or should be working on aren't always the things you're being evaluated on.

You and your boss should jointly define your key responsibilities and objectives, so you know how your performance will be measured. If you don't know this information, it will be difficult to schedule your day and prioritize your tasks in a meaningful way.

Job measurement process

Follow this process for the three to five most significant job responsibilities for which you are directly responsible, one worksheet for each:

1. **RESPONSIBILITIES.** List the job responsibility or category. If you have a job description, use that as a starting place. If not, keep track of everything you do for one week, and then categorize those activities into significant responsibilities (e.g., Customer Service, Research, Management, or Quality Control). There is a difference between a responsibility and a task. For example, "Participate in team decisions" is a responsibility; "Attend team meetings" is a task. "Communicate with customers" is a responsibility; "Write monthly ezine" is a task. "Obtain market visibility" is a responsibility; "Write article for trade journals" is a task. "Develop media relationships" is a responsibility; "Create press releases" is a task. The distinction hinges on the question, "Why do I do this?" The responsibility is high level, and the task is specific. One responsibility may carry five (or more) associated tasks. If you can eliminate one responsibility through clarification, you may eliminate several tasks. You carry out tasks to fulfill responsibilities.

2. **PRIORITY.** Rank your responsibilities in order of priority, with number one being the most important, according to your company (try to determine these jointly with your boss). This will help you spend time on tasks that have the highest payoff.

3. **TASKS.** Identify one to five major tasks associated with each responsibility.

4. **MEASUREMENT.** Determine the best way to measure each task. For example, for production, it could be units produced or number of sales. For quality, you could measure defect rates, rework, or inspection reports. For safety, you could measure worker's compensation claims, accident reports, or lost time. For employee relations, you could measure turnover, diversity goals, or absenteeism.

5. **PERFORMANCE STANDARDS.** For each task, define the minimum acceptable level of performance measured that demonstrates competency for each task.

6. **OBJECTIVES.** Using the SPAGHETTI technique, list at least one objective for each responsibility for the year. This is a key result you want to accomplish that makes an improvement, represents an innovative approach, or solves a problem related to that responsibility.

7. **PROJECT PLAN.** Each objective will have a specific project plan associated with it (see the next section for detailed discussion).

When you've created a worksheet for each job responsibility, schedule a time with your supervisor to sit down and review what you've created. Get input and gain consensus on your objectives. During the performance review at the end of the year, you can add comments to each one about any circumstances you faced, what results were achieved, and what rating you would give yourself on a scale of 1–5, with 1 being excellent results.

PREPARATION quiz item #5:

> 5. I maintain a list of projects to accomplish and break the larger ones down into concrete steps.

Short-Term Project Planning

Peter Drucker said the greatest task of work was to "define your work." Many professionals have given plenty of thought to *what* they want to accomplish ("increase employee morale," "strengthen client relationships"), but they haven't *done* anything about this or created a plan of attack.

Once you have written objectives requiring more than one step, you should translate them into a plan. If you don't, your objectives will remain pie-in-the-sky goals, could take much longer to achieve, or may not get done at all. Some objectives will have a single step, while more complicated projects and objectives can have many different required actions. When you're ready to move the objective into the present and work on it, it's time to create a project plan.

Here's the process:

1. Create a matrix on your computer or a piece of paper (see example next page).
2. For each objective, brainstorm all the specific action steps required to achieve it. Order is not important; don't worry about creating a logical sequence. Just get all your ideas down.
3. Once you've written out all the individual steps, go back and number them in order of completion.
4. Add corresponding start dates and deadlines for each step.

Project worksheet

Sample Objective: "I will get a more challenging and satisfying job as an engineer in a different industry with an increase of $7,500 per year by June 2004. I will buy myself that new truck when I land it!"

#	Action steps for this objective:	Start	Finish
3	Update resume	3/1	
6	Attend association and networking functions		
	a. Society for Human Resource Management	4/12	
	b. Chamber of Commerce	4/22	
	c. American Association of Industrial Management	3/29	
5	Check job bank weekly	4/1	
1	Search want ads	Daily	
2	Call networking contacts	Daily	
4	Complete certification training	3/15	6/2

You can make this matrix as elaborate as you need to. If you have a lot of long-term projects and objectives with many steps, you could create a matrix or worksheet for each to include:

1. Information needed (job market, requirements)
2. Resources (people, time, computer, contacts, money)
3. Problems/Solutions/Obstacles
4. Costs (tangible, intangible, short- and long-term)
5. Benefits (tangible, intangible, short- and long-term)
6. Backup plan and triggers (if plan A doesn't work, what's plan B?)

7. Delegates (who is responsible for each step?)
8. Dates of review/Milestones for each step

There are generally two problem behaviors associated with creating action plans:

1. **STAGNATION.** People talk about all the things they must do but fail to create action plans to accomplish those objectives. They stress about, think about, and talk about neat ideas, but they fail to outline a clear plan of attack, so they have a hard time moving toward their goals.

2. **BUSYNESS.** Some people rush around completing individual tasks, but they have no idea what objectives those activities support. They spend all day on the phone, answering email, and attending meetings, but haven't defined the objectives that are driving all the activity. They have a hard time measuring outcomes. For more advice on conquering "busyness," see Chapter 5, item 46, and Chapter 6, item 54.

Next, you will transfer the start dates you indicated to your monthly and daily task lists.

PREPARATION quiz item #6:

6. I conduct weekly, monthly, and yearly reviews of my plans.

Monthly and Weekly Review

Regularly reviewing your objectives is the most important part of "time management." Indeed, it is the foundation of creating the best use of your time each day. Many seminar participants have complained, "I don't have time to sit down and plan." My response is always, "You don't have time *not* to plan!"

Planning will keep you on course in achieving your goals and objectives. Abraham Lincoln once said, "If I had sixty minutes to cut down a tree, I would spend forty minutes sharpening the ax and twenty minutes cutting it down." Dale Carnegie told a similar story of two woodsmen that went something like this: Two woodsmen went to the forest to chop wood. They were to be paid based on how much wood they each chopped. One man worked hard all day, took no breaks, and only stopped briefly for lunch. The other chopper took several breaks during the day and took a twenty-minute lunch under a shade tree. At the end of the day, the first woodcutter was dismayed to discover the second had chopped more wood! He said, "I don't understand. I killed myself all day and never took a break. You even took a lunch and still cut more wood than I did! How did you do that?" His companion asked, "Did you also notice that while I was sitting down, I was sharpening my ax?"

Does it take time to sharpen the ax? Of course! But the time invested in the short-term has long-term payoffs, since you'll be more effective cutting down tress. Planning is the difference between being *reactive* or being *proactive.* When you don't plan, you end up reacting to the day's events as they occur, rather than being proactive in determining what you want to achieve.

What does a reactive day look like? You arrive at work in the morning with no clear idea about the day's activities. Things begin to happen—the mail arrives, the phone rings, people drop by. With a flurry of activity, you respond to these various demands. You put forth considerable effort, but at the end of the day you haven't accomplished anything significant. This approach is often referred to as firefighting or flying by the seat of your pants.

If you don't determine what you want to achieve, others will be perfectly happy to fill your time for you.

The solution is to learn to focus on task priorities and to accomplish them in order of importance. If you don't, there is a severe danger that the trivial, time-consuming activities of the day will push the critical few entirely off the calendar. (See item #9 later in this chapter on how to schedule activities.)

Yearly planning process

Frustrated by bad habits like smoking, overeating, being disorganized, or not exercising, many of us vow to change and make a New Year's resolution. We pledge, "This year, I'll walk on my treadmill three times a week." By May, however, your resolution and your treadmill are gathering dust in the basement. Feeling defeated, many people give up further attempts to change.

Making a decision to change just because it's New Year's Day isn't enough to keep you motivated for long. Lasting change means being prepared to make sacrifices. Are you truly willing to make the effort to kick a bad habit and start a healthy one? If so, you'll need to develop a plan of action and make the plan a priority.

Here is a suggested process to get you started:

1. Conduct an "annual review" before the end of December. First, take a moment to step back and appreciate all the things you have accomplished. Then read your personal mission statement to connect again with your values. Next, determine the things that you meant to do, change, or accomplish by the end of the year that didn't get done. Finish, delegate, or abandon any projects, wishes, or to-dos that have haunted you during the past year.

2. Select a *few* (two or three) things that you'd like to change or accomplish in the next year. Boldly state in writing what you *really* want in the coming year and are motivated to work toward. You could even create a storyboard, a visual representation, or collage of your goals complete with photos, clippings, and sayings.

3. Word your objectives carefully. Let's say your resolution is to relax more in the coming year. Try not to think of it as "This year I am going to relax." That's a big stressor! It forces you into thinking of the resolution as something you must do, not something you want to do. Make it sound gentler: "This year I'm going to explore different ways of relaxing." It also suggests more of a plan—you'll fulfill the resolution by experimenting with relaxation techniques. The first resolution sounds as if you're going to force yourself to relax by sheer willpower. If you set a goal to bench press 300 pounds by the end of the year and you only get to 275, it's hard to feel like you didn't make it. However, if you make the objective "I will be in top physical condition by December and lift as much as I possibly can during each workout," you're actually getting what you want from your routine, which is daily success.

4. Transfer pertinent due dates to a daily to-do list, monthly task list, or calendar (see item #7 for ideas). Make an "appointment" with yourself just as important as one with another person. Aren't your needs just as (if not more) important than those of others? If you're going to start taking aerobics classes at noon on Mondays, Wednesdays, and Fridays, write those days and times in your calendar.

5. Create reminder cards and post them around the house, on the bathroom mirror, on the dashboard in your car, etc. Use these to continually remind yourself about your goals.

Take small steps toward your goals, every day or week. If you can do just a little bit to get going, you'll soon feel the positive effects of change. Every little bit of change can lead to long-term healthy habits that last far beyond New Year's Day.

Monthly and weekly planning process

At the end of each month and week (preferably Friday afternoons), you should sit down and conduct two reviews:

1. FORWARD THINKING. Review your calendar and project plans to determine what you need to complete by the end of the month or week, as appropriate. What deadlines are approaching, what project steps should be started, what meetings you need to prepare for, what travel arrangements you need to make, etc. Write each specific task on a daily to-do list. You will need one daily to-do list for each day of the month. If you're using the Tasks feature in MS Outlook or a similar electronic to-do list, ensure that the "Start Date" field shows the day you will begin that activity. If you only fill in the "Due Date" field, you will see that item on your Task Pad every day. By filling in the "Start Date," the task won't appear on your list until that day.

2. REVERSE THINKING. Review the past week's daily pages for incomplete activities and missed items. Where did you leave a message and didn't get a return call? Where did someone cancel an appointment that you need to reschedule? What

didn't get done that needs to? When did you forget to send a thank-you present to a client? Make sure you moved any follow-up to the appropriate day for action. The most successful performers are not only self-starters; they are self-finishers as well.

PREPARATION quiz item #7:

> 7. I track my tasks, projects, and appointments effectively.

The HUG System

Everyone has a different time management system, a way of tracking appointments and to-dos. Some use paper systems; some use electronic systems. I don't believe there is one "right way" of tracking or one "correct" time management system. Regardless of your methods, your system must satisfy the "HUG" criterion:

H—HANDY: I call people who don't keep their time management systems handy "scrappers." They are easily identifiable by all the little scraps of paper everywhere: envelopes, sticky notes, even matchbook covers. That's because they don't carry their system with them to meetings or to lunch. Not having anything to write on, they grab the nearest available piece of paper (or write on a hand). Whether it's a PDA, planner, or notebook, carry your system with you at all times. Scheduling meetings or checking due dates can happen in the oddest of places. You might want to switch to a smaller system if yours is too cumbersome to keep handy.

U—USABLE: A usable system combines both your personal and professional lives. If you've ever tried to keep separate work and home calendars, you know you'll inevitably have conflicts. You might be at home talking to a friend on the phone, and she asks for a lunch date on Thursday. Not having your work calendar with you, you're not sure, but you think you might have an appointment. You schedule the lunch anyway. Then sure enough, you've got a conflict. Or at work, your team wants to schedule a brief meeting Saturday morning, but your home calendar is, well, at home. So you schedule the meeting, only to be reminded when you get home that your seven-year-old is in a soccer tournament that weekend. Keep your entire life in one place and carry it back and forth. Write your contact information and "Reward if found" with a dollar amount in the front, in case you should leave it somewhere.

G—GARBAGE-FREE: You should be able to take your planner, binder, or notebook, and shake it, without all sorts of papers falling out. Your system is not a briefcase. Data-sensitive items should be kept in a tickler file (see Chapter 3 on "Order"). Also, don't include unnecessary sections in your system. Get it down to the information you actually use. Just because your planner came with a tab for Finances doesn't mean you must force yourself to use that form (I keep mine in QuickBooks Pro). If you have your personal mission statement on the computer in a Word document, you don't have to handwrite it to put behind the Goals tab. In other words, personalize and tailor your system to your needs. It's taken me years to create the perfect planner that's just right for me.

If you do choose a planner, which should you use? (See Chapter 8, item #78 for a comparison of paper versus electronic planners.) I've tried many over the years, such as FranklinCovey, Priority Manager, Day-Timer, Day Runner, etc. They all have benefits and work equally well for different people. I personally have stuck with Franklin, because I like the forms and flexibility best. Check out your coworkers' systems, and ask how they use and like them before deciding on your own.

Important sections in your time management system

CALENDARS. There are a multitude of calendars out there, each one designed to fit different needs. A month-at-a-glance may be all you need if you have a couple meetings or appointments per day. A week-at-a-glance is helpful if you have many meetings and need more room to write. If you find the boxes on a monthly calendar are too small, you may want to use a weekly calendar. A page-a-day or two-pages-a-day is perfect for keeping a daily appointment page, your to-do list, meeting directions, and notes all in one place. Alternatively, you can create your own customized calendar. Use a word processing program to make a blank template, make copies of it, write in the days and months, three-hole punch it, and keep it in a three-ring binder. Computerized calendar programs, such as MS Outlook, save you from having to recopy your calendar; a few quick clicks will show the appointments monthly, weekly, and daily.

TO-DO LISTS. To-do lists are for keeping track of action items, not meetings or appointments. You should have two different to-do lists: daily and master. A daily to-do list is the first thing you see in the morning and the last thing you see before leaving. It keeps you focused and on-target throughout the day. A master to-do list is an ongoing list to keep track of things you might want to do someday but that you're not ready to move to your daily list. Lists let you write something down so you can forget it, allowing your brain to be less cluttered. For example, if you need a few items at the grocery store, you could make a list, run in, and grab just the items you need. Or you could walk up and down each aisle, looking at every product, hoping your eye will catch something and trigger your memory. If you get the shopping done a half hour earlier by using the list, you could be spending your time doing more important things.

A–Z TABS. A–Z tabs are great for tracking addresses and contact information. If you use contact manager software or an email program to track names and numbers, using a PDA and synching the data allows you to always have it accessible. But I also use A–Z tabs to track communications and lists. If you use a planner, purchase plain, lined paper in the same size. Write the name of each person with whom you communicate frequently at the top: subordinates who report to you, key coworkers, clients, your boss, spouse, children, etc. As you think of things you need to discuss with others, but don't have time to do immediately, simply turn to that person's log, filed behind the first letter in the last name, and make a note. When you have several items "saved up," you can call to schedule an appointment to review your thoughts. Or refer to this section in a scheduled weekly or biweekly meeting with subordinates. Also keep track of lists filed behind the letter of the category, such as goals, values, classes to attend, books to read, shopping lists, errands, gifts, chores, vacation ideas, purchases, birthdays, holidays, special occasions. Tailor this section to fit your needs.

PROJECTS. Keep a separate section for each large project. These can be business, home, or personal projects, such as developing a new sales presentation, coordinating the department picnic, redecorating the bathroom, etc. Use numbered tabs to track updates, deadlines, or any crucial information for each project. Keep a separate file for all related paperwork. Remember, your time management system is an organizer, not a backpack.

PERSONAL INFORMATION. I keep my driver's license number, my children's social security numbers, a list of books I want to read, ideas for stories for my speeches, blank paper, a time zone chart for calling clients, birthdays and anniversaries, insurance policy numbers, and other personal data in my planner.

PREPARATION quiz item #8:

> 8. I create and prioritize my to-do list each day.

What should I work on first?

I guess that many readers of this book are already fairly good time managers (high performers typically buy books like this because they want to get even better). You get a lot done. You are fairly efficient. You know how to make lists and check things off. So if you're such a hard worker and know how to get a lot accomplished each day, why do you often feel like you're spinning your wheels? Why is it that, when all is said and done, and a week . . . a month . . . a year goes by . . . you feel frustrated by all that is left undone? Why is it that all the things you *should* have done are *not*, but you *did* the things you *shouldn't* have? Put simply, you're not prioritizing correctly.

When faced with a long list of things to do and given a short block of time to complete something, you might look at your list and determine which task you can knock out right away. You decide to start that important project "in a little while." Then you go to lunch. Then you're either too tired or a crisis comes up that demands your attention. In the final analysis, you got nothing *important* accomplished that day. Weeks later, you feel defeated for having accomplished so little. Sound familiar?

Italian economist Vilfredo Pareto once observed that 20 percent of the Italian population owned 80 percent of the wealth.

Pareto's law, more commonly referred to as the 80/20 rule, has these interesting applications:

- 20 percent of your activities produce 80 percent of your value as an employee.
- 20 percent of an organization's employees produce 80 percent of its results.
- 20 percent of your product line accounts for 80 percent of your sales.
- 20 percent of your customers account for 80 percent of your revenue.
- 20 percent of your clothes are worn 80 percent of the time.

Maybe it's not always exactly that precise; perhaps it's 75/25 or 85/15, but the principle generally holds true. The 20 percent of your activities that produce 80 percent of your results are known as the "critical few." The 80 percent of your activities that only produce 20 percent of your results are known as the "trivial many." So if you have ten things to do, only two are really important.

You must identify your activities with the highest value and concentrate on improving those.

To do this, focus on the priorities of tasks and plan to accomplish them in order of importance. If you don't, there is a severe danger that the trivial, time-consuming activities of the day will push the critical few entirely off the calendar. In other words, to "leverage" your time, give less attention to activities that are urgent but unimportant and devote more time to those things that are important but not necessarily urgent. If left alone long enough, important things left undone will inevitably become crises.

Remember, the dilemma is *not* a shortage of time—it is a

problem of *priorities*. Would a thirty-hour day solve your time problems? Not really. Soon your thirty-hour day would be just as full with no fewer frustrations. You would still have a list of things you never got around to and a pile of unfinished books and projects. Do you have a "someday" pile at work? How about a "decide later" pile? Even if you did have more time, these would still exist because of habits you've developed. It's more complex than not having enough time or not managing your time effectively. Instead, it becomes a lesson in managing priorities and being disciplined.

There will *always* be more things to do than time to do them. Sometimes you must forgo something you would *like* to do in favor of something that *has* to be done to accomplish your objectives.

Determine your priorities using following matrix. The intersection of Value (Importance) and Deadline (Urgency) will determine the priority of your tasks. Here are some sample activities and their priorities:

	HIGH VALUE	LOW VALUE
DEADLINE	1. "Do it now" Customer interruptions Crisis Payroll Time cards Some meetings, email Deadline-driven projects Firefighting	3. "Gotta minute?" Improper delegation Drop-in visitors Unnecessary reports Unimportant meetings, email, phone calls, mail Others' "pet" projects Time wasters
NO DEADLINE	2. "I really should . . ." Hiring Training Procedures Long-term planning/prep Performance appraisal Mentoring Exercise Client needs assessment	4. "I really shouldn't . . ." Busywork/"Escape" Fun/easy/trivial Surfing the Net Some phone calls Time wasters Excessive TV Too much socializing

If left undone long enough, Quadrant 2 items will inevitably become crises. Successful people spend a good majority of their time every day in Quadrant 2, doing things that are not crises. With increased long-term focus on Quadrant 2 activities, the number of Quadrant 1 items would be reduced. Quadrant 3 items are largely time wasters and must be managed and controlled better. Quadrant 4 items can virtually disappear through self-discipline until such time as the priority changes.

PREPARATION quiz item #9:

> 9. I schedule my day realistically, manage it successfully, and consistently complete what I've planned.

My Schedule Blows Up Within Five Minutes

Do you remember those time management classes from the late 1980s? We were taught by someone like me how to schedule our days: Okay, from 8:00 to 8:15, I'm going to do this, from 8:15 to 8:50, I'll do this . . ." The tried-and-true methods no longer work. Planners, calendars, PDAs, Microsoft Outlook, to-do lists—none of these things allow us to meet all the demands placed upon us. Tools are helpful, but unable to accommodate the speed, complexity, and changing priorities inherent in what we are doing. We need new ways of thinking and working.

Effective daily planning permits you to realize more of your expectations and reduce your stress levels associated with, say, writing a check on the way to a wedding.

It's important to plan the next day *before* you leave your office in the evening or before you retire for the night. Why?

- You wake up to a purpose. With a plan, you have a picture of the day in your head in the morning. A clear focus will reduce your stress.
- You will know if you have made realistic plans for the day. If you find out your schedule is too full to accomplish the things that must be done tomorrow, you can delegate, delete, reschedule, or move tasks ahead a day.
- You avoid the dilemma of deciding, "What should I do next?" Constantly asking yourself this and sorting and re-sorting items takes time. If you've already made these deci-

sions, you simply start on the next task. As the saying goes, "Plan your work, and work your plan."

- You don't get insomnia. If you don't have a clear picture of what tomorrow looks like, you will lie awake and run those to-dos through your mind over and over.

Your time is probably very fragmented, and much of it is uncontrollable. The best starting place to improve your use of time is to determine the extent to which you control the time available to you. No one has total control over a daily schedule. Someone or something will always make demands on you. But nearly everyone has more control over their time than they realize. Even during structured "working hours," there are opportunities to select which tasks or activities to handle. Most people have about 2.5 hours discretionary time. The goal is to control 25–50 percent of your day. Hopefully, the ideas in this book will impact it by 12–15 percent. Some of your time will require attention to crises—my goal is to teach you to manage the portion of time over which you *do* have control. Here's the process:

1. Fill out a worksheet to determine total controllable time.

Number of hours you plan to work	8
Subtract meetings	3.5
Subtract uncontrollable time (based on a typical day, or adjusted for the day you know you'll have):	1.5
Routine activities	
Visitor interruptions	
Phone calls	
Crisis	
Estimate of total controllable time	3

2. Review/Build your to-do list.

- Items you didn't finish
- Systems-imposed activities
- Boss-imposed activities
- Peer- or subordinate-imposed activities
- Self-imposed activities

3. Prioritize your activities.

4. Assign pure-time estimates. If you could work on the task from start to finish and not be interrupted (which never happens), how long would it take?

5. Accomplish tasks in order of importance. When you have an interruption, you have already accounted for it in uncontrollable time. Handle it quickly and get back to your to-do list.

Here is a completed sample:

▼	Priority	Time	Item
	2	.25	Phoenix travel plans
	1	1	Newsletter insert
	4	.25	Call Kristin
	2	.5	Printer cleaning research
	1	1.5	Lucent workbook
	3	1	MS Fonts
	4	.5	Filing

With just three hours of controllable time, you won't be able to complete all your listed tasks. It's important to know that up front, so you are more focused on completing the high-priority items. When a meeting runs over or an unexpected event pops up, you can adjust accordingly.

PREPARATION quiz item #10:

> 10. I determine the best channel of communication to convey my message prior to sending it.

Should I Call a Meeting or Write an Email?

Email, voicemail, and conference calls have revolutionized how we communicate in corporate America and around the globe. In today's fast-paced business environment, companies depend on technology to link virtual teams across cities, states, and countries. Yet most companies don't provide training on how to productively communicate with these resources.

Whenever I find myself on the receiving end of an email volley, in which an email has repeatedly gone back and forth, I will simply pick up the phone and end it right there. Some people don't put enough thought into which technology they will select to effectively communicate their message. For any given purpose, one channel (or medium) will be more effective than another. Use the chart on the next page to assist you in your decision making:

Richest Channel ⟷ Leanest Channel				
Physical Presence	**Personal Interactive** (phone)	**Impersonal Interactive** (email)	**Personal Static** (voicemail)	**Impersonal Static** (letter, report)
Best for emotional, ambiguous, long, difficult messages			Best for routine, clear, simple messages	

The two main considerations are whether your message is:

1. INTERACTIVE OR STATIC: Should your communication be one-way or two-way? Interactive means a back-and-forth conversation; static means delivery of a message. What does your message require? Brainstorming and questioning require interactivity. Updates can be static.

2. PERSONAL OR IMPERSONAL: Personal means I can either see or hear you directly. Impersonal communication is in writing. Does your communication require you to hear or see another? Are you trying to build relationships? Will the tone of voice be important for this particular message? Are the ideas potentially confusing? Put some thought into whether *you* are a vital component of a particular message.

Some people dash off two hundred email messages a day without putting thought into what may be more appropriate communication methods; some companies, on the other hand, are in meeting overload and insist on meeting face-to-face when a simple memo would do. To avoid wasting time on the wrong technology, put some thought into the best choice prior to communicating:

CALL A FACE-TO-FACE MEETING ONLY WHEN PHYSICAL PRESENCE IS RE-QUIRED. If the meeting does not require problem solving, brain-storming, or input from employees, use an alternative way to share or distribute information. When the information shared is simply FYI, a face-to-face meeting isn't required. Could you send out a group voicemail, an email, or a memo? At the most, sched-ule a conference call and ask participants to submit project status in writing two days prior.

TALK VOICE-TO-VOICE WHEN A MESSAGE IS POTENTIALLY CONFUSING OR EMOTIONAL. Through the early nineties when you needed to ask a colleague a question, you simply got up and walked to his or her office or cubicle. Alternatively, you picked up the phone. Today, people don't even walk two doors down to converse; they just dash off an email. The downside is that people spend inordinate amounts of time staring at a computer screen rather than inter-acting with others, reducing a vital component of human inter-action. We also use email when we shouldn't and waste time. Before dashing off your next email, think about your purpose. If you have to deal with a problem with someone, a potentially con-fusing or difficult message, or an emotional message, don't send an email.

DON'T USE VOICEMAIL AS A WAY TO AVOID CONFLICT. Because of voicemail, the need to interact voice-to-voice or face-to-face is less essential. Can't you just *tell* when people didn't expect to get you "live" on a call? They almost sound disappointed and defi-nitely unprepared; they're poised to leave you a message and didn't really want to talk. Automation gives fewer opportunities to practice your interpersonal skills. And because of the rush-rush multi-tasking environments in which we operate, it's be-coming harder for people to actually sit quietly and focus during a personal conversation. The human touch may also be lacking when a company's automated system doesn't provide an "escape." When a colleague is sitting at her desk, resist the urge to call her voicemail. Get up and deliver your message personally. If you are a customer service professional, don't always answer your calls through your voicemail. Be a *real* person and relate personally with those on whom your business thrives.

Use the following sample reference chart to quickly think about the purpose of your communication before sending it.

FUNCTION	MEETING	PHONE OR CONF CALL	EMAIL	VOICE-MAIL	LETTER OR FAX
Brainstorming and negotiation	X	X			
Formality required	X				X
Informal, quick update			X	X	
Relationship building	X	X		X	
Distribute lengthy, complex info			X		X
Distribute simple, brief info				X	
Legal purposes; requires hard copy			X		X
Send detailed documents for review and response			X		X
Discuss documents you sent	X	X			

FUNCTION	MEETING	PHONE OR CONF CALL	EMAIL	VOICE-MAIL	LETTER OR FAX
Send urgent message; immediate response needed		X		X	
Familiar topic; little explanation			X		
Discuss project updates/status	X	X			
Corrective action or praise	X				
Share organizational message	X	X			X
Add personal touch to quick message				X	
Need open discussion on new policy	X	X			
Quickly send important update to many people; record required			X		
Ensure privacy	X	X			
Hear someone's voice to read between the lines		X			

CHAPTER TWO

Mastering the "R" in Productive

REDUCTION

BECAUSE A FINITE AMOUNT OF TIME IS AVAILABLE, if you want to get more done, the temptation is to go faster and work more hours. However, productivity is not about squeezing more into your days. This chapter will help you *reduce* things that waste your time, called "speed bumps." By eliminating speed bumps, you create the space to accomplish the important.

Speed bumps exist at organizational, departmental, and individual levels. For example, IBM wanted its employees to move faster, make decisions faster, and complete projects faster, to compete with the hungry startups that were gnawing on the edges of its business. Employees were so used to operating in the status quo, they were unsure exactly what that looked like. So IBM established a "Speed Team," consisting of successful project managers who had a strong reputation for pushing projects forward at a blazing pace. This team educated IBMers on the characteristics of fast-moving projects and taught them how to eliminate time wasters. For IBM, the speed bumps included administration, unnecessary levels of bureaucracy, too much red tape, and unclear priorities. *You* can also be a speed bump—the causal factor in wasting precious time. Each item in this chapter will outline a potential speed bump and give ideas for reducing its effects.

REDUCTION quiz item #11:

> 11. I eliminate the cause of most problems and avoid crises.

The Sky Is Falling

Jen, one of my newsletter subscribers, wrote, "Laura, I feel like my workday is completely out of control. I have a Palm Pilot and a huge list of tasks, but some days I barely have the time to even glance at them. How can I get my head above water and get to the point where I'm not spending every day just fighting the most current fire that has come up?"

Indeed, many people like Jen are good at planning their days, creating a to-do list, and outlining priorities. But when you get to work, everything, including your plan, blows up in the first ten minutes because others need you to do "very important" things. By the end of the day, you're frustrated by your inability to accomplish anything important.

Whose crisis is this?

There is a difference between an emergency and a crisis that occurs because of something that wasn't done. If you delay something long enough, you are contributing to a future crisis. By procrastinating, you often create the next crisis. The first time it happens, it's an emergency. The second time, you're an accomplice. Here's what you can do after every "fire."

CREATE A BACKUP PLAN. How have you responded to recurring problems in the past? What contingency plans have you put into place to make sure the crisis doesn't happen again? If your computer crashed and you lost all your data, I would assume that you now have a literal "backup" plan to ensure this doesn't happen again. For example, a reader told me, "Part of my job involves scheduling other people. When one of these people cancels, it becomes a crisis, requiring me to place many telephone calls, send emails, and endure lots of stress! This never fails to happen when I am up against a project deadline, or preparing to put on an event in the immediate future." This is the type of repeated situation that should always include a Plan B, scheduling a backup person in the event that Plan A fails. When the same thing is guaranteed to happen over and over, put a plan into place that will help you handle it better.

BE PROACTIVE. Another reader said, "My problem is that much of my time is spent on the telephone with my members who call with questions, so I'm putting out fires or directing them to resources." This comment begs the question: What systems have you put in place to proactively answer the questions people are asking? How can you help them easily find the information they need (through your website, newsletter, email updates, etc.)? Sometimes we are so busy putting out the fires, we never step back and evaluate what's lighting the flame.

LOOK IN THE MIRROR. What part did you play in creating this fire? To reduce time spent on crisis management, spend time doing long-term, proactive, important activities, rather than always responding to the urgent. Don't facilitate crisis at work by procrastinating until tasks become urgent. Spending thirty minutes more per day working on items that are high in importance but low in urgency would significantly reduce the amount of time you spend responding to crisis. Ask yourself, "What ideas, projects, and pro-grams—if implemented now or in the near future—would sig-nificantly impact the profitability or productivity of my staff or my organization?"

When a true crisis cannot be avoided because of changing pri-orities, unrealistic deadlines, or mistakes:

- Take a deep breath, ask yourself what needs to be done, and handle it in an orderly fashion. Stay calm and think clearly.
- How major is the crisis? Step back and look at the whole picture. Narrow the scope of the project if you must or eliminate some non-essential elements.
- Offer incentives. Get someone you know who will put forth additional effort. Offer a reward for on-time comple-tion.
- Ask yourself, "Whose crisis is this, anyway?" Seek alterna-tive sources or switch suppliers or players if someone isn't delivering on promises. Can you delegate the crisis to someone else? Don't be afraid to ask for help if needed.

REDUCTION quiz item #12:

12. I control and prevent interruptions.

Sorry Officer, I Didn't See the Red Light

With phone calls, hallway conversations, emails, and people "stopping by," how often do you get interrupted during the day? Let's say you interact with six people frequently throughout the day, and each one interrupts you in some form every two hours. With six stakeholders, that would be 24 interactions a day, or 120 a week, resulting in an average interaction three times an hour in a forty-hour week. If each interruption took ten minutes, you would spend 50 percent of your time on them. If you can't work for more than a few minutes without being interrupted, a small project could end up taking all day.

We've tried the extremes, which are (1) an open-door policy and (2) blocking off time for several hours and hiding from everyone. The open-door policy produces so many interruptions that it's almost impossible to get anything done. But if you're not available at all, a small problem you could have handled promptly turns into a crisis because you couldn't be reached. You need a balance between controlling interruptions and staying informed.

USE AN UNDERSTOOD SIGNAL. If several people in your department are having problems with drop-in visitors, agree on a signal that says, "Please don't interrupt unless it's an emergency." A manager I worked with at Coca-Cola had an open-door policy. He wanted his employees to feel comfortable talking to him about anything, anytime. Unfortunately, he rarely could find time to get his work done. At his next staff meeting, he explained the problem he was having. He said that when he had a deadline, he would put on his red Coca-Cola baseball cap. His door would remain open in case there was an emergency, but he would prefer employees didn't interrupt him during those times. He reported it worked like a charm. Get together with your department and agree on a signal everyone will use consistently. Installing curtains across the cubicle door? Turning your name plate around? Wearing orange armbands? Partially closing the door? One group I worked with found that coworkers respected the signal about 80 percent of the time. When I questioned the people who said others weren't respecting their signals, it turns out they *never* took down their signals. They were never available to their coworkers, so their coworkers simply ignored their signals. If you use this system, make sure you don't abuse it.

ESTABLISH CONDITIONAL INTERRUPTIONS. If you'd rather not use a signal, you can agree on which issues merit interruptions.

TYPE 1 ISSUES are those that require your input specifically. The world will stop until you are available to discuss it. Condition your colleagues to interrupt you only for these types of issues.

TYPE 2 ISSUES need only a quick "yes" or "no" answer and require just a little interaction. Have your colleagues "save up" these issues and check in with you once a day for five things instead of five interruptions with one thing apiece.

TYPE 3 ISSUES are those that could be answered by someone else; you're not the only person in the world who can help. Kindly request that people look elsewhere for answers to these issues. Avoid the "it's not my job" attitude; simply educate the visitor on the appropriate resource.

TYPE 4 ISSUES are already answered in print somewhere—like a procedure, guide, or employee manual—and don't require your assistance. People ask these types of questions when they're being lazy. Tell your coworkers clearly, "Please don't bother me with these issues."

SET ASIDE "DOWNTIME." Some companies have instituted a period of time every day when you cannot interrupt another employee, schedule a meeting, or answer your phone. Can you imagine having an hour and a half to yourself every morning? These "quiet times" can be used quite successfully. Allow employees to turn on their voicemail if they are up against a tight deadline. Work out an agreement with your colleagues to cover phones for one another at certain times to etch out a little uninterrupted time each day. You might consider closing your door (if you have one) when you truly need to concentrate. Establish fixed office hours when you can be interrupted.

SCHEDULE REGULAR CHECK-IN TIMES. Are you rarely available to talk? Perhaps people are interrupting you because they know they must grab you when they can. The solution is to schedule regular check-in times for updates from people you must talk to often. Have each person create a running list of things they need to discuss, so you can cover all the points at once. Pay attention to who interrupts you the most and chat about this new approach.

ALWAYS CHOOSE TO VISIT A COLLEAGUE IF GIVEN A CHOICE. Limit the number of people you invite to your work area. If you're scheduling a meeting, always offer to meet your coworker in his or her office or a conference room. This will keep you in control. You can excuse yourself once you accomplish your purpose. It is much easier to get up and leave than to remove people from your office once they've parked there. When you arrive at someone's office, don't ask questions like, "How are you today?" (Unless you really want to know.) The person will be more than happy to tell you. Start off with a pleasant, "Good to see you! I wanted to talk with you a little about the Smith file." When invited to sit, decline if you can, saying, "I've been sitting all day. I'd rather stand if you don't mind."

GO INTO HIDING. When I needed to put the finishing touches on this book, I knew I could never complete it if I worked in my office. So I would escape for three days at a time to my friend Kay Baker's house, where no one could find me. Without the daily office distractions, I finished my book. If you absolutely have to get away for a solid hour without being interrupted, find an empty conference room or borrow a vacationing colleague's office.

REDUCTION quiz item #13:

13. I handle drop-in visitors and coworkers effectively.

"Gotta Minute?"

Try as you might, you couldn't keep that person from talking to you. Short of barring the door or turning on your voicemail, interruptions are inevitable. The issue now becomes how to manage them once they do occur and keep a ten-minute interruption from becoming a twenty-minute interruption. What you do during an interruption is just as important as eliminating it. Controlling time taken up by visitors requires both courtesy and good judgment. Here are some suggestions.

BE HONEST. When someone says, "Gotta minute?" do they really mean *one* minute? Never! Respond, "Actually, I have just one. Will that be enough or can I call you back at three o'clock?" If someone enters your office and begins talking nonstop, wait until he or she takes a breath, then say, "Joan, I want to talk to you about this, but I've got my back up against a deadline right now. Would it be okay if I called you in an hour?" Let people see you write the appointment in your calendar so they feel heard. When you don't have time for an interruption and allow it to occur anyway, you're not doing either one of you a favor. That person isn't being heard because you're not listening, and you're not completing a high-priority item. Most people are happy to schedule a more convenient time.

USE VERBAL TACTICS AND BODY LANGUAGE. When someone barges into your office without knocking or asking if it's a good time to talk, stand to greet the person. When you remain standing, your visitor is unlikely to sit. State how much time you have from the outset. "I have seven minutes to chat," makes it clear that your time is limited. After your visit is over and it's time to move on, politely signal with nonverbal signs that it's time to go. Shuffling some papers, turning slightly toward your computer, or stretching sometimes works. If your visitor ignores your cues, say, "Well, that's it then! Thank you for stopping by." Simultaneously walk toward your colleague and edge toward the door.

BE ASSERTIVE. If sending these subtle signals—like tapping your pencil, continuing to write the email, or flipping through papers—still doesn't work, you have to speak up. The visitor is completely oblivious that this isn't a good time to interrupt you. Diplomatically deflect the conversation and request a postponement. Phrase things positively like, "Jane, I want to discuss this with you, but I need to get this agenda finished for a ten o'clock meeting." "I've got to get this in the mail by noon, so can I call you at three to discuss this?" "Can this wait until I complete this contract?" When you ask, ninety-nine times out of a hundred, you'll get a positive response. People don't want to be jerks; they just want you to know they need you.

PLACE A CLOCK STRATEGICALLY BEHIND YOU. If you do have to have a chair in your office, place a clock behind you in view of visitors. Every once in a while, turn around and glance at the clock. *When you glance at the clock is very important.* You should never check the time when the other person is talking, because it's rude. However, when you begin speaking, you can casually turn around while talking, check the clock, and continue speaking without missing a beat. This is very subtle and sends a message to the person that you are on a schedule and watching the clock.

PRACTICE THE "SLOW STROLL." You've tried everything. You started answering your phone and doing the work in front of you, but they *still* won't leave! Holy cow, are they slow or what? You could try putting down your pen purposefully, turning to face them, leaning forward, looking them right in the eye, and saying, "Thanks for dropping in. You'll have to excuse me now because I need to get this project finished." If that *still* doesn't work, simply stand. Give in. Interrupt them blatantly and say, "Hey, why don't you accompany me while I go grab a cup of coffee." Start walking toward your door, placing your hand on their arm to guide them if you must. Keep walking. They will follow you like a calf, still talking. Walk quickly to the coffee machine, get some coffee, and say, "I've got to run to the restroom! See you later!" Then make a quick getaway!

REDUCTION quiz item #14:

14. I refuse requests I don't have time for.

Just Say "No"

When you have boundaries, you can say "no" in a way that doesn't feel like "no" to the other person. Boundaries allow you to not be the bad guy and feel guilty. When a client asks me to drive over for a ten-minute meeting, I can say, "I hold phone appointments at absolutely no charge, but if I drive over, I will have to charge you for consulting time." Clients are more than happy to talk on the phone after that, but the decision was theirs, since I gave the choice back to them in a way that maintained the relationship.

Here are ways to say "no" in a positive, professional manner:

FIND CREATIVE WAYS TO STATE YOUR BOUNDARIES. If someone asks you to lunch and you just can't find the time, you might politely say, "Ordinarily that would be fine, but it just doesn't fit into my schedule right now." Learn to set boundaries with your boss too! When your boss asks you to take on yet another huge project say, "Right now I'm working on that database project you assigned me. I'm afraid if I take on something new, it won't get done on time. However, I am willing to do this new project. Which do you prefer?" Ask your boss what the relative priorities are for the different pieces of work on your plate. That's a reasonable way to call your existing workload to your boss's attention, and you won't be fired for pointing it out.

SAY "NO" IN A WAY THAT IS POLITE AND FROM THE HEART. Practice it often! Don't be too passive and let others violate your rights, but don't be too aggressive either and violate others' rights. Here's a good phrase that works for me: "Thank you so much for asking, but that just doesn't work for me right now." Then smile, look the person in the eyes, and *be quiet!* You don't need to rationalize or explain. What can they say to that? If they try to object, just keep repeating, "That doesn't work for me right now." It's friendly, but firm.

How can you politely say "no" to someone? Try these:

"I don't have time for that right now, but thank you for thinking of me."

"I'll be able to do that if I can get you to do the first part of the project for me."

"I can't do that for you right now, but if you can wait until Tuesday, I'll be able to help you out."

"Ordinarily, I'd love to be involved in something like that. But I'm up to my eyebrows in other commitments and won't be able to take that on. I'd be happy to serve in an advisory or consultative capacity, but I can't be an active committee member."

"I regret that I just don't have the time right now to give that the attention it deserves. Someone else will be far better suited than I right now."

"I appreciate your vote of confidence, but I can't work it into my schedule right now."

"I'll be glad to handle that for you. However, I can't get to it until I finish X, Y, and Z. That will be . . ."

Sticking to your guns

I've listened to countless people lament that they simply don't have enough time in the day. Many of those people have a jam-packed calendar because they can't say "no." Others prey on them, because they know a people-pleaser can never refuse. Perhaps you're afraid of losing control on something for which you may eventually be held responsible. It's time to get realistic and determine if the demands on your time have exceeded your ability to handle them. Time to go back to your mission statement and say "no" to anything not supported there.

Who should you say "no" to? Your boss, your friends, your spouse, yourself . . . anyone who tries to bust your boundaries. Take a close look at how much time you could save for yourself next week if *this week* you started being honest with people about things you don't really want to do.

Be realistic! Your friend is not going to hate you if you simply can't swing the time for a shopping trip this Saturday. The world will not stop revolving if you don't chair the PR committee. If you've been asked to bring homemade cookies for your son's preschool party, offer to bring juice, plates, or silverware instead. Think of other ways to accommodate requests made by others. If what you offer is not good enough, the requestor will ask someone else. Good! At least you've done your part.

Saying "no" does *not* undermine your authority or competence. Your credibility is actually enhanced when you honestly tell people you lack the time or the interest.

First, it makes you seem more desirable (we always want what we can't have). Second, you ensure that you don't perform tasks in a slipshod way, making you appear less competent in the end. Three, you'll have more time to devote to the tasks that return the highest value for your time. So flex that "no" muscle, create your rules, and make sure others stick to them.

REDUCTION quiz item #15:

15. I recognize and eliminate personal shortcomings that lead to decreased departmental and organizational productivity.

It's Not *My* Fault!

Why does your organization care about employee productivity? In order to be successful, your organization must both make money and save money. To make money, it must find and keep customers. To save money, it could reduce benefits, staff, or salaries; it could lower the quality of its products; it could cut costs and expenses. Or it could improve employee productivity. That makes sense.

Why should employees care about productivity? The main reason is so that they don't get laid off. But the main benefit is that by becoming more productive, overworked employees can get the same amount of work done in less time and leave the office earlier than before. Employees get a life, and organizations get to keep them. This is truly an amazing connection.

You see, an organization is a living, breathing being, made up of living, breathing beings. It's a complicated ecosystem. If you think of your company as a rain forest or a life cycle, it has complex interrelationships. One part affects the other parts. When the worms stop doing their job, the lions suffer. When the lions stop doing their job, the worms suffer. When one part of the system is "sick," it affects the whole.

In a seminar I recently taught, I posed this question to the group: "What happens to you every day that keeps you from doing what you know you should be doing?" I told them I was assuming they were all hard workers, had good intentions, and knew what they should be working on. So why wasn't the work getting done?

Incredibly, their answers *all* focused on other people, the organization, or systemic issues (external factors):

- Unimportant meetings
- Crises and emergencies
- Frequent interruptions
- Unnecessary email volume
- Excessive socializing
- Understaffing and unrealistic expectations
- Ineffective communication

In other words, these were the areas in which the organization was "broken" and accepted and perpetuated "sick" behavior. But remember that an organization is a living, breathing being, made up of living, breathing beings. So I pointed out they had only identified external factors and asked the question again. "What happens to you every day that keeps you from doing what you know you should be doing? This time, focus on yourself and the interrelationships in the organization. What do you do *personally* that causes the above?"

Silence. Then, slowly . . .

- I suppose I interrupt people too . . . it's kind of the norm around here.
- Sometimes I procrastinate on important projects I know I'm supposed to be working on and end up creating the crisis myself.
- I blame the company for a culture that expects long hours, when I actually don't work on high-priority activities until the end of the day, which forces me to stay late.
- I sometimes send personal and inappropriate emails to others, rationalizing that "others do it, too."
- I gripe about the meetings around here, but I secretly relish the mental breaks from work.

And so on . . . It was incredible. Once we managed to shift the focus of the conversation, we got *real*. The group realized that some things that felt uncontrollable or seemed to be caused by other people were really within their own spheres of influence. Individual members acting out these behaviors actually created the whole.

We're not talking about major shifts in productivity here, because it's impossible for anyone to be productive 100 percent of the time. We're talking about a few percentage points of improvement from each employee that would result in increased profitability, retention, and employee satisfaction.

So start with yourself and spread it to others. Take some initiative. Let the system work. Ask yourself what areas you are buying into and where you are actually supporting the problem behaviors you notice organizationally. If a Time Cop came and handed out tickets for productivity failures, where and when would you get a ticket? It's only when individual people notice, challenge, and implement changes in personal habits that real productivity growth occurs systemically.

REDUCTION quiz item #16:

> 16. I avoid spending time in irrelevant, unnecessary meetings.

Where Minutes Are Kept and Hours Are Wasted

A survey respondent told me, "Outside interruptions and meetings are my big time eaters. I have literally spent entire days in meetings. I not only get nothing done at my desk, I also inherit additional work. I suppose if I could wish for one thing it would be fewer meetings. Hey, I can dream, can't I?" Yes! Let's dream a little. Wouldn't it be nice to have a pass that says, "Get Out of a Meeting Free"? Here are some ideas for reducing time spent in meetings:

CONSIDER THE TIMING. If you're someone with the ability to call a meeting during a certain time, seriously consider the best time to hold it. It's often eye-opening to do a prime-time graphing activity with your staff or the people normally in attendance (see Chapter 4, item 31). You'll find corporate America has trained most people to be "morning people." Our natural energy cycles cause us to be "up" or have "prime" time first thing in the morning. Unfortunately, many people insist on holding meetings at that time. Some kinds of meetings are good during prime time, like those involving brainstorming, problem solving, or strategic thinking. Routine staff meetings, project updates, or information-only meetings should be held during lulls in productivity. Similarly, a brainstorming session on Friday afternoon at three o'clock will probably not yield the best results.

REDUCE TIME SPENT IN UNIMPORTANT MEETINGS. Can you send an alternate? Can you call the meeting chair and ask to report first, and then explain that you have another meeting on its heels and you need to depart in a timely manner? Can someone tape record the meeting for you to listen to in your car?

Help the group stay on track

- Require an agenda. If one isn't sent two days prior to the meeting, ask for one.
- Use a timekeeper to keep the meeting on target. When something comes up that's not on the agenda, place it on an easel pad labeled "parking lot." If time remains at the end of the meeting, parking lot items can be discussed. If no time remains, the items are placed on the next meeting's agenda. Keep meetings focused, tangent-free, and moving.
- Start and stop on time. I had a boss once who began his meetings at 4:17 p.m. No one dared be late to a meeting with such an odd time. We were always there by 4:15, and he started promptly two minutes later. Open with a quick, friendly greeting, and then move directly to the purpose of the meeting. Don't allow an exceedingly long social hour.
- Eliminate any discussion that involves only two people. They can schedule a one-on-one later.

REDUCTION quiz item #17:

> 17. I eliminate all unnecessary responsibilities or tasks that belong to someone else.

Why Am I Doing This Again?

An executive director for an association wrote, "I would like to know how to explain to a board of directors (I have many bosses) exactly how much I am responsible for on a daily basis without having to write a list. I'm not trying to justify my existence; I would like them to realize their expectations are so great, I need more staff and/or they need to determine the priorities."

Unfortunately, most organizations hear the battle cry of "too much to do and not enough people" far too often. No matter if I'm presenting a seminar to a small company, huge corporation, nonprofit group, or government agency, employees are complaining of understaffing. If you want to build a case to bring in some help, you've got to have some proof that you're simply not whining. Hard data will be necessary if you don't want to sing the boss the same old song. Even if you don't need to make a case, it's valuable to see where you're wasting time and can plug productivity leaks.

We have a new, big mall in Denver called Colorado Mills. It's laid out so it basically makes one big circle, divided into quadrants called "neighborhoods." When you enter the mall through any of the outside doorways, you will see a directory of the mall. Let's say you want to go to Ann Taylor to buy a new blouse. You can look under "Clothing, Women's" and see you need store number 325. You can easily find the number through the color-coding system, so you know where you want to go. Inevitably, you can't find the little person labeled "You are here." "Where am I?" you ask.

If you have no idea where you are, you can't figure out how to get where you're going. The mall has lots of little shortcuts and passageways, so if you know Point A and Point B, you can plot the shortest distance. Without knowing the starting point, you can randomly set out in any direction. Eventually, you might bump into Ann Taylor, but it will sure take you a lot longer.

A time log is the best way to determine where you are so that you can plot the most efficient course to get where you want to go. The time log helps you with the question "Where am I?" By knowing "You are here," you can more quickly draw a line from where you are to where you want to be.

Procedure for creating a time log

Day of Week:			Date:
Time	Activity	Comments	Priority
7:00			
7:30			
8:00			
8:30			
9:00			

1. Create a table like the one shown here on your word processor (or email me at Laura@TheProductivityPro. com, and I'll send you a template). List the hours you work in half-hour increments.

2. Record activities at least every half hour. Be specific. For example, identify visitors and record duration and topics of conversation. Entries might look like this:

Email (continued) = 10 minutes
Bob Jones stopped by = 15 minutes
Travel to branch office = 40 minutes
Phone call from Judy = 15 minutes

Write a comment on each activity that might be useful in assessing how the time was spent. Did something take longer than usual? Why? Were you interrupted? For example, on the travel to the branch office, you could write, "Unscheduled—dealing with emergency."

3. Keep the log for a minimum of one week. Avoid vacation or holiday weeks.

4. Be honest. Only you will have access to this information. Don't "fudge" or go several hours without making a notation. If you know you're going to cheat, don't keep the time log in consecutive days: skip a few days in between to ensure you're recording information correctly. You're only looking for patterns.

5. Carry a copy of the log with you wherever you go.

6. Once you've completed seven days of time logs, go where you won't be interrupted, spread them out on a table, and study them.

Referring to your time log, ask yourself the following questions:

- Which part of each day was most productive? Which was least productive? Why?
- What are the recurring patterns of inefficiency? (i.e., I searched for a file, someone kept interrupting me, waiting for something, etc.)

- Where did the process get bogged down?
- Where did I procrastinate or allow enjoyment to override a priority task?
- Which activities do not contribute to achieving at least one of my objectives? How can I change this?
- On average, what percentage or work time am I productive? (Be honest) What is my reaction to this figure?

Look at the activities you wrote down that consumed or controlled your time. Ask yourself:

- Was that task **necessary?** Was the information useful to someone? Only do the essential tasks.
- Am I the **appropriate** person to be performing this task? Am I doing work beneath my skill level? Is there someone else who can handle it? Look for activities that should be given to others.
- Is there a better, more **efficient** way of handling this task? Do I need a new procedure? Can I automate it? How can I handle recurring activities?
- Can I **eliminate** a task? Have you ever looked back in retrospect on a completed task and realized that, had it gone undone, there would be no consequence? When you're faced with too much to do, assess the tasks by asking, "What would happen if I simply didn't handle this?" If the answer is "nothing," don't do it.

If you can demonstrate that you've spent the majority of your time working on very high priorities, and you're still not able to get everything done, you might have a case for bringing in additional support. You will also know where you are, so you can plot the most efficient way to get where you want to be.

REDUCTION quiz item #18:

> 18. I get rid of everything I don't need or use and live simply.

Living the Simple Life

We enter this world owning nothing and knowing only how to eat, sleep, and breathe. From then on, life gets complicated. We want stuff, so we buy stuff. Then we have to clean the stuff, fix the stuff, and store the stuff. The pile of stuff grows larger, requiring a bigger house in which to keep the stuff. Suddenly, we have no time to eat, sleep, and breathe.

A September 2000 study, "Economic Apartheid in America," shows that the more Americans spend, the less satisfied they seem to be. Of those who earn more than $50,000 a year, only 5 percent say they've achieved the American dream. Ironically, that's the same proportion found among those who earn less than $15,000 a year. Moreover, Americans use twice the energy and produce twice the waste as most Europeans. American life expectancy and literacy rates—key quality of life indicators—are only a few percentage points higher than those in the Indian state of Kerala, an area with a GNP of less than $400 per capita, compared to more than $20,000 in the United States.

Such statistics support the "less is more" simplicity movement. We may have more timesaving devices than our grandparents ever dreamed of, but our harried twenty-first-century lives have left us with less free time than ever. Thirty years ago, experts were reassuring us that with the advance of technology, our biggest challenge would soon be what to do with all the leisure time we were going to have. Unfortunately, life has become so complicated and busy for most people that the idea of leisure time is just as outdated as those experts' ideas. We live in a hustle-bustle world in which we don't know our neighbors, don't have time to cook dinner, and don't go on vacation without our laptops. Simplifying, however, is not always simple.

Do you long to live more "simply," but you don't know what that means or how to begin? Here are some tips and principles to help you simplify your life and have more energy to spend at the office:

GET RID OF YOUR JUNK. While I was at her home writing, my friend Kay got inspired to conduct a major clutter cleanup project in her garage. It took both of us to haul the *huge* container of trash she'd created to the curb. I asked her if she had any advice to offer my readers. She said, "I'm a big-picture person. When I looked at all my junk, I had a tendency to say, 'There's no way. I can't get this done.' My self-talk made me feel overwhelmed. Then I told myself, 'You don't have to do the whole thing; you just have to look in *that* box.' Then slowly, one box after the next, I got it done." When I asked how she felt, she said, "Light as a feather, unencumbered, and excited. I can wrap presents, and do laminating and other things in my storeroom, now that it's not full of junk." (See Chapter 3, item 29 for ideas on systematically decluttering an area.) Getting rid of your junk frees up valuable physical space, but more important, it frees up mental energy, so you have more of it to devote to your family and work.

GET RID OF YOUR DEBT. Don't equate "living within your means" to deprivation. For example, most Americans don't have the cash or the time to purchase gifts for everyone on their holiday list. How many times have you charged expensive items and spent five months paying for them? See if you can break tradition this year by drawing names or just sending cards. Save time by creating a newsletter and including it with your cards, rather than repeatedly handwriting the same dull inscription.

Look at where cutting back on spending can actually result in more quality time together. Spending time playing Monopoly on the floor with your children can be more rewarding than sitting in a movie theater with no interaction.

REDUCTION quiz item #19:

> 19. I delegate properly; I rarely do tasks that others are capable of doing.

Can You Take This Off My Plate?

Do you work ten hours a day? Do you take work home on weekends? One symptom of overwork is improper delegation. Productive people know how to get help and delegate. John F. Kennedy surrounded himself with smart people and told them about his goal. He said, "Within ten years, we're going to put someone on the moon." He never told anyone *how* to do it, but it happened anyway. Delegation is an extension of your own hands: the more you can multiply your hands, the more successful you can be.

The great poet Virgil said long ago, "We are not all capable of everything." Those who *try* to do everything themselves don't accomplish nearly as much as they want to, because time and energy are not limitless. U.S. presidents who were skillful delegators, including Lincoln, Eisenhower, and the Roosevelts, were praised for having effective administrations, while "lone rangers" such as Cleveland, Harding, Polk, and Carter were criticized for lackluster performances. Carter was obsessed with details; he even monitored scheduling of the White House tennis courts! Polk's management philosophy was to "supervise the whole operation of the government," even to the point of meeting daily with Washington's street repairmen. Only forty-nine years old when elected, Polk emerged from the presidency an old man at fifty-three and died of heart failure fifteen weeks later. He was what Harry S. Truman called "a four-ulcer man in a five-ulcer job."

Delegation is an indication of your trust and faith in others. But many people resist delegation with the battle cry, "If you want something done right, you have to do it yourself." It's natural that you have mastered many tasks in your climb up the corporate ladder. You may even be the resident expert in your department, capable of doing almost any job better and faster than your subordinates can.

What if a football coach insisted on suiting up, jogging onto the field, and replacing the quarterback? What if the symphony conductor left the podium and demanded the first chair's violin? What if the neighborhood soccer coaches sidelined the kids and took the field themselves? Of *course* you are capable of doing it yourself.

What can delegation do for you?

DELEGATION FREES TIME FOR OTHER ACTIVITIES. You can now focus on important activities, like strategic planning, policy making, and goal setting. Specialization is needed in so many situations that no one person can successfully handle decisions across the breadth of an organization.

DELEGATION DEVELOPS FOLLOWERS. Employees coached through increasingly difficult assignments grow in confidence, professionalism, and job satisfaction. Work you perceive as unimportant might give someone else important opportunities for on-the-job training.

BOTTOM-LINE SAVINGS. Each job is completed at the lowest and least expensive level. Delegation is efficient and cost-effective. Your company is most likely paying you a higher salary than the person hired to answer the phones. Never do anything that can be done just as well by someone who is paid less.

FEWER WORK DISRUPTIONS. With careful training and delegation, employees can carry on the work of the department even in your absence. You can (gasp!) go on a vacation.

TRUST BETWEEN MANAGERS AND SUBORDINATES. Cooperating on delegated assignments opens channels of communication and creates a climate of cooperation. People want to feel they are making an important contribution to the organization. Employees feel like part of the process when they have contributed to decisions that affect them.

You should always retain broader management duties such as overall planning, policy making, goal setting, and budget supervision, as well as work that involves confidential information or supervisor-subordinate relations. If you have someone to delegate to, consider assigning the following types of work:

- Decisions you make most frequently and repetitively
- Assignments that will add variety to routine work
- Functions you dislike
- Work that will provide experience for employees
- Tasks that someone else is capable of doing
- Activities that will make a person more well rounded
- Tasks that will increase the number of people who can perform critical assignments
- Opportunities to use and reinforce creative talents

If there is another person who can handle it, stop doing it. Let others perform something they are 80 percent as capable of doing as you are . . . because it's a mistake to believe you can do it 100 percent perfectly. Be open to new, innovative ways of tackling projects and spend your time on activities you value highly.

REDUCTION quiz item #20:

> 20. I keep socializing during work hours to an appropriate level.

You Need to Be Quiet Now

A reader asks, "How do I draw some boundaries for myself at work without being offensive or coming across as uncaring? I tend to get sucked into everyone's problems. I catch myself doing the same thing to other people (rambling on about my whole life). How can I go about excusing myself without cutting people off and offending them?"

Socializing during work hours is a difficult issue because not all of it is unproductive. Given today's emphasis on teamwork, socializing is essential for communication, coordination, and conflict resolution. When the conversation has high value and time constraints, the discussion is essential. However, when the discussion has low value and becomes excessive, it loses its value. Especially when you enter the realm of gossip or negativism, you've overstepped the boundaries of what is appropriate. When you continue a conversation long after your business is complete, you are letting your boss, team, and organization down.

Especially important in this situation is to listen to your intuition and self-talk, which will tell you when you've overstepped your limits. If you say to yourself, "Okay, I've been here long enough. I really need to get a move on," don't stand there for ten additional minutes. Listen to your subconscious mind signaling you to act.

Let's say you've promised your family that *this* Friday night you're not going to be later than 5:30 p.m. so you can all go out together. At 5, you head for the door, and someone stops you to talk. As that person talks and talks, you sense your frustration starting to build. When these feelings kick up, your mind says, "I can't talk to you right now!" But you don't want to hurt the other person's feelings by abruptly saying, "Gotta go!" So what do you do?

1. **ASSESS THE SITUATION.** Is this person a friend whom you truly care about, who is telling you his mother just went into intensive care, or an acquaintance filling you in on her latest sailing trip?

2. **DECIDE.** Should you set limits and get out of the situation, or should you change your priorities?

3. **ACT.** You have to choose to do what will meet your needs. The hardest part is often getting the words out. Say, "Dorothy, I'm sorry I need to interrupt you quickly before you go on. I literally only have three minutes, because I'm running out the door to meet my family. Should we chat tomorrow, or was your story only going to take another minute?"

Putting limits around socializing is an important way to recover time for more important things. You must always remember that the promises you've made to yourself and others are more important than someone else's desire to chat. Conversations can be postponed; your family's disappointment cannot.

CHAPTER THREE

Mastering the "O" in Productive

ORDER

ORDER RELATES TO YOUR LEVEL OF ORGANIZATION. It's how well you control the paper, email, reading material, and information into and out of your office. Order is your ability to sort, filter, and process information effectively. It's also your ability to *find* what you want, when you want it. It's how tidy your work areas look, inside and out.

I believe a messy office is a career detriment. I've heard many negative comments about messy desks, such as, "Joan's office and her work are so sloppy." People equate messy desks with messy work. Not fair, I know, but perception is reality. My HR clients have flat-out told me: "I'd promote someone with a tidy office over someone with a messy office any day."

A seminar participant wrote, "My time management abilities are fair but could certainly be better. I interface with several agencies and outside individuals on a daily basis, which tends to keep me moving from issue to issue. With a little more organization, I could be more productive."

ORDER quiz item #21:

> 21. I realize that some people aren't "born" more organized than others.

The Organized Person: Genetic or Environmental?

One of the questions I'm frequently asked is, "Are you born with the gift of organization, or do you pick it up from watching your parents?" Half believe that if you're not born with the genetic "organization gene," you're out of luck.

First of all, I doubt organization is genetic. My brothers were slobs. In fact, my mother made them keep their bedroom doors shut so that their messes wouldn't bother anyone.

But my father swears I was always organized. Even as a young girl, I had "systems." My stuffed animals lived on my bed in a specific order during the day and on my toy box in another specific order at night. I never left the house without making my bed. I actually folded and put my clothes away. I had a precise order in which I got dressed, brushed my teeth, and combed my hair, in exactly the same sequence. However, when I took my first office job, I had no idea what to do with all the paper, magazines, files, and project information littering my desk. I wasn't born with a genetic predisposition toward labeling and classifying files, and neither were you.

The argument for the environment

Perhaps, then, it's environmental. My mother could never throw anything away. She washed and reused Ziploc bags. She used a teabag over and over again until no color came out of it (I can still picture that shriveled little teabag on the stovetop).

My father was also a huge packrat. He's a retired Air Force colonel, so I moved frequently during childhood. I remember certain boxes that Dad moved from house to house to house. He never opened them. He just kept putting a moving sticker on top of the other moving stickers and carrying it along. I recall asking, "Dad, why don't you just put that box out for the garbage collectors instead of moving it? You've never opened it!" His response was, "I can't! There might be something valuable in there!" If you have no idea what's in the box and have never looked for the item, how can it be valuable?

Did I pick up those packrat tendencies from my parents? Nope. I am the queen of tossing! If I haven't used something in a year, I give it to charity.

Truly, organization is neither entirely genetic nor environmental; it's learned.

Organization is a skill that can be taught, just like riding a bike. I honestly believe anyone can become organized with the proper training. Over the years, I've recognized, however, that not everyone can and should organize the same way. Getting organized is a process of trial and error and persistence.

Benefits of being organized

I took my first "time management/organizing" class in 1988. I was so excited by what I learned and it so transformed my productivity that my career from that point on was devoted to the art and science of productivity. I wanted to change other people's lives in the same way mine was changed. Through organization, I found:

- freedom from chaos,
- more flexibility and creativity,
- higher productivity,
- lowered stress levels, and
- less expense of money, time, and overall resources.

Being organized will give you more control over your life and time. Getting rid of clutter is *more* than just being efficient, *more* than being more productive on a daily basis, and *more* than a way to lower stress. Being organized is a key way to find the time and the self-control to start achieving more of the things you want to do. I assure you that digging out from under and staying on top of the clutter in your life *is* possible. And the bonus—once you know how and have your systems set up, it is actually *easier* to be organized than to be disorganized!

ORDER quiz item #22:

> 22. I keep a clutter-free work surface.

Orderly Surfaces: Who Cares?

If you are overwhelmed and mystified about where to put all those memos, reports, drafts, bills, magazines, letters, and miscellaneous documents that come to you, you're not alone.

Some people try to justify their disorganization by appearing as if they are disorganized *on purpose.* They say things like, "I have a great system. I just let things go and if it's really important, someone will call about it." Others tell me they have no *choice* but to be disorganized. One woman told me in defense, "But I'm *creative,* you see. Creative people are naturally disorganized." I don't agree. I've known many creative, right-brained people who were highly organized; they simply had different systems. You don't *have* to be creative and disorganized, *if* you are motivated and willing to learn.

Let's make another important distinction: "Neat" does not necessarily equal "organized." Let's say, for example, that someone you care about is coming to your home or office, and your desk or dining room table is so full (and has been for so long) that you don't even remember what the surface looks like. You sweep your arm across the surface, dumping all the contents into a container, throwing it under the bed or in the closet. You have "neat," yes, but do you have "organized"? Of course not. You could be a neat, disorganized person. Or you can be organized and not neat, but you will experience several problems.

An organized office:

- **SAVES TIME.** In my experience, the average professional spends at least thirty minutes a day just looking for things. Many people work longer hours to compensate for this wasted time.
- **ALLOWS YOU TO FOCUS.** When you are surrounded by clutter, it's difficult to concentrate on the task before you. Most people have one to two weeks of work on their desks *right now,* assuming they don't get anything else to do today.
- **ALLOWS OTHERS TO FIND THINGS IN YOUR OFFICE.** It's frustrating for coworkers to try to locate items in your office when you go on vacation or stay home sick.
- **LOWERS YOUR STRESS LEVELS.** People with a cluttered office report having anxiety, and being overwhelmed and frustrated. Your environment directly affects your moods, atti-

tudes, and emotions. Stress-related illnesses cost the
United States $300 billion per year.

- **DISTILLS THE IMPORTANT FROM THE UNIMPORTANT.** Without a system, you will deal with large amounts of extraneous material. Just as we only wear a small percentage of our clothes,
we only use a small percentage of information that crosses
our desks.

An organized desk sends this important message to other
people: "I've got it together." Visualize your desk in your mind.
What does it "say" to others? That you are overwhelmed by work?
That you are disorganized and therefore not too competent? That
you obviously have trouble making decisions, since you can't decide what to do with anything? The next time someone walks
over to your cluttered desk and makes a joke about the mess, you
might want to listen. Regardless of what excuses you offer, your
desk says a great deal. Your newly organized desk will now say
that you are professional, competent, decisive, efficient, productive, and in control. No matter what you've seen on coffee cups,
a clean desk is *not* the sign of an empty mind.

ORDER quiz item #23:

> 23. I know how organize "pending" items or papers requiring
> future action.

Honey, Where Did You Put the Plane Tickets?
Have you ever filed a piece of paper so well that you hid it from
yourself? "I just wanted to put it somewhere safe," you explain.
Many people are unsure where to keep important papers. If you

pick up a piece of paper and say to yourself, "I need to act on this, but not for two more weeks," you don't want to file it, do you? What would happen then? You'd forget to do it! Out of sight, out of mind.

Where do you put a agenda for a meeting two weeks away? Where do you put an invoice so you remember to pay it in three weeks? Where do you put those plane tickets you don't want to lose? Where do you put the birthday card (that you managed to buy on time) so you remember to send it? If you're like most people, you put it on your desk! Where you can see it. Where the piles grow as if you'd poured fertilizer on them and soon cover the birthday card.

Bad habits

First I'll tell you where *not* to put an action item. You don't want to file it in your permanent files, because you'd forget to take action. You don't want to put it in a stackable tray because "out of sight" becomes "out of mind." You don't want to carry it around in your organizer for two months because you'll become weighed down by paper. You don't want to tack it on your bulletin board because soon you'll become blind to it and forget it's there.

You need a system that will remind you which papers require your action *today* and allow you to *forget* the rest until their time. What's the answer? This indispensable system is called a "tickler file" (also called a calendar file, a bring-up file, a suspense file, or a pop-up file).

A tickler file reminds us about items needing our attention each day. Think of it as a calendar for paper. Compare it to a well-managed, well-sorted in-basket. It contains papers that are pending, need your attention, or require you to act in some way—papers you can't toss, delegate, file, or work on right now.

Your tickler file stores what *would* have been piles sitting on the desktop, the credenza, or some other surface.

Here is the procedure for creating one:

1. Obtain forty-three hanging (Pendaflex) folders. Label thirty-one folders 1 through 31 for the days of the month; label the remaining twelve January through December. Hang them in an accessible file drawer, a file box or container, or an expandable file. The only requirement is that it be close to your work area. Put the numbered folders behind the current month, similar to a calendar. The current month is the first folder, and the current day is the second folder. The rest hang in order. For example, on March 15, your file would look like this, front to back:

March

15
16 . . .
31

April

1
2 . . .
14

May . . .
February

2. File any papers that are pending or require your action (assuming the above arrangement).

   • A conference registration ticket for June 3 would be filed in the June folder (months act like holding files for anything further than 31 days out).

- Plane tickets for July 4 would be filed in July.
- A printed email message requiring your action next week would be filed in the appropriate day.
- A meeting agenda for March 20 would be placed in the folder marked 20.
- A copy of a written delegation item due March 28 could be filed in the folder marked 24 to remind you to follow up with the person.
- A birthday card for April 11 would be filed in April 7 or 8; a birthday card for May 18 would be filed in the May file.
- An invoice due on March 31 could be filed in March 25 or 26 (or, if you pay all your bills at the same time, the bills would all go together on the date you want to pay them).
- A return merchandise slip could be filed two months out so you remember to compare it against your credit card statement.

When deciding where to file papers, always ask yourself, "When do I need to see this item again so that I can complete it before it's due?" Don't file items on the day they are due unless you can do it that day! Some items have fixed deadlines; others require you to pick the next action date. If you have an item that qualifies for the calendar file but is too big, put a note in the file that refers to the location of the material, such as on your bookcase or in a file cabinet.

3. At the end of each day, plan for the following day. Before you leave work or before you go to bed, take out the folder for the next day. For example, on March 15, you would remove the folder marked 16. Take out the contents and refile any papers you're not going to get to. Move the empty folder behind the next month. Record the tasks on your to-

do list. Put the papers in a "priority tray" (not your in-box) on top of your desk. At the end of the day, reevaluate any paper left in the priority tray, and refile in the tickler file. On the last day of each month, review the next month's folder and sort the contents into the numbered folders.

Putting the tickler to use

A tickler file is the single most important thing you can use to organize your papers (email systems will be discussed in Chapter 8). It allows you to pace yourself better, eliminates piles from surfaces, and keeps all your reminders in one place. After you adjust to it, you gain confidence that items filed out of sight will pop up again.

Customize and tailor the contents to fit your individual needs. Find a system that works for you. For example, you can use two tickler files (one at work and one at home), or you can transport personal papers from home and incorporate everything into your work file. Frequent travelers can use an expandable accordion file that fits in a briefcase.

The biggest thing you can do to goof up a tickler file is to forget to look in it! Purchase a page-a-day cartoon calendar and put one cartoon in each daily folder. Each day, post that day's cartoon. If you notice the cartoon isn't current, you'll realize you've forgotten to check your tickler file.

24. I maintain organized and orderly files; I can find essential information when I need it.

Piles and Piles of Files

Most people dread filing. I say "most" because I have actually met some strange individuals who enjoy it. I've even tried hiring them to do my filing for me! Here are some of the common complaints I hear about filing:

1. I don't know what to call this file.
2. I don't remember what I called the file, so I create a duplicate.
3. I'm unsure about the order and placement of my files in the drawer.
4. My filing pile gets so large it becomes overwhelming.
5. My files are like black holes—once a paper enters, it's rarely seen again.

If the above statements sound familiar, your files need improvement. Here are some questions to ask yourself: "Does it take me longer than three minutes to find something in my files?" "Have I ever filed anything so well that I hid it from myself?" "Are any of my file folders straining from the weight of the contents?" If you can answer "yes" to any of these questions, keep reading. I can't promise this section will make you *enjoy* filing more, but it will make the task more *manageable*.

First of all, not all files are created the same! You shouldn't attempt to have one large filing system, but multiple systems based on their content and frequency of use. There are actually four different types of files.

ACTIVE/DYNAMIC FILES. These files are accessed once a day at a minimum. A good example is the tickler file. Active files move and change; stuff doesn't just "hang around" in there. Because of the frequency of use, active files should be kept in immediate proximity to you, preferably in a small filing drawer to your immediate left or right.

PROJECT/CLIENT FILES. These files are accessed a minimum of once per month. Examples include meetings you attend frequently, committees in which you're active, reports you run at least once a month, and newsletters you write each month. Because you access them frequently, they should be handy and readily accessible in your office. Each time you begin a new project or join a new committee, label a new manila folder. Many people keep project files in a "step" file on the desk. Others use the other desk drawer. Still others use hanging file racks that sit on the desk, with hanging files (Pendaflex) instead of manila folders. Large reference documents that you refer to while using a project folder can be kept in binders in your bookcase.

REFERENCE/PERMANENT FILES. These files are accessed a minimum of once per year. Examples include completed projects, prior-year budgets, personnel information, and other records. Because you don't need to access them very frequently, they don't have to be immediately on hand. You can put them in a filing cabinet in the back of your office or in a lateral file behind your chair.

ARCHIVE/HISTORY. By definition, these files haven't been accessed in more than a year. Take a deep breath . . . and store these items outside of your office. Purging is essential. The only alternatives to purging are getting bigger office space, adding a room to your home, or buying more filing cabinets. Throw away or recycle any unnecessary duplicates, outdated draft copies, and otherwise unnecessary materials *before* you clutter your life with more filing cabinets. If you haven't touched a file in four weeks, move it to your central files instead of keeping it at your desk. Once a year, archive the central files you no longer need except as a record of history. For example, move all your tax returns and related receipts/documents to archive files in your basement. Keep only current information in your central files.

Additional filing tips

USE A NOUN AS THE FIRST WORD IN THE FILE. One of the biggest problems we face in filing is that we title our files as we speak. In the English language, an adjective always precedes the noun (English is one of the only languages that does this). For example, if you had several insurance files, you might call them "Automobile Insurance," "Homeowners Insurance," and "Medical Insurance." When you file these alphabetically, they promptly become separated and spread out in the drawer. Even worse, you can't remember, "Did I call that 'automobile' insurance, or 'car' insurance?" You would logically want to go to *one* place in your files to find all information related to insurance. So a simple solution is to put the *noun* first, such as "Insurance, Auto"; "Insurance, Homeowners"; "Insurance, Medical." It looks funny, but when you file alphabetically, all of your insurance files will be together. You can title files by subject, by name, by customer, by project, numerically, geographically, or chronologically—whatever best fits your needs. Ask yourself, "What is this file *about*?"

USE SUBCATEGORIES. Most people have either too few or too many files in their filing system. Start with a major title for a new project, such as "Party, Christmas." When the folder gets to be about two inches thick, sort it into subheadings such as "Food, Facilities, Invitations" using manila folders. If the contents are too large for a manila folder, place another hanging folder immediately behind the main folder. Identify each file by its own name, and then file alphabetically in your file drawer. Just remember to file papers in the broadest possible category. Thick files are easier to deal with than thin. Instead of having numerous files with only a few pieces of paper in each one, consolidate all related materials under the most practical major category.

COLOR CODE. If you have a large quantity of one type of file—clients, projects, forms, and administrative files—assign each type a different color to make the system easier to use and more attractive. Identify each major section of your files by color: Clients—orange, Projects—yellow, Forms—green, Administration—red, etc. Use whatever colors make sense to you. Color-coding makes accessing files and refiling easier and less time-consuming. It also can help identify misplaced files.

ADD INFORMATION CONSISTENTLY. When you add information to a file, don't just stick it anywhere in the folder or you will have to dig through the entire file to locate a particular piece of paper. Consistently add information to the front or back of the folder to create a chronological order. It doesn't really matter which method you choose, so long as you're consistent. I prefer to file paper in the front of the file. That way, when I open a file on my desk, the papers on top are the most recent.

FILE AT LEAST WEEKLY. Once you have your system set up, don't let your filing build up. That's what causes trouble. If you wait a month before filing, your pile is a mile high, and it's hard to catch up. File at least once a week on a day and at a time when you experience low energy.

ORDER quiz item #25:

> 25. I sort, process, and store information quickly and easily.

The "6-D" Information Management System

You know you need to learn this method

- if you use your email and voicemail to store things you need to do but don't have time to address right now;
- if your brain swims with all kinds of ideas and things you need to do;
- if the location of the stacks of paper on your desk determines their contents. (The upper left-hand corner of the desk means something different from the upper right-hand side of the desk. And, of course, items angled sideways carry an altogether different meaning.); or
- if you are constantly searching for things. You find yourself saying things like, "I know it's right here."

Each piece of paper, each idea in your head, each email, each voicemail, and each fax is simply a piece of information. There are only six things that you can do with any piece of information:

1. DISCARD. Get rid of it. Permanently. Many people have a fear of dumping. Have you ever said, "I'd better keep this because you never know . . . it might come in handy sometime"? Or, "I threw something away once, and wouldn't you know it, I needed it again the very next day?" We've all had this experience before. However, remind yourself:

   - This doesn't happen often, compared to how many times I discard paper and never need it again.

- Because I have not organized in a long time and my backlog is severe, I probably wouldn't have found it again anyway.
- Almost everything is replaceable and I could get another copy if I really needed one.

2. **DELEGATE.** Refer the item to someone else. Get it going "out the door" to that person right away. We cannot manage by doing it all ourselves in the Information Age, so give away as much as possible.

3. **DO.** If you have enough time to complete, review, sign, or reply to the item, do it immediately. Then get it going back out the door to the requester. This step is generally for action items that will only require two to five minutes to complete. Investing the time now will save time in the long run because you won't review the item over and over again.

4. **DATE.** If you can't work on an item immediately, determine when you need to see it again and put in your tickler file. Keep bulky reference information in a binder on your bookcase or in a hanging file, and just put a reminder in your tickler. Email can be printed and filed it in your tickler or moved (dragged) to your task list.

5. **DRAWER.** File things you can't toss, delegate, or act on (project information or reference items only).

6. **DETER.** Halt the information; keep it from getting to you in the first place. Stop any reports, memos, letters, minutes, catalogues, magazines, and junk mail that you don't need or have time to read.

If you think of these options each time you look at a new piece of information, it will create one seamless system, rather than several disjointed methods for individual items. The chart below lists the six Ds with equivalent action steps.

Six Ds	Paper	Email	Voicemail
1. Discard	Toss, shred, recycle	Delete	Delete
2. Delegate	Route, interoffice mail	Forward	Forward
3. Do	Complete in 3 minutes	Reply	Respond
4. Date	Tickler file	Print and file in tickler or move to tasks or move to calendar	Write on to-do list, phone log, in planner, or create new tasks
5. Drawer	Project file or "to be filed" bin for reference files	Save in personal folder or on hard drive	Transcribe and file in appropriate file
6. Deter	Get off distribution lists	Use filters or unsubscribe	Change your greeting

Getting started with the "6-D" system

1. Get your organizing equipment ready. Surround yourself with the trash can, recycling bin, envelopes, routing labels, tickler file, planner, "to be filed" folder, phone, and pen.

2. Get your hanging file folders and set up the tickler file.

3. Post a three-by-five-inch card with the six Ds printed on it. Process new information (paper, email, voicemail) through the 6-D system.

4. Take thirty minutes each day to organize old piles of information.

5. Start with your paper in-box, because it's usually the newest. Touch each piece of paper and run it through the 6-D system.

6. Start sorting through the miscellaneous piles of paper that have accumulated in your office, thirty minutes at a time.

7. When your paper piles are gone, start going through old emails, bottom up, and run them through the 6-D system. (For ideas on reports, articles, or other reading items, see Chapter 7, item 61. For more email tips, see Chapter 8, item 76.)

ORDER quiz item #26:

26. I discard information quickly and easily.

Conquering the Fear of Dumping

When you pick up a piece of paper, do you say, "I might need this again someday?" If you have a difficult time throwing things away, you are suffering from the fear of dumping!

The "Depression" mentality

Some of this fear of dumping was programmed into our heads as children by things our parents taught us. During the Great Depression, our grandparents or parents were taught that everything had value. Reuse everything. Never throw anything away. Waste not; want not. Eat everything on your plate, because the poor children in China are starving! Sound familiar?

Were those messages valid and important back then? Absolutely! Our well-meaning parents raised us and passed those messages along. Now we find ourselves in the middle of the Information Age, where we discover that the Internet gives us anything we could possibly want, right at our fingertips. We are operating on old truths and principles that aren't valid anymore. We have created a society of packrats who can't throw anything away! This phenomenon has been dubbed "the Depression mentality."

Changing the wiring

Part of getting organized is learning to rewind the old tapes we're playing in our heads and rerecord them with messages that are more productive for today's realities. That means asking these tough questions:

- Do I really have time to read this?
- Is this something I'm going to need in the near future?
- What's the worst thing that could happen if I throw this away?
- Can I get another copy if I need it?

Some people think they have the only copy of this item. With today's huge paper and electronic distribution lists, that's rarely true. In my years of teaching productivity, I believe it comes down to ego. "It would be so embarrassing if I needed this again and had to go ask somebody for it!" Who cares! It takes a lot less time to ask someone for one item than to file two hundred you'll never need. You've got to get tough with tossing. The biggest key to getting organized is being ruthless about what you decide to keep. If once a month or a couple of times a year you say, "Darn, I probably should have held on to that," then you've succeeded. I'd much rather have you err on the side of throwing too much away than not enough. Because what's the alternative? Keeping more than you need and investing too much time, energy, and resources into saving things.

Perhaps your company or the government requires you keep it; perhaps it's part of a customer's file; perhaps it is pertinent information for a project you're working on. No problem. But if you don't have a good answer to the question "Why should I keep this?" then toss it.

Good candidates for tossing include:

- Catalogues you never order from.
- The envelope your mail came in, after you make sure you have all the pertinent information.
- A cultural arts calendar for your local community center. (You have never once attended an event there, but someday maybe you will.) If you did decide to go to an event, you could get the information by calling the center, checking the website, or opening the newspaper.
- Most everything labeled "bulk rate."
- Utility and other service statements. Once you verify that your payment was received, you can toss last month's statement. Unless you are self-employed and can write a por-

tion of your home expenses off as business expenses, only keep the current statement. Any other information you require can be obtained simply by calling the company.

- Articles you read and loved and cut out. If you file that article away, are you ever going to read it again? Read it, weep, laugh, tell your significant other about it, stick it in the mail to a friend, or pat yourself on the back because you had the exact idea two years ago. Then get rid of it.

ORDER quiz item #27:

27. I touch paper only once; I'm very decisive.

The Paper Shuffle

Indecision, by its very nature, causes clutter and creates pile-ups. Many of the piles on your desk and old messages in your email represent decisions you've put off.

The keys to successful information management are:

Having a "home" for each type of information • sorting the information using the 6-D system • deciding immediately where each item belongs, and • putting it away immediately.

You don't have to *do* anything with it; you do, though, have to put it where it belongs. *Any* decision is better than no decision at all. You can always change your mind later.

SUPERGLUE RULE. The first time you pick up a piece of paper from your in-box, you have to pretend it has superglue on it. It's now stuck to your hand, and you cannot put it down until you do one of the six Ds. The same concept applies to email and voicemail: the first time you read a message or listen to a voicemail, you have to pretend that it's "stuck" to your eyes or ears. You can't save it in your in-box; you must be decisive about where it goes. If this helps, remember "OHIO"—Only Handle It Once.

START-TO-FINISH RULE. Do you ever sort a big pile into smaller piles and then go back through the smaller piles again? If you read an item and think, "This needs to go to Joe," don't put it into a "delegate" pile. Immediately pick up a sticky note or routing label, dash off a quick note, put it in an interoffice envelope, and get it going out the door to Joe all in one step. Get used to doing things from beginning to end. By cutting out the intermediary steps, you'll save lots of time.

EMPTY INBOX RULE. The key is to keep your in-boxes empty each day—paper, email, and voicemail! Again, you don't have to complete all the items; you simply have to put them away.

ORDER quiz item #28:

> 28. I avoid using sticky notes or scraps of paper to record phone messages or tasks.

Are You a Scrapper?

Another area of organization deals with all those little pink telephone slips, messages, and sticky notes you accumulate all day. Have you ever found yourself unable to understand your own scribbled notes or unable to even locate a message taken earlier in the day? Do you ever have trouble remembering if you returned a phone call or if someone called you back? Some people miss appointments or forget to return phone calls because they cannot locate the original message.

My husband, John, used to be a great example of this. He is

the director of marketing and operations in our company. Before John came to work with me, he was a letter carrier for the U. S. Postal Service. He dealt with thousands and thousands of individual pieces of mail and magazines and packages every day. His daily to-do list looked like this: 1. Deliver the mail. He had a pile of mail there in the morning; he delivered it; it was gone. He didn't take work home at night. (They'd come after him if he did!)

His new focus on marketing mainly involved phone calls, sending out materials, following up with clients, and tracking any telephone or email contact. It quickly became obvious that he had no previous organization or time management training. I recognized that he was a "scrapper." He wrote miscellaneous notes to himself all day with phone numbers and reminders to call people. Covered with sticky notes, his desk looked like a sea of yellow.

Consolidating your system

The "separateness" of this scrapper system made it easy for him to get disorganized. Where do you keep all those pieces of information? In John's case, I taught him to use a paper planner (we prefer FranklinCovey), and he got used to keeping it handy and available at all times. You've got to create some sort of system that lets you immediately capture important information. (See Chapter 1, item 7, for more ideas.)

Sticky notes shouldn't be used for phone calls or messages. They also shouldn't be used for anything that requires your action or that you want to keep as a permanent record. Well, then, what *should* they be used for?

- To write down a fax number (if you stick it to the back of the document, you can type it in while it's facedown in the machine)

- To make comments on a document (contracts, letters, proposals, reports, etc.) when you can't mess up the original
- To use in a team meeting for flowcharting or brainstorming, where pieces of the process need to be easily and quickly moved around
- To write common messages ("At lunch," "Please do not disturb," "Working at home today," "In a meeting," etc.) to post on your office door or cubicle wall
- To remind you to do something as you're leaving your house in the morning, such as "Don't forget to pick up mail" or "Pack Meagan's lunch"
- To create a separate list that can be carried with you, such as grocery lists, errand lists, and shopping lists
- To write affirmations to yourself or thank-you notes to stick on a coworker's computer screen
- To bookmark pages in a cookbook, magazine, or catalogue, so you can refer back to the pages

ORDER quiz item #29:

> 29. I know the contents of every cabinet, drawer, and storage space in my home and office.

Poisoning the Packrat

Do you have a drawer at work you hate to open? A closet at home that gives you shivers? Get these areas under control once and for all! The question is, how?

What process do you currently use to organize an area? If you're like most people, you will pull everything out of the drawer or closet, dump it on the floor, attempt to sort and organize it, run out of time and steam, and shove it all back in again!

Now you have a half-done project, and your drawer or closet may even be more disorganized than before.

The five-box method

Instead, plan a one-hour de-clutter assault. Get five sturdy boxes and label them.

PUT AWAY—Contains items that should be put away. Use this box for items that are in the wrong place, such as shoes left in the middle of the living room, a sweater that belongs to a friend, or dirty dishes in the bedroom. Use the last ten minutes of the allotted time to empty the box of its contents. Wander through the house putting items where they belong. Or, place the route box in a high-traffic location when you're done. Post a "lost and found" notice over the box, advising owners that items unclaimed after forty-eight hours will be donated to charity. Then do it! Watch how fast items get put away.

GIVE AWAY—Contains items that are in good repair that you no longer want, need, or use. If the item has not been used or worn in a year, there's a good chance it won't be used or worn in the future. Give these items to charity, or if the item is too good to give away, sell it at a garage sale. What is clutter to you may be valuable to someone else.

STORE—Contains items you don't use on a regular basis that need to be boxed up for storage. These items will be used infrequently, but they have a high likelihood of being needed again. Examples are holiday supplies, maternity clothes, and children's toys. You may need to divide the contents this box up into several individual boxes when you're through, or sort contents into appropriate already existing storage boxes. If you are storing important items, like photos, birth certificates, and wills, you should purchase a fireproof box or move them to a safe deposit box. Ask yourself, "If my house burned down, what could I *not* replace?"

TOSS—Contains items that are broken, old, worn, or in bad repair. This is the throwaway box. Also toss items if you don't know what they are, where they came from, or why you have them. This could include items like keys to cars you no longer own, padlocks you don't know the combinations to, business cards with wrong phone numbers, pictures of people you don't know, and dead ink pens.

BELONGS HERE—Contains items that will go back into the drawer, closet, or cabinet you're organizing. What a concept! Something might actually be in the correct location. Keep it in this box until you've sorted out the other items. Then spend another de-clutter assault organizing it back into the proper place.

Deciding what to keep

Ask yourself:

- Have I used it in a year?
- Would I save this if my house were on fire?
- Does this item have personal value to me?
- When is the last time I held it, remembered I had it, or used it?
- Do I keep it stored out of sight?
- Might I need this again in the future?

Eventually, *everything* may come in handy sooner or later. If you answered "no" to the first five questions and hesitate on this last question, just get rid of it.

Your "work space"

DESIGNATE YOUR HOME OFFICE. Find an inviting place in your home as your "office" to pay bills and sort mail. Just make sure it's convenient. If it's just never convenient to get there, it's likely that piles intended *for* the office will start forming in some other part of the house. Your desk should also be kept away from family traffic patterns. Don't sit down to pay your bills at the kitchen table knowing that your kids or spouse will be trooping by and interrupting you. Get creative in the placement of your home office. Some ideas I've heard include a walk-in closet converted into a home office, an unused alcove, a desk on a stairwell (where the stairs curve around before going up another level), a portion of the entryway or hallway (if it's large enough), a hideaway computer hutch in a seldom-used formal dining room, or an enclosed porch.

OFFICE ARRANGEMENT. The most ideal shape is a U or L shape. You don't want to have to turn completely around or get up to get what you need. A U shape lets you easily access your main work surface, computer and fax, and layout area for today's work and larger reference documents. A layout area doesn't have to be a piece of furniture. It could be a wall shelf or the top of a credenza or filing cabinet.

THE LAW OF REAL ESTATE. The surfaces on your desk are very valuable. Think of them as real estate. For any item to live on the surface of your desk, it has to pay rent. To pay rent, an item must be touched or used every day. For example, if you have a three-hole punch and don't punch papers with it every day, it should go in a drawer. Try hanging personal items on a wall or shelf or bulletin board rather than putting them on your desk.

ORDER quiz item #30:

> 30. I have a systematic plan to stay organized.

Principles for Organizing Success

Staying organized requires ongoing practice and planning. Here are tips to help you further reduce your amount of "stuff"—and stress!

De-clutter ideas

USE A TIMER. When it's time to begin your organizing task, take one item out at a time and put it into the appropriate box. If you're going to organize for one hour, set an egg timer for fifty minutes. When it buzzes, use the last ten minutes of your organizing session to put items away, put the charity items in the car, throw out the trash, and put boxes into storage.

FOCUS. Concentrate on finishing one organizing task at a time. Don't flit about like a butterfly, doing a bit of this and a bit of that. If you don't focus, you'll end up with a bunch of half-organized areas throughout your home or office and never get one thing quite finished.

When organizing, think of yourself like a postage stamp—stick to one thing until you get there!

When you're putting things away from an organizing project or de-clutter assault, *do not* stop to tidy a drawer or clean a closet. Just put the item in the right room or drawer and schedule the next de-clutter assault for another time.

ONE IN, ONE OUT. I used to have a huge collection of sweaters (gulp, about a hundred). "Hey," I rationalized, "I live in Colorado!" I soon realized that my hobby was creating a closet hazard. So I bought a beautiful Lane cedar chest and made a deal with myself that I could keep only the sweaters that would fit into it. So

I crammed about fifty in there, took a deep breath, and donated the least desirable ones to charity. Now before buying a new sweater, I give serious thought to which sweater would have to go.

TIME TESTING. Tag each of your clothing items with a date one year from now. As you wear each item, take the tag off. Anything left hanging in your closet that still has the tag on it when that date arrives goes! Also label every odd kitchen appliance with a piece of masking tape on the back. Again, write a reasonable date within which you must use the item or get rid of it.

USE CONTAINERS TO STORE SIMILAR ITEMS. Things that go together should be stored together, at home and work. Find boxes, baskets, toolboxes, and totes to organize common items such as batteries, crafts, makeup, home repair kits, tools, art supplies, cleaning supplies, gift-wrap, or fishing gear. Use duffel bags to store sports equipment, one sport per bag per person.

USE THE "BULLETIN BOARD" TECHNIQUE. Remember how our teachers used to change the bulletin boards every season and holiday? It instantly changed the "look," "feel," and "flavor" of the classroom. In the same way, you can change your home seasonally. Label boxes with the seasons or holidays, and rotate the knickknacks, collectibles, and heirlooms several times a year. This way they'll be "new" all over again, and you won't be overwhelmed by the amount of stuff in your home.

All of these tips and organizing techniques aside, I believe *the* most effective way to control clutter is to *say NO*—when someone offers you a piece of furniture or clothing or books or a new magazine subscription or anything you really don't want or don't have room for. Unless it's a major find, pass on it. That's why we have Wal-Mart. When we need something, we can go get it, rather than keeping things around "just in case." Don't play librarian at work or try to be the hero. Keep infrequently used items out of your office and retrieve them when needed.

CHAPTER FOUR

Mastering the "D" in Productive

DISCIPLINE

ARE YOU PERSISTENT IN COMPLETING your high-priority tasks *without* getting sidelined by menial activities? Do you put your nose to the grindstone each day, or do you only work hard when you're in the mood? Do you have a set of rules for yourself that govern your behavior and activity?

Discipline refers to your ability to maintain consistent, productive behavior. Many people tell some form of "I do really well one day, but then I get into a funk and can't get back on top of things." Sure, everyone has an "off" day. If you are self-disciplined, however, you exhibit *consistent* focus in your day-to-day work, even if you don't feel like it. Strive for the self-control and confidence gained when you enforce your own rules!

If you need work in this area, this chapter will show you how to correct and regulate yourself for the sake of improvement and personal productivity. You will learn to do what needs to be done and exercise restraint over your own impulses, emotions, and desires. Sometimes working on the *right* thing doesn't mean doing the *fun* thing. To be an exceptional performer in your organization, focus on high-value output, based on your job requirements.

DISCIPLINE quiz item #31:

> 31. I know my natural energy cycle and work effectively during peak times.

Taking Advantage of Your Prime Time

People have a natural time during the day when they feel "up" (prime time) and a natural time when they feel "down" (down time). Knowing which is which for yourself is an important productivity enhancer. During prime time, your brain is "on," your batteries are charged, and you're able to focus. During down time, your brain feels "slow"; it's difficult to muddle through your work.

I view my energy level like the dimmer switch my husband John recently put in our bathroom. People don't operate at "Off" and "On." They don't run full-tilt all day then sleep all night. It's not "0 percent" and "100 percent" but rather various levels all day. Most people tell me they can perform at optimum levels four to five hours a day.

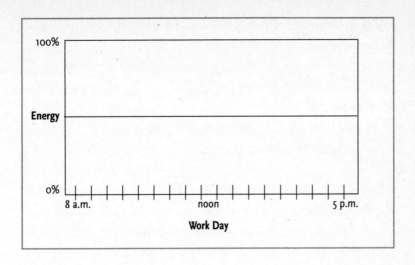

First, let's chart your energy levels. In the table above, notice that the vertical axis is marked "0%" to "100%" to represent your energy level as a percentage. The horizontal axis is marked in one-hour increments. If you arrive at work earlier than 8 a.m., please cross that out and write in your regular start time. Similarly, if you don't leave at 5 p.m., please cross that out and write in your end time.

Now plot your energy cycle. Think about where your energy level is when you first arrive at work in the morning. Draw a dot on the vertical axis where your energy level intersects with time. As the day progresses, draw a series of dots horizontally to show how your energy ebbs and flows. Then connect the dots and analyze your line chart.

Draw a dotted line at about the 75 percent energy level mark across your line drawing, above which represents your peak-productivity zone. Write these exact time ranges out to the side of your graph. These are your "expensive" hours because your brain is capable of doing higher-level activities in that range compared to other times during the day. It's important to know when you're in prime time because then you can get so much more done. Focus on:

- tasks of high value or importance
- critical decisions
- problem-solving or brainstorming activities
- complex or detailed thought

When you work on these activities during down time, it takes much, much longer and is much, much more painful than during prime time. But the last thing you feel like doing when you're "up" is working on a report, writing a proposal, or analyzing figures. If you wait until your energy is going down, though, you've lost the opportunity to get the task done quickly. The trick is self-discipline. Resist the urge to do "fun, easy, trivial" things or talk to your friends during your prime time.

I actually have two prime times: morning and early afternoon. When I'm in prime time, I need to make marketing calls, because I need to be "up" and on top of the conversation. I also respond to Requests for Proposals (RFPs) sent by prospective clients in prime time. I want to write quickly and succinctly. My prime time is the key opportunity for that work.

Similarly, I listen to my body when I'm in down time. When I feel my energy level waning, a quick glance at the clock usually tells me why. I know I need to get up, stretch, and perhaps go for a quick walk around the block, eat an energy snack, or make a cup of tea. Then I go back and work on different activities, not necessarily ones with low priority, but those that don't require the brainpower of the prime time tasks. Sometimes, I purposely let voicemail pick up my calls when I know I'm in down time and won't be as articulate as I'd like to be with a client. If I don't listen to my body's signals and respond appropriately, I get a rip-roaring headache, preventing me from taking advantage of my second prime time.

Once you know when your prime time is, protect it for all you're worth! Listen to yourself and rest when you're "down."

DISCIPLINE quiz item #32:

> 32. I'm good at controlling perfectionism, realizing that some things are "good enough."

My Way or the Highway!

Have you ever delegated a task to someone, then taken it back because the person didn't do it the "right way"? Which of course is *your* way, because your way is the perfect way. You may suffer from the disease of perfectionism. Do these phrases sound familiar?

"If I let someone else do this, it won't be done correctly."
"If you want anything done right, you have to do it yourself."
"If you can't do something right, it's not worth doing at all."

If you hear yourself saying these things, be careful. It's true that if you truly believe your way is the only "right" way, you're going to garner resentment from others. If you demand that people perform your way, according to your perfect standards, many people will be content to let you do things *your* way, leaving you wondering why you have so much on your plate! Yes, perfectionism will make you crazy and others around you nuts as well.

I know. I am what I fondly call a "recovering perfectionist." I've learned not every task deserves my best effort. One reader said it beautifully: "I need help learning when to say 'Enough.' Every 'A' doesn't have to have a '+' after it, and every 'Wow' doesn't have to have a '!' after it. I don't want to say that I am a perfectionist—I see it as striving for excellence and not wanting to settle for less. I think this can be detrimental to my time management and frustrating for my colleagues and bosses."

I think my kids may have helped me "recover." When Meagan, my first-born, was too young to clean up after herself, I would clean up her playroom at the end of the night. The books would go back into the bookcase, on the correct shelf, in order by size, height, and topic. Crazy, huh? Did that increase customer satisfaction in some way? Now that I have three kids, as long as they stuff them back on a shelf somewhere, I'm happy, because it's fine the way it is.

High standards versus unrealistic expectations

One of the early lessons I learned was to distinguish between a high standard and an unrealistic expectation. Some things require high standards and have to be done "just so." Most expectations we impose on others, however, are simply picky-picky standards without merit.

There's a big difference between being disciplined, careful, and attentive, and being obsessive. The difference is in focusing on the *purpose* of your efforts. Look at everything in terms of the big picture. To the extent that the details enhance and promote your overall purpose, give them your time and energy. To the extent that the details detract from, or even replace, the original purpose, let them go.

A seminar participant told me that his mother was so obsessive when he was a kid that he couldn't play ball on the grass because it would mess up the lawn. She also was a perfectionist about keeping her house clean. They had a white sofa in the living room, but he couldn't sit on it because it might get dirty. If a chair was out of place slightly, he had to move it back. He couldn't play freely, his friends were uncomfortable, his family didn't feel at home, and she was a wreck. Nothing is more wasteful than worrying and fretting over trivial details.

Keep your life's purpose clearly in mind, and make the details your servant rather than your master. Eliminating picky-picky standards will make life more bearable for everyone involved.

When the situation *requires* high standards, keep your expectations high. For example, if you overheard a pilot saying, "Well, I landed nine out of ten planes last week," you'd worry slightly if that person was piloting your plane. As a professional, you must demand the best if it's required. In other situations, when it *really doesn't matter,* be flexible and let small mistakes go. Ask yourself, "Is this acceptable?" Perhaps a team member performed a task differently than you might have, but it was perfectly satisfactory given the circumstances. Learn to trust and let others do the work their way, even though it may not be the way you would have done it.

Becoming flexible

ASSIGNMENTS. I had a boss who prided himself on his writing ability and insisted on reviewing every single document we wrote, even internal memos circulated only in our department. They came back littered with red marks. But the only thing that changed was style. Was it really necessary for him to change my writing style, sentence structure, and word choice to reflect his preferences? He should have asked himself, "Is this document technically correct? Is it understandable?" If it's acceptable, who cares how it's worded! It's no wonder he worked sixty hours a week and had a heart attack.

HOUSEWORK. Do your high standards in housework keep family members from helping you? Are you not satisfied even when they help? Does your young son offer to set the table, and instead of being easygoing and flexible in your standards, you berate him because the fork is in the wrong spot? See if he ever takes the initiative again.

RELATIONSHIPS. Have you ever managed to claim a small victory by getting your sweetie to pay the bills or perform a small chore, and then complain that he or she did it incorrectly? I have a friend whose husband offered to go to the grocery store (normally her responsibility) so we could get a cup of coffee. Upon our return, she rifled through the bags and started berating him for buying the wrong type of peanut butter, getting cheese curls, and not using the coupon she had cut out. At some level, isn't peanut butter just peanut butter? When good enough will do, let it go.

Benefits to the recovering perfectionist

When you're able to let go of small things instead of being bothered by them, there aren't as many situations that provoke you to speak up. You'll feel no need to mention the occasional blooper; you just let it pass. Strive toward performance criteria that are adaptive, realistic, and attainable. When good enough will do, leave it alone. People will appreciate not having to conform to your way of doing things. People don't like being told they have to change or that they're not good enough. Role model high standards when appropriate, and others will be inspired to follow your example.

Besides letting up on others, we must let up on the demands we place on ourselves. Perfectionism is not a positive character trait, to be worn like a medal. By its definition, perfectionism is unattainable. So if you call yourself a perfectionist, you have a particularly unrealistic standard for your behavior. You will *never* achieve the levels you demand of yourself. Your attempts at perfectionism will affect your feelings about yourself in negative, undesirable ways. You inflate the importance of mistakes, critical feedback, and minor flaws. You distort their significance. Instead, relax. You're bound to make mistakes. Learn from them, and then let them go. You'll find you're able to accomplish much more as well.

DISCIPLINE quiz item #33:

> 33. I avoid putting things off or waiting until the last minute.

Can We Talk About This Later?

Well, I guess we've put it off long enough. Time to talk about a tough issue. A reader asks, "Laura, I work hard all day, I'm organized, and I control time wasters. So why can't I seem to get on top of things?" Hmmm . . . could it be that you're busy working hard on the *wrong* things? Do you have a little nagging voice in your head saying, "I've got to get started on this"?

Upon further discussion, the explanation for his less-than-stellar productivity was a lack of discipline in doing what he knew he should be doing. He's like many of us. We put off doing what we know we should be doing and have an impending sense of doom hanging over our heads all day . . . week . . . month.

It's human nature to avoid pain. When you put off a task, it rewards you twice: first, you get to do something else more fun and second, you don't have to do the undesirable chore. When the task comes back to haunt you, though, it only punishes you once. So it's easy to see why procrastination wins out! Unfortunately, in the end, the cost of putting things off far outweighs the reward. The pain is ultimately worse than the pleasure you derived from procrastinating. You end up operating in perpetual crisis mode, a consistent state of drama.

Here's a quick quiz. Let's say you have a to-do list with only ten items on it for the entire day. You get a period of time in which to accomplish one thing on your list. What do you do first? If you are like the majority of folks, you'll pick something easy, something fun, or something trivial . . . something you can check off. Doesn't it feel good to check things off? It gives you a real sense of satisfaction. Another block of time, another item checked off! Wow, look at that. You're already one-fifth of the way through the list. It's now the end of the day. Let's say you have nine out of ten items checked off. The one that's left is the most important item, the hardest, the yuckiest, or the most valuable. The one you've been putting off for a week.

"But look how productive I was!" you argue. "Nine out of ten things checked off my list!" You may have been brainwashed to think that productivity equals check marks. Therefore, you must learn to detach your sense of accomplishment from "completions." Productivity does not equal quantity. Instead, use the value of the items completed as your gauge. If you completed four out of ten items, and one of the four was the most important of all, you were more productive than if you completed nine but left out the most important one.

Your worth as an employee will consistently outpace your coworkers' worth if you spend your time focusing on the critical few tasks that lead to the highest performance, value, and output.

Convinced you need to stop procrastinating? Here are a few questions and tips to get you started:

IS THE TASK OVERWHELMING? Forget waiting for a "block of time." That no longer exists. Instead of viewing the task as one huge project, break it down into manageable chunks you can schedule over a period of a week or two. A twenty-hour project can be seen as ten two-hour tasks. Getting it down on paper can help you see how to best approach the project. The key is to do *something* to move toward completion. If you need to focus without interruption, it's best to not work in your office.

IS THE TASK UNAPPEALING? Perhaps the task is boring or tedious. Post written reminders to yourself where you will be sure to see them: your bathroom mirror, car dashboard, or refrigerator. The rule is, If the sticky note falls off, you're still procrastinating. Schedule a five-minute appointment with yourself to begin the chore. When the designated time arrives, start working on the task. If you feel like stopping at the end of five minutes, you can stop. The only rule is you must schedule an additional five minutes for tomorrow. When you begin to see some progress, five minutes soon becomes ten, fifteen, twenty . . .

IS THE TASK TRIVIAL? If you're rewriting an item on your to-do list for the third day in a row—*stop!* Before you transfer that task, ask yourself why you haven't completed it. Perhaps other tasks with higher priorities have justifiably pushed it away. If the task seems unimportant, quickly do an analysis to determine if you can justify your procrastination. If the task is trivial, completely remove it from your daily to-do list and add it to your master to-do list. Review your master to-do list each month to see which items have changed priority. If you don't have to look at the item every day, you will stop feeling guilty and stressing out over not getting it done.

IS THERE NO ACCOUNTABILITY IN COMPLETING THE TASK? To solve procrastination for good, find yourself a "ruthless friend" (a person who likes you, but not too much). This could be a colleague, friend, coach, or your mother. Say what you're going to do, by when. Ask that person to remind you at set intervals and bug you about your progress. Sometimes going public creates self-imposed pressure to perform.

Jot down three things you've been procrastinating on (item), why you've been putting it off (cause), one idea about how you can get started (action), and by when you will have the task completed (due). Writing an action plan or giving yourself a good swift kick in the pants may be just what you need!

DISCIPLINE quiz item #34:

> 34. I force myself to slow down when necessary; I know speed can be counterproductive.

What's the Rush?

Elbert Hubbard, who wrote the famous essay "A Message to Garcia" in 1899 said, "If you want work done well, select a busy man; the other kind has no time." Peter Drucker topped it off with my favorite quote of all: "Nothing is less productive than to make more efficient what should not be done at all." Warp speed isn't required for every task; in fact, some things need to be done slowly. The only person who ever had his work done by Friday was . . . Robinson Crusoe!

When I landed my first job at TRW fresh out of college, I worked with a woman who resembled a celebrity being pursued by the paparazzi. In my naïveté, I thought she must certainly be a very important person. I later discovered she was considered one of the worst performers in the department and was sick quite frequently.

Why do people always have to be in such a hurry? When feeling rushed and frantic, they make more mistakes, deal with others poorly, and lose their ability to think clearly. When I conduct a training seminar in an organization that operates at a continual frenzy, people describe high stress levels resulting from poor de-

cisions, distrust, dishonesty, low morale, and dysfunctional meetings where no one can agree on a direction.

When you work, be unhurried but undeterred. Consciously
chosen, slowness is not the opposite of speed. It's the middle path
between *fast* and *inert,* the two extremes of time. It's simply being
normal. When you surrender to the apparent impossibility of the
tasks that will *never* be done—like filing, laundry, dishes, and
email—you get the feeling that you have time.

Decide, on purpose, *not* to be busy when it really doesn't matter. There's a season for everything: crops are harvested in the fall
and planted in the spring, babies are born and people die, and after day comes night. I'm not encouraging you to give up your
beeper, your cell phone, your email, and your voicemail. Just remember there are times to be busy and times to be still.

DISCIPLINE quiz item #35:

> 35. I determine what I will accomplish each day, rather than al-
> lowing other people to dictate my schedule.

Quit Bothering Me!

Today's employed professionals are feeling more overworked and
overwhelmed than ever before. Why? Start with the Internet and
add email. Get fewer people to do more work for longer hours in
tiny workspaces. Add efficiency and overtime demands coupled
with unrealistic deadlines. Throw in high stress levels, no time
with family, and reduced budgets. Stir and simmer. The result: a
lot of wigged-out employees.

That's the new reality. You can stay in your situation and do
nothing (that's not working). You could leave ("Are you crazy,

Laura, I've got a kid in college!"). You could try to change your employer (a futile effort—stress is everywhere). What you're left with is the possibility of changing your behavior.

Time management is self-management, activity management, and priority management. It's about you in relationship to the things you choose to do and people you choose to interact with.

We need new rules of engagement to help us deal more effectively with other people.

ELIMINATE THE "BABY DIAPER" SYNDROME. As you move up in responsibility and leadership, you'll have more people who want to proudly show you what they've "made." Because of low self-esteem, they need you to reinforce their importance. These people "CC" you on every email they send, clogging up your in-box with hundreds of messages. They hit "Reply to All" and send annoying "Me too!" or "I agree!" messages, adding nothing to the discussion. They schedule you for meetings where your approval isn't required; you're just there to smile at them.

We *must* get out of this "CYA" (need I spell it out?) mentality and cut down on the politics. Communicate to people that results will speak for themselves. Trust them to make decisions within their limits of authority and come to you only when they have problems. Mention the waste of time caused by CYA activities in your next meeting. Talk about the proliferation of courtesy copies on email. Give examples (without naming names) of the type of items you do *not* need to see. I guarantee you this will cut down on a lot of your wasted time. Don't feel guilty. Don't make excuses.

YOU AREN'T A BARTENDER OR SPOUSE. The workplace isn't a bar. We don't whine over our beer here. If you're a group or department leader, when employees come to you with a "problem," ask them about alternatives and their recommendations. If they have no idea, send them away until they come to you with alternatives. If they have alternatives and no recommendation, ask, "What would you do if I were on vacation for two weeks?" Develop problem-solving, creative employees who are capable of making decisions without you. If you don't, you're training them to believe that they aren't smart or capable enough to think for themselves or make decisions without your wave of approval.

When you read these guidelines, please don't gasp and think, "How rude! This would never fly. Others would never allow it." In my experience, your coworkers would be relieved if everyone abided by these rules. Share these time savers at your next staff meeting. Discuss some ideas with your boss. Initiate some changes.

Remember this: you train people how to treat you. If you continue to allow people to do things, you are implying permission and consent. It's your responsibility to open your mouth and request a change. Enforce changes a few times, and people will treat you differently as a result.

DISCIPLINE quiz item #36:

> 36. I work productively from my home office and avoid distractions.

Home, Sweet Home

Part- or full-time telecommuting is becoming more and more popular. After the September 11 attacks, many of my corporate HR clients fielded increased requests from employees to work from home. No surprise there. Telecommuting seems quite attractive, but many an employee has tried and failed with this arrangement. While it's nice to be free from the frequent interruptions you experience in a traditional office, working at a home office comes with its own set of distractions. Do you have what it takes to succeed?

Having discipline means that you're aware of your personal weaknesses and create rules about what you may and may not do during the day. After working from home for twelve years now, I've developed some working-from-home rules:

CONSTANTLY REINFORCE YOUR WORKING SITUATION. When friends call me in the middle of the day, I cheerfully say, "Hi! I'm so glad you called. I'm right in the middle of something; can I call you back after seven tonight?" My astute friends have finally figured out I won't talk during the day, unless it's an emergency. Similarly, if a family member calls, I tell them I'm busy with a deadline and I'll call back tonight. Just as we don't expect our employers to call at 9 p.m., we must set boundaries with our family while working.

ANSWER YOUR PHONE PROFESSIONALLY, AS YOU WOULD IN YOUR TRADITIONAL OFFICE. Even if you have only one line, answer it in your business voice during work hours. Say hello, and the name of your company or your name. This says to the caller that you're at work, not sitting around watching the soaps. I absolutely do not let any children touch my business line.

ALWAYS REFER TO THE PLACE WHERE YOU WORK AS YOUR OFFICE. I don't work from home. I work from an office in my home, one that is just as valid as an office in a big corporate center.

GO TO THE DOOR TO ANSWER NEIGHBORS' REQUESTS WITH A PORTABLE PHONE TO YOUR EAR. Whenever neighbors come to my door, I bring my portable phone and pretend I'm in the middle of a phone call with a business associate. I cover the mouthpiece and whisper, "I'll call you back." Instead of calling them back in five minutes, I call back after seven and apologize for the delay, saying that daytimes are really busy with work, but now I'm free. It's a friendly way to send a message. (Now I've told on myself; I hope they will laugh when they read this.)

DRESS FOR WORK. Media images may tell you it's okay to stay in your pajamas all day when you work from home. But some people just don't work productively if they don't get dressed. If *you* can, fine, but if you know you can't, get yourself ready first thing. As a bonus, dressing for work creates a professional image that will be a signal to your family that you are in the *office* and ready for *work*. I certainly don't mean you should wear a suit and tie, but getting neat and clean makes most people feel more professional.

GIVE SPECIFIC "BUSINESS" REASONS FOR TURNING DOWN REQUESTS. When someone approaches you with an unwelcome request on your time, turn him or her down by saying something like "I'd love to, but I have a major client presentation that day" or "Sorry, but I'm just finishing up a proposal." The message you're trying to convey is that your office is a place of work.

Your personal rules will vary a bit, but you've got to determine what they are and commit them to writing. Some people enjoy the flexibility of working from home occasionally so that they *can* get out and do some personal things. You can do a load of laundry or run an errand if you allot yourself the time and make up the hours in the evening.

What will your rules be? What will contribute to your success? What things must you stop doing in order to become more successful and more productive? Open a blank document and start typing!

> 37. I handle common, routine tasks on a daily basis so things don't pile up.

Clutter Control

Handling common tasks on a daily basis will keep them from getting out of hand. You may avoid doing certain things, because you dread the task so much. You might be doing it *too* infrequently, and it's more of a chore than it has to be.

FILING. If you put off this task long enough, it will seem like you poured fertilizer on the piles: they keep growing and growing. When you go to find a document in your files, you've got to search through the filing pile instead. When asked, most people tell me they do filing about once a month and absolutely dread the task. If you file each and every day, it won't pile up and only takes a few minutes. If you have something to file, put it away immediately without even setting it down. Who wants to spend hours filing when you can invest a few minutes a day, and it will never get out of hand?

TIDYING YOUR OFFICE AND HOME SHOULD IDEALLY BE DONE DAILY. I always put things away at the end of the day. How many times have you put something down "just for now," and that item was still sitting there a week later? Temporary places often become permanent places. It's better to put it away while it's in your hand, than to allow the clutter to accumulate in large piles.

LAUNDRY. With five people in our household, our laundry pile soon reaches the ceiling if we don't keep up with it. It only takes a cumulative fifteen minutes to toss a load in the washer, put it in the dryer, and fold the clothes as you take them out. After wasting a couple of Saturdays whittling down our laundry pile, we're more aware of the need to hack at it daily.

CLEANING. My housekeeper cleans our house every other week. However, after one week, the bathroom can get, well, gross. The glass shower doors start showing spots, mildew grows, the mirrors get spotted, and the toilets . . . need I explain that one? So I do some minor one-minute tasks daily, and the bathroom never gets yucky between cleanings. I spray shower cleaner on the doors and walls after every shower. I spray mildew cleaner on the grout at the bottom of the shower, so mildew never appears in the first place. I use pre-moistened disinfectant wipes to quickly wipe the countertops in bathroom and kitchen. I immediately dry any water splashes on the mirror and counter with a hand towel. With a few minutes invested each day, I'm able to keep the house tidy and presentable.

DISCIPLINE quiz item #38:

> 38. I arrive at appointments and meetings on time; in fact, I'm typically early.

The Early Bird Catches the Worm

A quiet amusement of mine is to watch the expression of people who arrive late for my time management seminars. Tails between their legs, these people shuffle in sheepishly mumbling something about traffic, while their friends tease, "How can you be late for a *time management class?*"

The number one complaint I receive from managers who hire me to coach their staff on performance is something along the lines of "the inability to meet deadlines, is always late, is constantly running behind, or he/she forgot."

There are actually three types of people I see:

1. "Late" people are typically perpetually late, for everything.
2. "On time" people typically arrive a minute or two ahead or behind the goal.
3. "Early" people are rare and generally arrive early to everything.

The legend of Victor Borge's famous comment in concert sums it up nicely. He was well into his performance when a woman came in late, fighting her way through the rows to her seat near the front. Borge stopped playing and as she proceeded—trampling over people, rustling, and disturbing her way to her seat—he said (much to her chagrin, as all eyes focused on her ill-timed arrival), "Excuse me, excuse me, excuse me." After she sat down, he walked over near where she was sitting and said, "Where are you from, ma'am?" "Fifty-seventh Street," she said. "Well, lady, I'm from Denmark and I was here on time."

People are much more irritated by lateness than we ever realize; it can dampen everything from promotions and raises to friendships. Late people crowd us, physically and mentally, all the time. We all hate the fact that their lateness undoes our schedule and disrupts our day. Showing up late for work or sending something in late, no matter how well done, still means a black mark against you.

I'm an Early, not because I'm so incredibly productive, but because I've discovered the benefits of being one and choose to be. For one of your productivity goals, I'd like to encourage you to become an Early. Why is it important to be early?

- You get the first choice of many things.
- You gain admiration and respect.
- You are able to relax and not sweat.

- You get good press and publicity.
- You get time while waiting to relax or read.

Being an Early makes you look competent and lets others know you can be depended on. Being a Late, however, makes people wonder if you'll come through this time. You'll always be bringing up the rear, never totally trusted, no matter how skilled you are. Even if you're an On Time, that's typical and boring. It just doesn't stand out. It's okay . . . just expected . . . yawn. Don't be simply "average."

- Being late says "I can't make deadlines." Being early says "I don't need deadlines."
- Being late says "I'm out of control." Being early says "I'm in control."
- Being late says "I can't look beyond the moment." Being early says "I look ahead."

So how do you become an Early? It has nothing to do with setting your watch five minutes fast and "fooling" yourself, because psychologically, you know it's five minutes fast and make up for it anyway. Keep your clocks on the correct time. It's less about time management and more about planning. In fact, this simple, inexpensive principle will actually *prevent* 50 percent or more of your "time management" problems.

Instead of thinking, "I begin speaking at 9 a.m.," my thoughts are this: "I should plan on arriving at 8 a.m. to set up and get prepared." Then I have to figure out how long it should take me to get there at eight, not nine! If I do arrive early and have some free time, I'm prepared. I have bills to pay, magazines to peruse, or thank-you letters to write. Before you relax each night, have your clothes selected, school papers signed, lunches made, briefcase packed, and schedule outlined.

Best of all, become an Early and you won't have "deadlines." They will become unnecessary because you've already completed things early. Deadlines were made for people who would not get things done without them. Work for the completion of a project or task, not for the deadline. Deadlines are often irrelevant, because the task gets put off until the deadline when it could have been done much sooner. Telling yourself you're "more creative under pressure" is just an excuse to procrastinate and becomes a self-fulfilling prophecy.

DISCIPLINE quiz item #39:

> 39. I avoid workaholism; I rarely work more than forty hours per week. I don't take work home with me, on vacation, or to bed.

Work to Live, or Live to Work?

Are you a conscientious employee, or are you compulsive about work? "Overwork is this decade's cocaine, the problem without a name," says psychotherapist Bryan Robinson, author of *Chained to the Desk: A Guidebook for Workaholics, Their Partners and Children, and the Clinicians Who Treat Them* (New York University Press, 1998). Workaholism, Robinson says, is "an obsessive-compulsive disorder that manifests itself through self-imposed demands, an inability to regulate work habits, and an over-indulgence in work, to the exclusion of most other life activities." Just as alcohol consumes the alcoholic, work consumes the workaholic. The clearest indication of workaholism, he argues, is simply the inability to turn work off.

On average, I'd say the professionals I interact with in the workforce put in between forty-five and fifty-five hours per week, even more if I factor in work at home and on weekends. According to the International Labor Organization (ILO), workers in America put in more hours than workers in any other country in the world. Something to be proud of, 'eh? Working 24/7 has become a badge of honor, a sort of competition. Is it time to question whether it's a badge worth wearing?

Characteristics of workaholics

Here are some common workaholic traits from recent research.

PERFECTIONISM: exibited by one who never feels like the work is "good enough," and labors long and hard to create optimal results.

TIME COMMITMENT: the amount of time one devotes to work; workaholics are so time-committed to their jobs that they tend to put less effort into spouse and family, friend, and leisure activities.

JOB OVER-INVOLVEMENT: one who devotes himself or herself wholeheartedly to productive projects and prefers to make constructive use of time; may even define job-unrelated tasks as working activities because workaholics often blur the distinction between business and pleasure.

STRESS: workaholics experience higher levels of stress than other individuals and may ignore the continual physical effects of stress on their bodies.

In addition to these research-based characteristics, I've observed some telltale signs of overwork in my seminar participants over the years. Here's a little quiz. Place a "Y" after each statement that fits you and an "N" after each statement that doesn't fit you:

1. I'm resentful of people who take time off.
2. I'm often absentminded; I forget my keys, deadlines, or commitments.
3. I don't have time to meet friends for lunch.
4. I have various physical ailments, including sleep problems, lingering colds, headaches, high blood pressure, etc.
5. I eat too much.
6. I don't exercise.
7. I'm no longer able to laugh at jokes; I feel I've lost my sense of humor.
8. I feel irritable and especially impatient toward people who interrupt my work.
9. I actually feel restless if I'm less than constantly busy.
10. My refrigerator is almost always empty, because there's no time to shop.
11. My thoughts about work preoccupy me all the time, even when I'm not working or when I'm trying to sleep.
12. I work extremely hard all day but wind up frustrated by what I haven't accomplished.
13. I feel tired all the time and generally lack energy.
14. I rarely turn my cell phone off.
15. I'm not involved in any volunteer activities or hobbies; work is the main thing that gives me pleasure.
16. My family and friends say I'm just not myself.

If you answered "yes" to more than five of these, you're a serious candidate for burnout and could be a workaholic. Realizing that you have a problem is the first step toward getting the help you need.

On the road to recovery

Unfortunately, workaholism has severe consequences:

- When studying the children of self-described workaholics, researchers found significantly higher rates of depression and anxiety for these children than those of non-workaholic parents.
- A survey by the American Academy of Matrimonial Lawyers cited preoccupation with work as one of the top four causes of divorce.
- Workaholics evidence more destructive behavior: more alcohol abuse, more extramarital affairs, and more stress-related illnesses.

How do you recover from this syndrome?

JOIN A LOCAL CHAPTER OF WORKAHOLICS ANONYMOUS (WA). WA is "a fellowship of individuals who share their experience, strength, and hope with each other that they may solve their common problems and recover from workaholism." To find a support group in your area, contact Workaholics Anonymous, World Service Organization, P.O. Box 289, Menlo Park, CA 94026–0289 or call (510) 273–9253.

CREATE A CLEAR LINE BETWEEN WORK AND FAMILY ACTIVITIES. Schedule events with your children, significant other, and family. Put each event on the calendar to force yourself to do it. Exercise. Volunteer.

PRACTICE GOOD MATH. Don't add a new activity to your life without eliminating one from your schedule that demands equal time and energy. Make some sacrifices in favor of your true priorities in life.

UNPLUG FROM TECHNOLOGY. Discipline yourself to check your email only a few times a day. Turn off your cell phone at home (unless you're an on-call doctor). Do you have to check your email early in the day, all day, and late at night?

Ultimately, the challenge is not yours or mine alone. As long as our culture rewards and honors those who work endless hours, and denies the cost of such choices, any individual attempts to shift the balance will remain an uphill battle. It might be time, inside and outside corporate America, to question whether the benefits outweigh the costs of permitting work to occupy more and more of our lives.

DISCIPLINE quiz item #40:

40. I work hard and put "my nose to the grindstone" every day.

An Honest Day's Work

Now, there's a difference between being a workaholic and working hard. You don't have to be addicted to your work, but you can still put in a hard day's work. Just watching the typical sitcom on television is comical to me, because the workplace is portrayed as a place to have sexual relationships, gossip, and play practical jokes. Pretty much, people deal with their personal life and only occasionally is any of this interrupted by anybody actually working. I don't want you to consistently work ten-hour days, but you should work hard during the eight hours you are there.

One survey of Fortune 1000 CEOs revealed that they are such dysfunctional time managers, so controlled by daily events and others, they average less than sixty minutes a day of productive work. (Pretty scary, when you consider how much they're paid.) Many entrepreneurs have similar problems. You might be your own boss, but you might be a pretty crummy one. I've received phone calls from some of my speaker buddies lamenting that business is bad. I ask them to describe their typical day, and after they tell me about sleeping in, going to the gym, having lunch with their mom, taking a nap, etc., I always ask, "Yes, and how many contacts did you make on Monday to generate new business? Tuesday? Wednesday?" You have to work, plain and simple.

What does hard work look like? Work looks much different today than it did in years past. My great-grandfather knew what it meant to work hard. He worked his dairy farm in Louisiana and hauled hay all day long, making sure the cows got fed.

Today, working hard means you're using your brain:

- Creating new ideas
- Implementing marketing plans
- Writing new policies
- Making difficult emotional choices
- Learning new skills
- Changing jobs
- Facing your fears
- Inventing new systems or products
- Making decisions when you don't have all the data
- Overcoming obstacles
- Taking risks
- Figuring out how to do things better

Hard work is anything that requires you to push yourself—not just show up at work, punch the clock, go through the motions, and leave. When I read about highly successful people in magazines, I'm often amazed by how many work *fewer* hours than the average person. Some people can run an entire company that does amazing things on thirty-five hours per week. They aren't working longer than you are and aren't necessarily smarter than you either. They succeed because they work hard and know when to play.

When you go to work tomorrow, really work hard. Make the effort, your future is worth it.

CHAPTER FIVE

Mastering the "U" in Productive

UNEASE

A POLICE OFFICER ON TRAFFIC PATROL one day was driving up a steep hill on a two-lane highway. All of a sudden, the traffic practically stopped in front of him. Rounding the bend, he noticed a line of traffic that extended for about a mile. He drove ahead on the shoulder to find the problem's source. At the front of the line he noticed the lead car was going very slowly. He clocked it at 22 mph. He pulled behind the car, put his lights on, and pulled the driver over. The driver rolled down her window; the office saw a little old lady with three other old lady passengers. He said, "Ma'am, do you realize you were going 22 mph?" "Oh, yes, exactly," said the little lady. "The speed limit sign here says 22." "I see what the problem is," said the officer. "That sign says this is Route 22. The speed limit is actually 55 mph." "Oh, thank you," the lady replied. The officer looked into the car and noticed the other three women were drawn and shaken. He asked the driver, "Is everyone okay in there?" "They will be," she said. "We just got off Route 119."

Do you feel like you're on Route 119? According to a nationwide office productivity study conducted by Xerox and Harris Interactive, most people work more than sixty hours a week, and over 33 percent work on weekends. The "faster, cheaper, do more with nothing" approach has created a workplace in which workers are always in high gear. This work style reduces productivity and increases stress. This chapter will help you reduce your stress level, steer you off the fast track, and guide you to Route 22 (or at least Route 55).

UNEASE quiz item #41:

> 41. I determine the sources of my stress and work to eliminate things that drain my energy.

You Want to Know What's Bothering Me?

Have you ever noticed how much energy it takes to stew about something? Stress is your body's response to an undesirable situation. When you experience an event you perceive as stressful, the stress hormone adrenaline is released. Your heart beats faster, your breath quickens, and your blood pressure rises. Your liver increases its output of blood sugar, and blood flow gets diverted to your brain and muscles. You're now ready to "fight or take flight." After the threat passes, your body relaxes again.

You may be able to handle an occasional stressful event, but when it happens repeatedly, the effects compound over time and can have negative effects on your health. Long-term, stress has been shown to cause heart disease, ulcers, high blood pressure, and low immunity.

You have a virtual energy in-box and out-box. You either reduce stress with energy deposits or increase stress with energy drains. Some people expose themselves to constant energy drains. To reduce stress, you must seek to minimize things that sap your energy:

TIME COMMITMENTS. When I began my professional speaking business in 1992, I joined seven different professional organizations to expand my network of contacts. After a year of attending all those meetings, I dreaded the thought of going. I stepped back and evaluated each one of them in terms of my return on time: "What do I receive from this membership?" "Is my investment of time and money worth the benefits I receive?" "Has this organization directly impacted my bottom-line?" *Everything* can have *some* benefit to your career. Ask yourself what *specific* benefits you can trace to your involvement with an activity and determine its worth. I quit all but three associations, to which I still belong today.

CHRONIC WORRYING. Worrying can be a big waste of time. Legitimate worries are real concerns and are actually problems to be solved. Other worries may never happen, such as, "The company lost money this quarter. I wonder if that means we're in trouble and I'm going to lose my job." This type of worrying is often a symptom of insecurity and reflects a lack of self-confidence. Worrying about the future causes nervous fatigue and can destroy your focus. So make an appointment with yourself to worry. Start a brainstorming session with "What should I do about . . ." and write down possible solutions. If you discover there's nothing you can actively do to reduce your concerns, it's probably not a worthy thing to worry about. Promise yourself you'll worry about it when and if it happens. You can only afford to spend time and energy on legitimate concerns.

INTERPERSONAL CONFLICTS. "I simply cannot stand that man." "I can't believe she did that." Unresolved conflict dissipates your mental strength, causes tension and fatigue, and is self-destructive. Ongoing anger wears you down emotionally and leaves you feeling out of control. Instead of letting conflicts eat at you, determine the most expedient way to resolve the situation. You could choose to give in to the other person. You could settle on a compromise and give up something to get something. You could develop new alternatives, so that both of you still reach your goals and feel good about the situation. You always have a choice in how you handle a conflict. Choose the best reaction and let go of the situation.

DEMANDING FRIENDSHIPS. Friendship is a delicate balance of give and take. When you're having a rough time, you need support. Sometimes your friends need you. In the end, it all balances out, right? But what if it doesn't? I've had people in my life that took and took and never gave back. I no longer have friendships with those people. Friendship isn't psychotherapy.

The above items are all examples of things that sap your energy. There are many more. You can create a T-chart that lists "Things I enjoy" on one side and "Things I dislike" on the other. Once you identify the things that sap your energy, you can identify possible ways to eliminate them. The important shift is to recognize that you have choices and options in the way you live and respond to stressful situations.

UNEASE quiz item #42:

> 42. I take personal responsibility for my own stress levels.

It's Not My Fault!

Often our current situation is so stressful that we can become helpless. We convince ourselves that this is the existing condition; this is just the way it is; we are victims of the situation; and think there is nothing we can do to reduce stress.

Here are some of the complaints I frequently hear from these "victims":

- I can't take lunch because I don't have time to eat.
- I can't go to sleep now because I need to catch up on house-work.
- I need to work late each night because that's the only time people don't interrupt me.
- I can't plan tomorrow because I don't have time today.
- I can't keep up with my email, so I'm going to stop trying to learn how to organize it better.

We blame our companies, the world, and other people for our condition and lack of productivity. I've trained at companies and discovered that it's the norm to work until 7 p.m. But I also soon discovered that there wasn't a lot of work going on until about 10 a.m. People would think, "Oh well, I'm going to be here until seven anyway," so they were unproductive most of the morning. The corporate culture at these companies was actually *encouraging* people to be unproductive instead of getting to business first thing and leaving at 5 p.m. Employees buy into it, "accept" it, and train themselves to be unproductive. They complain about the interruptions, but do nothing to prevent them. They sit there, steam, seethe inside, and take it on the pretense that "I don't want to be rude."

You don't have to accept your situation, your craziness, and your lack of productivity. You can change it! Stop believing you have no control over your stress. You may enjoy wallowing in self-pity. You may think you're controlled by circumstances and the situation. Breaking out of that comfortable place is scary, but it must be done.

Accepting personal responsibility

Responsibility is about exerting personal choice. It's going out and creating what you want. Every choice you make has an end result, positive or negative. If you choose to get organized, you choose not to settle for chaos. If you choose to be late, you choose to miss out. If you choose to drink too much one evening, you choose to feel bad the next day.

We are responsible for how our lives turn out, which can be tough to accept. When we like how things are turning out, it's quite easy to say that we are responsible for our success. But when things aren't so good, we're quick to point fingers at other people and place blame on them. Whatever is happening in your life is a direct reflection of all the choices you have made to this point. If we make *different* choices today, we'll get *different* results tomorrow. Try to change your perception. Step back and ask yourself if you're playing to a self-induced drama. What might happen if you refocus your attention on positive, proactive experiences and open your thoughts to opportunities instead of problems?

UNEASE quiz item #43:

> 43. I control my stress and emotions by monitoring my self-talk.

Change Your Feelings by Changing Your Thoughts

When something upsets you, how long do you stay upset? By understanding how emotions are created, you can change the stressful feelings you don't want, instead of thinking, "This shouldn't bother me."

There are four parts to any outcome (derived from rational-emotive behavior therapy, developed by Dr. Albert Ellis):

1. EVENT. Something happens.
2. INTERPRETATION. You decide what the event means to you. Your brain interprets the event, and you actually "say" something to yourself.
3. EMOTION. You experience some sort of feeling (happiness, sadness, anger, or fear) that's logical for your interpretation of the event.
4. BEHAVIOR. You respond in some way as a result of the emotion. You do or say something, generally an observable behavior.

For example:

1. A bear jumps out of the woods.
2. You say to yourself, "Yikes. A bear."
3. You feel fear.
4. You run.

Now you *know* you're not supposed to run. Your brain tells you you're terrified, and that's the most common reaction. The four steps happen in that specific order. You wouldn't just start running, then feel afraid, then tell yourself there's a bear in front of you. Your brain created the fear for you, so you could activate your flight-or-fight response. *This is important:* The *bear* didn't create your fear, because it has no direct wiring to your brain. You (or your brain) created the fear, as you do with all emotions.

Here's another illustration:

1. John gives me a beautiful new watch (event).
2. I think, "How sweet! He loves me!" (interpretation).
3. I feel happy (emotion).
4. I give him hugs and kisses (behavior).

Versus:

1. John gives me a beautiful new watch (event).
2. I think, "I wonder what he wants?" (interpretation).
3. I feel suspicious (emotion).
4. I say, "All right, what did you do?" (behavior).

What was exactly the same in that example? The event. Yet there were two different outcomes. Have you ever noticed how two people can experience the exact same thing and have completely different responses? Something that generally makes you come unglued may not bother another person. You wonder, "How can he be so calm!"

As a professional speaker, I travel a few times every month. I have incredible empathy for people who are afraid to fly, because I used to be one of them. However, once I finally understood how the fear was created, I was able to change my thinking and reduce my fear.

Let's say the plane hits turbulence (event), and someone next to me thinks, "I'm going to die. We're going down" (interpretation). So the person feels fear (emotion) and clutches the armrest and turns white (behavior). Instead, when I feel the turbulence, I think, "It seems a little bumpy today, but this is completely normal," and not feeling so anxious, I continue reading my newspaper.

So when I felt happy in the first gift scenario, who caused that? I did. When I felt suspicious in the second gift scenario, who caused that? I did. When a person sitting next to me in an airplane experienced turbulence and felt fear, who caused that? He/she did. When I felt the same turbulence and remained calm, who caused that? I did.

Who causes you to feel the way you do? *You do.* Events don't cause anything. They are completely neutral. If turbulence *caused* stress, then every single person on the airplane would experience stress, and that's not what happens. *You* cause yourself to feel every emotion you feel and enact every behavior you do. You can determine your attitude and act accordingly—simply by assuming personal responsibility. No one can make you feel angry, or guilty, or happy, or inferior, or bored, or afraid, or anything, without your complete cooperation and participation.

A key factor in reducing stress is to gain control over your emotions by learning to change your thinking. In the same way you learn, you can unlearn, and consciously think new thoughts when you encounter a potentially stressful situation. Many people think the only way to change your emotions is to get someone or something else to change. When you know you're in charge of your emotions, you become very powerful. You can change the way you think and thereby change the way you feel.

Map out your stressful situations

Now that you've identified some of your negative thought patterns, you can work on creating new thoughts for the next time you get into that situation. Write out the following:

Event: _____ _____

Your usual thinking: _____

Resulting emotion: _____

Your normal reaction: _____

For example, I used to experience a lot of stress at the end of the day. Work was over, the kids were home from school and daycare, and everyone was a bit tired and cranky. Meagan would do what most eight-year-olds do: talk incessantly. Johnny, who was four, was whining and practicing his favorite word: "no." James, my two-year-old, was crying to be held. I could feel my blood pressure rising as I had three children talking, whining, and crying at the same time. So the map would look something like this:

1. The five o'clock meltdown hour (event).
2. My usual thinking: "Don't they ever stop talking? I'm going to lose my mind. I just cannot take this" (interpretation).
3. Anger and stress result (emotion).
4. I yell, "You kids knock it off!" (behavior).

Yikes. That's not quite the outcome I wanted! To change my reaction in this situation, I must change my emotion. If I want to change my emotion, I must change my thinking. To change my thinking, I must replace negative thoughts with positive thoughts that are more constructive and will give me a better outcome. I may not completely eliminate my anger, but I can reduce it.

So now my thoughts go something like this: "Hang in there, Laura. If you just focus and listen to Meagan for two minutes, she'll be happy and will move on to other things. Keep smiling and nodding your head, Laura. You can do this." And sure enough, if I pay attention to my kids and focus on them instead of myself, they manage the transition better.

In the same way, you can brainstorm new thoughts to replace the old ones. Get someone else's input in this stage, because your thoughts are automatic. It is often hard to come up with alternative thoughts.

UNEASE quiz item #44:

44. I think positively and maintain a great attitude.

The Grass Is Always Greener

What is attitude? It's your manner or disposition that reveals your feelings or beliefs. It's how you look at things. If you generally view the world negatively, those beliefs will typically show up in the way you behave. You can create stress with this "stinking thinking." If you want to change your attitude, you first must identify your negative thought patterns. Here are some of the common patterns of stinking thinking:

- IMPATIENCE. "I can't believe he hasn't answered my email yet." This causes you to be less tolerant of others. You judge others by your own high standards and when they do not perform as quickly or as well as you expect, you frequently stew inside and lack peace.

- RIGIDITY. "This table isn't set correctly; this napkin is out of place." Inflexibility places tremendous burdens on your inner self. Rigid people nearly always seem to be looking for something to be upset about.

- PERFECTIONISM. "I cannot believe I had that typo in this report." This is a form of rigidity. You become overly disappointed in yourself when you make a mistake.

- INABILITY TO RELAX. "I don't have time to take a ten-minute bath." You're always on the go. Constant pushing can lead to stress and exhaustion.

- EXCESSIVE COMPETITION. "I cannot believe she got interviewed on that show and not me!" instead of, "What can I do to get that spot next time?" This thought pattern adds pressure that will ultimately result in stress to you and others around you.

- LACK OF HUMOR AND ENTHUSIASM. "Whatever. Who cares." A sour attitude breeds stress. A humorless person is generally one who is seething inside and full of self-reproach and self-contempt.

- MENTAL HOPELESSNESS. "There's no use." This is the end result of frequent unhappy moods and loss of hope. It can lead to utter despair and saps your recuperative strength to the point you cannot recover. Depression often requires medical intervention.

- CONSTANT SELF-CRITICISM. "Can't you get anything right?" "I can't believe you said something so dumb." Negative self-talk erodes your confidence and ability to perform at optimum levels.

How to stop the stress cycle and change your reactions

When a stressful event happens that would normally make you react, do the following:

1. **FREEZE.** Recognize it's happening. Don't start thinking in the same old way.

2. **THINK NEW THOUGHTS.** Purposefully think the new thoughts that you brainstormed, replacing the old thinking with the new.

3. **REPEAT.** Over and over if necessary. Sometimes you have to drag yourself out of your thinking. This can take a while. Count while thinking. Choose to wait before you react. Feel the emotions changing or declining.

4. **DECIDE.** Choose how you are going to respond or behave, rather than stressing out.

Work through every situation that triggers your stress. When you notice yourself getting worked up over something, let that be the next scenario you need to map. Through practice and motivation, you can become a more positive thinker and keep yourself from stressing out in negative situations.

UNEASE quiz item #45:

> 45. I manage my stress well; stress doesn't affect my productivity at work.

No Pain, No Gain!

Too much or too little stress can have a negative impact on your productivity. What's that? Can you have too *little* stress? Yes! You need to have some stress in your life. You cannot get rid of all stress; in fact, some stress is desirable, even necessary. Without good stress (sometimes called "eustress"), you wouldn't even get out of bed in the morning. Humans experience good stress as motivation, drive, desire, and ambition. Some people who don't have enough stress in their lives perform poorly at work from boredom or lack of challenge. You also don't want too much negative stress (sometimes called "distress" or "burnout"), because it too can result in diminished performance. You have to strike a happy medium with a moderate level of stress.

If you plotted the stress-productivity relationship, it would look something like this:

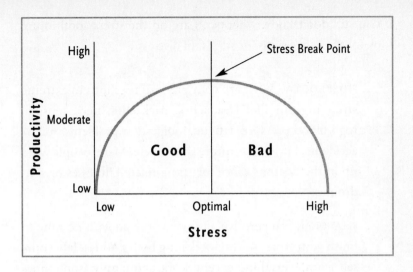

Most people I've met since I began conducting productivity seminars in 1992 are on the high end of the stress continuum. They feel overworked, overstressed, overwhelmed, and overcommitted, and their stress levels are potentially destructive. Here are some descriptors in each of the different areas of the chart:

Low stress	Optimal stress	High stress
Overqualified	Competent	Busyness
Passive-aggressive	Calm	Temper
Absent-minded	Keen memory	Forgetful
Withdrawn	Enthusiastic	Negative attitude
Bored	Motivated	Blaming and irritable
Lethargic	Alert	Fatigued
Indecisive	Excellent decision making	Poor, snap judgment
Minimal effort	High energy	Edgy, jumpy

If you still don't know where you are on the stress continuum, look for these five signs, or stages, of distress:

1. PHYSIOLOGICAL: What are your physical reactions to extreme stress in your life? Headaches, backaches, neck tension, high blood pressure, fatigue, indigestion problems, minor accidents, lowered immune system, etc. Many people wind up in the doctor's office for stress-related illnesses or syndromes.

2. RELATIONAL: You perceive a heavy workload with no time to finish your work, so you work long hours. You isolate yourself from everything except work and family (sometimes even family). Your friend asks you out to lunch, and you say, "Lunch? I don't have time for lunch!" In fact, you don't have time for friends or the things that used to give you joy. You pull out of all volunteer and personal activities, and your personal relationships decrease.

3. CEREBRAL: Your brain feels like it's just not working anymore. You have so much to do, you can't think. You make errors in your assignments, and it's extremely difficult to focus or concentrate. Time seems to drag in this stage; you find yourself watching the clock a lot.

4. EMOTIONAL: This is a stage of severe sadness or anger. I witnessed an employee in this stage throw a handful of paper clips at a coworker and burst into tears. Some people develop addictions, trying to escape through drugs, alcohol, affairs, or excessive spending. In this stage, you will see missed deadlines, minimal productivity, and possibly clinical depression.

5. **SPIRITUAL:** You feel hopeless, helpless, and totally empty inside. You may want to make drastic changes because you feel your life is so awful. You have the urge to quit your job, leave your spouse, and move to Hawaii to become a beach bum.

If you recognize any of these symptoms in yourself, you are on the high end (the distress side) of the continuum.

Please note that it's normal to go back and forth between eustress and distress. When you're working on a particularly demanding project and putting in long hours, you might stay in physical burnout for a couple of weeks. But when the project's over, you should be able to pull yourself back to eustress. The worry begins when someone seems unable to get out of the downward spiral and stays constantly in distress. The stress becomes destructive.

It's important to identify these stages in yourself so you can practice better self-care and stress-reduction techniques. It's also important to be able to watch for the stages in others and intervene when your coworkers, friends, or family are losing it. When you're in a particularly stressful time in your life, it's more important than ever to take care of yourself.

> 46. I feel cool, calm, and collected, rather than hurried, rushed, and tense.

Insane, Busy, Crazy

I love the line from the song "Circle of Life" from *The Lion King:* "There's more to see than can ever be seen / More to do than can ever be done." It's the law of time. We get an inner twinge that says, "There's not enough time in the whole universe to do what you want or need to do." The twinge prods you to rush around like a maniac. Many people are perpetually hurried, harried, busy, and tense. We are synchronized with the hurried clip of contemporary society. We're living in a rhythm that goes snap-snap-snap.

Besides being a recovering perfectionist, I'm a recovering hurrier. I skipped a year of high school and completed both my undergraduate degree and MBA by the age of twenty-one. When people ask me, "Why did you do that? What was your hurry?" I don't have a good answer. I simply did everything as if I were running a race. I pushed to accomplish *it.* Eventually, though, it felt like a race to nowhere. I've since learned to be more purposeful in putting my energies into things that make sense. Sure, I'm still committed to success, but it's a different kind of success. It takes discipline to ensure my time includes my husband, my children, and my service to my church. I try to remember that life isn't about the race.

I recognize myself in so many people. Professionals thrive on adrenaline and busyness. They often only have goals for the sake of racing toward something. When they achieve a goal, they still aren't happy. They simply set another goal. "I'll be happy when . . ." They are very *busy* people. In fact, busyness has become a type of competition. "How are you?" "Busy!" "Oh yeah, I'm so busy." "I'm just going insane." "Oh yeah, me too, I've totally lost it." Like this is something to be proud of! Larry Dossey, in his book *Space, Time and Medicine,* described this distinct pathology as "time sickness." Victims of time sickness, Dossey says, are obsessed with the notion "that time is getting away, that there isn't enough of it, and that you must pedal faster to keep up." The trouble is, the body has limits that it imposes.

Emotions as a lighthouse

So how do you stop rushing around? Use your *emotions* as a guide, because they will signal you when something needs your attention. Like a lighthouse at sea, they are warning signals that tell you when something is wrong. When a boat sees the beacon through the fog (warning: you're too close to shore), it decides on a remedy (get away), and takes action (steers the boat back out to sea). You, too, need to go through this three-step process:

1. HEED THE WARNING. Be aware that you're rushing around. When you feel irritated, frustrated, and impatient, *stop.* Listen to your emotions. Your emotions provide valuable information you should use as a prompt. Check out what your body is saying to you. Emotions are an alarm that prompts you to make needed changes.

2. DECIDE WHAT TO DO. Challenge a few of your assumptions, change or clarify your priorities, alter your behavior, set limits, get out of the situation. You're in charge of how important things are to you, and you can reorder them if you want to.

3. ACT. If you commit to doing one more thing and it makes you want to throw up, change your mind. It's never too

late to go back to someone and say, "I know I said I would do this, but I've reconsidered. I decided it just doesn't work for me after all." You may have to repeat that mantra several times. The other person may be disappointed, but you have remained true to yourself and your priorities.

Gaining control of your time allows you more time to do what you want to do. A *Time*/CNN poll found that 65 percent of people spend their *leisure* time doing things they'd prefer not to do. What's the point in leading a "full life," if you don't have the time and energy to enjoy it? Make it your goal to spend time on the activities that are meaningful in your business and personal lives, instead of rushing around being busy with things you don't really care about.

UNEASE quiz item #47:

47. I maintain a good sense of humor and take things lightly.

Lighten Up!

My father is a retired colonel in the U.S. Air Force. He was very loving but also could be quite stern. If he asked, "Do you think that's funny?" it was definitely *not* a good idea to say, "Yes, I do." So I quickly learned when to wipe that smile off my face. When I took my first corporate job, I had a boss who would comment to anyone caught laughing, "Stop fooling around and get back to work." The message was "If you're having fun, you can't be working."

A Burke Marketing Research survey, however, found that 84 percent of personnel directors believed that employees who have a sense of humor do a better job than those lacking that quality.

Managers not only value humor in employees, many seek to hire employees with a sense of humor. Humor on the job has also been linked to a better bottom line. Research shows humor results in:

- Increased productivity
- Better communication
- Improved morale
- Reduced absenteeism
- Enhanced problem-solving skills
- Diffused tension and anger
- Stronger teams
- Reduced medical costs

It's critical to have a sense of humor *and* produce it during stressful situations.

What is a sense of humor? It's the way you look at things; it's your attitude. People with a sense of humor have the ability to take their jobs seriously but take *themselves* lightly. They can find humor even in tense, stressful situations. Humor combats stress and allows you to shift your perspective.

I'm not suggesting you turn your workplace into a comedy store, but you can work hard *and* laugh hard while accomplishing important results. To regain your sense of humor, practice some humor strategies. When something stressful happens, try one of these tricks:

SQUISH THEIR HEADS. When someone is annoying you, use your thumb and pointer finger to look at that person's head from a distance and pretend you're "squishing" it. Only try this when someone isn't looking. If someone is grumpy, do it in front of him or her as a joke. Subtle signal!

BECOME YOUR FAVORITE TELEVISION STAR. When in a stressful situation, think, "Now how would Bart Simpson react to this?" Put your favorite cartoon character or comedian in the situation and look at it in a different light. Just imagining what could happen can give you a chuckle, making the whole situation less annoying.

PRETEND YOU'RE SWATTING A GNAT. Gnats can't bite you but are definitely annoying. Some people are like that. If people bug you, swat at an imaginary gnat buzzing around your face. Silly, yes, but it makes you feel better and leaves you with a smile.

CREATE AN "I LOVE ME" FILE. When you receive a thank-you note from a friend or colleague, put it in a three-hole page protector and add it to your binder. Keep funny cartoons, email jokes, photos, or anything that makes you smile in your binder. When feeling stressed, you can read it to diffuse your tension.

Wouldn't it be great if you could create this sense of fun, camaraderie, and spontaneity throughout your department? Laughter is contagious—why not infect the whole company! Here are some things my client organizations have done:

Nextel routinely hands out stress toys and squeezies in their call centers. The HR director organizes mini-carnivals on the floor, festivals in the parking lot, and game shows. The employees get treated to an occasional movie and popcorn.

The Denver Water Board sponsored a desk organization contest for national Clean Off Your Desk Day, held in early January. We took "before" pictures of people's offices. We then offered a series of seminars and gave participants a week to organize their offices. I came around and took "after" pictures. I blew the "before" and "after" photos up on big posterboards and hung them in the employee cafeteria. Employees voted on the "most improved" and "most organized" offices. Prizes were given out to the winners. It was a blast!

Holiday Builders, a homebuilder based in Florida, hired an ice

148   Leave the Office Earlier

cream truck to arrive during an off-site seminar. Who can be stressed out when you hear the ice cream truck coming down the street?

Programs like these can lower stress, increase productivity, and boost employee morale. Create a culture of positive people and fun! Make it your goal to help others in your company laugh more.

UNEASE quiz item #48:

> 48. I refuse to let stressful situations or people bother me.

Get Off My Planet!

Think about the situations, events, or people at work that stress you out. Then determine which of those things will go away. An important stress tool is the ability to recognize *normal* stressors that are part and parcel to the industry, organization, or job you're in. Once you realize that some things exist with you or without you and will continue to exist once you're gone, you stop taking them so personally.

Many jobs are inherently stressful. I held stress management seminars for the correctional officers at the Department of Corrections in Canon City, Colorado. We started the day talking about the things that stress them out. One man told me, "I'll tell you what's so stressful about this place. Everyone around here is so darn negative! There are negative people everywhere!" I had to try hard not to laugh. Doesn't that strike you as funny? So I said with an odd look on my face, "But . . . this is a *jail.*" Everyone laughed. If I went to work as a correctional officer, I would *expect* negative people to be there. It's a normal stressor. The "customers" don't want to be there! You don't want repeat customers . . . the décor isn't the best . . . need I go on?

When you recognize what little you can personally do to change a situation—it just *is*—you become desensitized to it. You observe, "Yep, look at that, it's happening again." Oh well. Shrug. You can become less sensitized to your job stressors with some practice.

- If you're a bank teller, don't complain that you can't get anything done because people are always interrupting you.
- If you're a customer service agent, don't complain about angry people with complaints.
- If you're a teacher, don't complain about children being noisy.

These things will never go away. It's part of the job. Neither will people at work who bug you. Think of them like a piece of furniture. You could go somewhere else, but the stress won't go away . . . it'll just be different. So figure out if these *types* of stressors are ones you can handle, and make the appropriate mental adjustments.

A final thought on this topic: Don't judge people when they're in a bad mood. You've probably had one yourself in the past twenty-four hours! Most important, don't take a bad mood personally, even if someone tries to blame you for it. You are responsible for your behavior, not for someone else's thoughts about it. In other words, you are responsible for how you dress for the weather, but not for the weather itself. You will be amazed what this shift in thinking does for your stress levels.

> 49. I control my temper at work and don't demonstrate anger.

Combating Desk Rage

Road rage, air rage, trolley rage, bike rage, and appliance rage . . . "Rage" is the word of the moment. Desk rage or office rage has America's corporate trenches resembling tryouts for TV's *Survivor* or *Weakest Link*. Have you personally yelled at another employee? Or got angry enough to throw something—a handful of paper clips . . . a sheaf of papers . . . a phone . . . or a bare-knuckle punch to the wall?

Here are some examples from my corporate clients:

- One employee blew up during a corrective action session. She came across the desk at the HR manager, pointing, yelling, and calling her a liar.
- When angry, one employee would throw his office equipment at the walls of his office, frequently damaging other equipment and making holes in the wall.
- Two engineers had to be physically separated after they almost came to blows over the procedure for filing paperwork.
- The IT department reported a record number of broken keyboards from people banging them with their fists.

Recognize when your anger is starting to rise:

- Become aware when you are no longer engaged in a constructive discussion.
- Monitor body signs that signal escalating anger: headache,

pounding heart, sweating palms, tense jaw, clenched hands, inability to listen, and racing thoughts.

- Monitor your self-talk for negative thinking like "I'm going to lose my mind" or "I cannot stand that woman." Telling yourself negative things about others or the situation only escalates anger.

- Leave the situation if you need to. Say, "I think we need a ten-minute break so we can get some perspective and try a different approach here."

- Find appropriate ways to blow off steam. Take a walk, exercise, squeeze a ball, or take deep breaths.

Here are some suggestions to reduce desk rage. For managers:

TREAT THIS BEHAVIOR SERIOUSLY. Begin with a reprimand or warning. "Unbridled anger is completely inappropriate in the workplace. It makes others extremely uncomfortable or upset. It also makes you seem unprofessional and lacking in self-control."

ENSURE ADEQUATE STAFFING. Since overwork is the number one cause of desk rage, try not to pile too much on one person. Watch for signs of burnout such as excessive absenteeism, clock watching, distractedness, and emotional trouble.

GIVE EMPLOYEES ENOUGH ROOM TO WORK. Employees who work in cubicle environments show higher stress levels than those who don't. Don't overcrowd the cubicle area or give the bigwigs offices that are just as big or bigger than in the past, while the minions get stuffed into smaller and smaller places.

CONFRONT EMPLOYEE AGGRESSION. If the supervisor yells and screams at the assistant, the assistant will yell and scream at other coworkers. What is modeled gets repeated. One hostile employee can poison a group and be the cause of turnover.

For employees:

REQUEST HIGHER CUBICLE PARTITIONS TO REDUCE NOISE. Low-level noises such as voices, the clicking of keyboards, and the hum of the photocopier elevate stress hormones in the body.

TAKE ADVANTAGE OF EMPLOYEE ASSISTANCE PROGRAMS (EAPS). EAPs help employees deal with stress levels. Often people need professional help.

USE CARPOOLS AND BUSES. Employees may arrive at work with road rage, which can make desk rage more severe.

FIND PLACES AND PROGRAMS TO DECOMPRESS. Time Warner Cable allows its workers to do yoga twice a week on-site. TravelersExpress MoneyGram brings a massage therapist on-site several times a month. Denver Water has private rooms where workers can shut the door and nap. Get creative!

WEAR BUSINESS DRESS. The casual nature of the dress code may affect the mentality of appropriate business behavior. If you are dressed too casually, your behavior might also be too casual. A 2002 study by Men's Apparel Alliance showed that one in five companies reinstated a more formal dress code in the past year. A *Working Woman* magazine survey of one thousand companies showed almost 50 percent of respondents believed that casual dress led to tardiness and decreased polite behavior.

ATTEND A SEMINAR ON EMOTIONAL CONTROL AND COURTESY. Companies may soon begin to hold training seminars on manners just as they do sexual harassment and discrimination. Clients hire consultants to help them cope with stress and rudeness that are as commonplace as water coolers and copy machines in today's workplaces. Whether it's brushing by someone in the hall, calling your assistant incompetent, or cutting in line for the fax machine, corporate rudeness takes its toll.

Do your part in maintaining low stress levels in your work environment. Watch your anger and find appropriate ways to blow off steam. Don't contribute to desk rage!

> 50. I flourish in the face of constant changes in my life and don't get anxious.

The Wisdom to Know the Difference

A *USA Today* survey polled ten thousand Americans with this question: "How many times per week do you think of quitting your job?" I was surprised to hear three times a week! When asked why they thought about quitting, the number one response was "stress." Well, everyone has stress; that's nothing earth shattering. The survey probed deeper and revealed that people are missing a sense of certainty. Uncertainty is like getting out of bed at night to get a drink. You know the edge of your dresser is jutting out, but you can't see it. You take a step and grope around, nope not there; you take another step, nope not there. When you're not clear where the next step is, it creates anxiety.

Think back on your life five years ago. Where did you work? What people were there? What technologies did you use? How was your organization structured? What was your workload? On a scale of 1 to 10, how would you rate the level of change in the last five years? What will the next step be? Project yourself two years into the future. How would you rate the changes you think will occur in that time? Probably just as tumultuous. Don't look for a safe harbor to wait out the storm, because there is none. Change will continue to occur at lightning speed. To keep your stress level low, find a way to be "change hardy," so it doesn't impact you so dramatically.

In 1903 the Wright brothers made their historic maiden flight, which launched the whole world of aviation. In 1969 the Apollo moon landing took place. Of course, these were two significant events in aviation history. Most aviation historians believe the most significant event between 1903 and 1969 took place on October 14, 1954. It was on this date that Chuck Yaeger, for the ninth time, entered his Bell X1 rocket airplane. He was airlifted by a B-29 to a great height and then dropped. He experienced a free fall for about 500 feet, and then he fired his rockets. He took his plane to 42,000 feet, accelerated to a speed of 700 mph, and sustained that speed for twenty seconds, breaking the sound barrier. Most experts thought it was impossible to break the sound barrier without destroying the aircraft. But Chuck Yaeger found that, though his plane shook violently as he neared Mach speed, the ride was as smooth as glass.

Similarly, pushing past your own limits is not going to be as hard as you think. You have to break your own sound barrier and the fears in your life. You might even discover it's as smooth as glass at the end. Until things smooth out, how do you get through the change?

REALIZE WHAT YOU CAN CONTROL. You have control over your life. You have control over the friends you choose, how you approach love relationships, and the path your career follows. You decide for yourself what's right and what's wrong, whether you should stay in this weekend or go out, whether to vote Democrat or Republican. You decide who to see, what to wear, and what to eat. However, you have very little control over the government, economic policy, the rise and fall of the stock market, Mother Nature, international events, and your company's direction. Accepting "what is" means realizing you can't control certain things and to stop trying.

TAKE OWNERSHIP IN THE CHANGE. You don't even have to *like* the change—you don't have to believe it's a good idea. But you are supposed to do everything you can, in your particular job, to make the changes a success story. If you're going to remain part of the team, you need to play for the team.

DEVELOP A REPUTATION AS A FIXER—NOT A FINGER-POINTER. Every organization needs people who are willing to find solutions, not complain about problems. People who are valuable and successful in times of change are flexible, objective, and creative. They welcome the challenges of problem solving. When they have a complaint to relay, they also have suggestions and options for a solution along with the problem.

Serious change requires serious courage. It's so scary that most of us don't even know how to approach it realistically. When people think of changing their lives, they often think in terms of huge, dramatic gestures. Ever dream of moving to the mountains and becoming a hermit? Extreme thinking like this can effectively destroy your ability to make constructive changes in your life. If you are a responsible, albeit burned-out, thirty-nine-year-old professional with a spouse and two kids, you may occasionally have thoughts about heading for Hawaii, but it isn't likely you'll abandon your family, your career, your dog, and your golf partner. The good news is that you don't have to head off to the islands to have a better life. You only have to accept what is, take personal responsibility for what you can change, and learn to accept what you can't control.

CHAPTER SIX

Mastering the "C" in Productive
CONCENTRATION

I WAS AN AVID READER GROWING UP. I've read the *Little House on the Prairie* series probably thirty times and an unknown number of Black Beauty and Nancy Drew novels. I remember sitting for hours in the corner of our living room in my daddy's favorite recliner, absorbed in the stories. Occasionally my mother would come striding into the living room, upset: "Didn't you hear me call you?" I would look at her strangely and, as I came back to reality, answer sincerely, "No, Mommy, I didn't." And that was the truth!

That level of concentration is hard to achieve today. So many things compete for our attention in the workplace that it's often very difficult to concentrate. This chapter will improve your ability to stay on target and focus on the task at hand.

CONCENTRATION quiz item #51:

> 51. I have my office set up for maximum productivity and mini-
> mum distractions.

Who's That?

You need privacy when discussing sensitive issues or require a period of time to concentrate. The way your furniture is laid out,
amazingly, can have a big impact on your ability to concentrate.
Most employees just take whatever was handed to them, in
whatever configuration, and accept it. With a myriad of alternatives to setting up your office space and furniture, what are some
considerations?

TURN AWAY FROM BUSY HALLWAYS OR DOORS. Humans are curious,
so when someone walks by, it's our nature to look up to see who
just passed. If people are wandering around looking for someone
to bother, they will catch your eye and smile. Not wanting to be
rude, you smile back. They enter your office and ask the death
question: "So, how's it going?" Congratulations, you just bought
yourself an easy ten-minute interruption. One solution is to rotate your desk or change the layout of your cubicle so that your
back faces the door. If someone walks by and sees that you are
busy, they are *less* likely to interrupt you (but not always). If you
can't rotate your desk, work at an angle or face a corner. Use a
computer screen or cabinet to block your corridor view.

REMOVE ALL CHAIRS FROM YOUR OFFICE. A chair is an invitation to
sit down (especially comfortable padded ones). If there are no
chairs, a visitor cannot park in your work area. When someone
unexpectedly drops in, simply stand, extend your hand, smile,
and ask, "What can I do for you?" The person will notice this busi-
nesslike response and cut the visit shorter than if he or she could
lounge. Keep a padded folding chair tucked out of sight. If an is-

sue is important enough, you can pull out the chair and invite your visitor to sit—but only if you have the time.

CREATE A U SHAPE. A U shape lets you easily access your main work surface, computer and fax, and layout area for today's work and items that won't fit in your tickler file. This is the most ideal shape, so you don't have to turn completely around or get up to get what you need. A layout area doesn't have to be a piece of furniture—it could be a shelf hung on the wall with brackets. The shelf can go above a piece of furniture, giving you added space on that furniture surface.

USE GLASS. If you have to put up walls to get some privacy, use glass. You can close interior blinds when privacy is needed, and open them when you want more interaction. Glass keeps the workplace looking "open," while providing a better balance between the need for privacy and the need for interaction.

CONCENTRATION quiz item #52:

> 52. I avoid wasting time by daydreaming.

Are You Dreaming?

You're staring out your office window . . . lost in thought about your upcoming dinner party . . . when you jerk back to reality: "Oops, where was I?" you think, as you look down once again at the report on your desk. You've been daydreaming.

Daydreaming can be a real productivity bandit, especially when you're supposed to be focusing on a higher-priority project. Excessive daydreaming can waste precious time that could be better spent on other things. But daydreaming isn't always bad. There's a difference between true daydreaming, as the brain's response to overload or boredom, and thinking time that may lead to promising ideas.

How do you ensure daydreaming time is productive time?

DON'T USE DAYDREAMING TO PROCRASTINATE. Daydreaming can be a good tool for transitioning to a new project during the day. It gives your brain a chance to change gears. Figuratively, your mind puts away the file on the last task, takes a break, and gets ready to open a new file and begin work. However, if you find your mind wandering when you're supposed to be concentrating on a task, self-discipline is required to stay focused.

SELECT YOUR DESIGNATED "DAYDREAMING PLACE." Some of my best ideas come to me when I'm flying, when my body and brain are still. Taking time in a place with no distractions gives your brain the opportunity to discover creative ideas and new solutions to problems. You may find walking the dog, washing dishes, driving in the car, exercising, or reading the perfect time to develop new processes or plan projects.

SPEND AN APPROPRIATE AMOUNT OF TIME. For the most effective brainstorming, choose a place or activity that takes no less than fifteen minutes and no more than sixty minutes. You want your brain to have time to rummage through the closets of your mind, but not so much of it that you're wasting it unnecessarily.

APPROACH YOUR DAYDREAMING PLACE WITH PURPOSE. Before you go to your daydreaming place, have a problem ready to mull over in your mind. Without the normal distractions, your brain will be free to explore new possibilities. By the end of your walk or plane ride, perhaps you will have discovered an innovative solution to that issue.

USE PAPER TO CAPTURE THE RESULTS OF DAYDREAMING. By writing down your ideas, you won't immediately forget them, and you can see them all at one time. Now you can look for relationships among your thoughts. Ask questions such as, "What causes X?" "What are the results of X?" "With what things is X related?" "What's behind this?" "Is this leading anywhere else?" "Who else might be affected?" I like to use a mind map with clusters of items, details, examples, and lines connecting them.

People don't often allow themselves the opportunity to think about challenging situations, because they're going ninety miles an hour all day long. And our culture and current work ethic don't condone thinking time. But effective daydreaming can synthesize the volumes of information that flow across your desk, the phone lines, and through your brain every day.

CONCENTRATION quiz item #53:

53. I remember things easily; I'm rarely absentminded or forget where I put things.

What Am I Doing Here?

You walk into a room, look around, and think, "Now, why am I here?" The older I get, the harder it is to remember important birthdays and appointments. But neuroscientists now say that memory loss *does not* go hand in hand with aging; it's more likely caused by our lifestyles, lack of sleep, and stress.

Busy people need good memory skills to help them remember details. But it's hard to concentrate when a hundred thoughts flood your mind every minute. Having a sharp memory can be as simple as using good memory tools.

WRITE IT DOWN. When I'm doing dishes in the evening, I'm forced to stand still for a few minutes. It's during this time that I remember small details about things to do. Since my office is in my home, I can dash over and record the thought in my planner. Some people prefer an electronic task list and type a note to themselves.

KEEP A RUNNING LIST. For errands, chores, and grocery lists, keep a note under a magnet on a hidden side of your refrigerator. Add to it each time something comes to mind or you throw away an empty container. When it's time to shop, you simply grab the list and off you go.

CALL YOURSELF. What if you think of something you need to do at work the next day but don't want to think about it all night long? Just phone your office and leave yourself a message on your voicemail.

USE A VOICE RECORDER IN YOUR CAR. I frequently come up with great ideas while driving, but it's dangerous to write. So I use the record feature on my cell phone (or you can purchase an inexpensive voice recorder) to record thoughts and reminders. The Record feature is also great for remembering where I parked or a phone number I saw on a billboard.

SCHEDULE EMAIL REMINDERS. Your email software or free email reminder services on the Internet will send you an email when important birthdays, anniversaries, or events are approaching. Free services use the Web to send you wake-up calls and other reminders via telephone. You set the time, date, and phone number for each reminder.

CHECK THE REMINDER BOX. In most email programs and electronic task lists, you have the option of setting a reminder to pop-up and notify you about an upcoming meeting or action item that's due.

POST A STICKY NOTE. I often write a note and stick it to my door so I don't forget to do something on the way out. Reminders such as "Bring James's diapers" or "Mail letters" or "Buy birthday gift" trigger my memory first thing in the morning.

When my husband misplaces his car keys, it's generally because his mind was on something else when he put them down. The kids will be arguing, or he's busy thinking about dinner, or he's talking on the phone. Sure enough, he'll lose his concentration at the moment he most needs to remember. If this sounds like you, a few retention techniques will help.

TAKE THE TIME. If you can't recall where you put the bag containing the shampoo you just purchased, pause and retrace your steps. Close your eyes and think back to the minute you arrived home. When was the last moment you remember having the bag in your hand? If you think you left important meeting notes in a coworker's office, think about the route you took and whom you spoke with. Who was there with you? Do you remember any particular sounds indicating the room you were in?

TALK TO YOURSELF. It's best to have a set place to deposit particular items, like the remote control, your purse, or your briefcase. If you're putting something down "temporarily," literally say the word "stop" in your head. Then purposely say, "I'm putting my keys on the coffee table."

REPEAT. We forget people's names as soon as we hear them because our minds were thinking about the next clever thing to say rather than what that person said. When you hear, "Hi, I'm Betty," repeat, "Hi, Betty, I'm Laura." Then use the name again, "Betty, where do you work?" At the end of the conversation, "Betty, it was a pleasure chatting with you." By using Betty's name three times, you are far more likely to remember it when you see her later in the evening.

USE PICTURES. When you look at someone, create a picture in your mind to help you remember. If you meet someone named

Paul, think of a ball on his head when you look at him. Someone named Mary could be holding a lamb. Joe would have a crab pinching his nose if you think of the restaurant Joe's Crab Shack. The sillier it is, the easier it will be to remember.

ASSOCIATION. This method involves linking one object with another and creating mental associations. By not forgetting things, you won't waste time or repeat a trip to the grocery store. Let's say you're driving home and your spouse calls and says, "Honey, please stop by the store and pick up tomatoes, milk, and allergy medicine. Since you can't write it down, create associations with things in your car. The car seat is holding tomatoes, milk is on the backseat, and allergy medicine is in the glove box. The wilder the association, the easier it is to remember. If you open the milk jug, and tomatoes fly out and hit you in the face, you'd probably remember that!

A bad memory doesn't have to come with old age. Try a few of these memory tricks and you will be amazed at your excellent memory. You'll be more efficient, since you won't waste time trying to remember things, and small details won't slip through the cracks.

CONCENTRATION quiz item #54:

54. I focus on a priority project without getting distracted.

Busyness Versus Productivity

A seminar participant said, "There are times when little details build up and I begin to lose focus. When I lose focus, I tend to flit around from one item to another without completing one thing." This reminded me of a butterfly, flitting around from flower to flower.

There is a fine line between ineffective distractedness (flitting) and effective juggling. The former is created by default, and the latter is created by design. The ineffective type is called a "butterfly" and the effective type a "postage stamp." A butterfly randomly flits from task to task. A stamp sticks to one thing until it gets to its intended destination.

Do you have half-done projects all over your office and your home? Do you get distracted easily and tend to blow like the wind in many different directions? You might be a butterfly. Butterflies have the sensation of having worked hard from being so busy, but they don't stay focused and concentrate on what must get done.

Stamps, on the other hand, are purposeful in their activities and can juggle many things. They get one thing started, and then purposely switch to something else for a time. They know when and why to switch back to the original task. They don't let themselves get distracted by brain traffic, emails, or interruptions.

How do you become less of a butterfly and more of a stamp?

PRACTICE. When you know you're off task, get into the habit of self-correction: "I really shouldn't be doing this right now. Get back on task!"

WRITE DOWN DISTRACTIONS, BUT DON'T FOLLOW THEM. If you think of something that needs to be done while you're working on a higher-priority task, write it down (paper or electronic) to remember it, then get back to the task at hand.

AVOID YOUR KNOWN DISTRACTIONS. Personally, I love to surf the Net and read the latest news. When I'm working on a high-priority project, I don't allow myself to launch my browser. I close Outlook so incoming email doesn't distract me. I make sure I've got a fresh cup of coffee before I begin so that I don't have an excuse to get up and go to the kitchen (where I might find something "important" to do).

DEFER INTERRUPTIONS. Resist the urge to check email that just came in. Ask a friend who drops by if you can come by and visit at lunch, because you're right in the middle of something important.

PRIORITIZE. Each day, ask yourself, "If I could only accomplish three things today, what would they be?" or "What would I need to accomplish today to feel good about the day when I leave?" Make sure to do those things first.

Self-correct yourself with a quick reminder "flit-flit!" when you're being a butterfly. Try to imagine yourself, instead, with a postage stamp on your head, focusing on priority tasks.

CONCENTRATION quiz item #55:

> 55. I focus on one thing at a time; I don't multi-task or attempt to do too many things at once.

Watch Me Juggle Fifteen Things!

What are you doing right now while you're reading this? Monitoring a screen for stock figures? Ordering office supplies online? Installing a new piece of software? Carrying on instant message conversations with three coworkers? Eating your lunch while working on a proposal? If you're like most professionals today, you're probably multi-tasking. As technology increasingly tempts people to try several things at once, many have embraced multi-tasking as a valid way of increasing productivity.

I'd like to clear up two multi-tasking myths:

MYTH: MULTI-TASKING IS "DOING MORE THAN ONE THING AT A TIME." No, it's really switching back and forth very quickly *between* tasks.

The conscious mind is actually incapable of doing more than one thing at a time. For example, let's say you're typing an email and a coworker walks in and starts talking to you. Can you give the same amount of attention to constructing the email as you can to listening to the person? No.

MYTH: MULTI-TASKING ALLOWS YOU TO INCREASE YOUR EFFICIENCY AND PRODUCTIVITY BY WORKING MORE QUICKLY. Not so, according to newly released results of a scientific study in multi-tasking. Scientists have discovered some hidden costs of what they call "task switching." Research done by Rubinstein and Meyer, authors of "Human Perception and Performance" (*Journal of Experimental Psychology*, August 2001), indicates that multi-tasking, in fact, *reduces* productivity. They determined that for all types of tasks, subjects lost time when they had to switch from one task to another. Multi-tasking involves deciding to switch tasks, making the switch, and then getting warmed up on what you switched to. For example, let's say you're banging away on a report on your computer. Then the phone rings and you answer it. When you hang up, there is a lag between the moment you return to your document—where you say, "Okay, where was I?"—and getting your train of thought back. In effect, you briefly get "writer's block" as you go from one task to the other.

Stop multi-tasking and start focusing instead.

DEFLECT DROP-INS. Don't get sidelined by interruptions. If you're working on the last-minute details of a report for a meeting that starts in thirty minutes, don't accept a drop-in visitor's request to "ask you something really quick." When people say, "Gotta minute?" they never mean just one. Deflect the interruption by saying, "Hi, Donna [don't pause], I really want to talk with you about this, *and* I'm preparing for a meeting that begins in just a few minutes. Can I call you at three?"

DON'T OBEY YOUR THOUGHTS. Many times you interrupt yourself.

You're sitting at our desk, concentrating on an important project, when all of a sudden you remember you forgot to tell Chris about a project update. So you get up or pick up the phone or dash off an email to tell Chris. Then you go back to your desk and start working again, only to get another thought. "Oh, that's right!" you say, and you do that. Stop! Don't listen to your brain or you will never complete what's in front of you. This is why so many people have half-done projects all over the place!

COMMUNICATION LOGS. Grab a three-ring binder, some loose-leaf paper, and A–Z tabs. Create a separate sheet for each person you communicate with frequently. File the sheets behind the first letter of their last names. When your brain reminds you of something, log it on the person's sheet and go right back to what you were working on. When a person's sheet has several thoughts "saved-up," call that person and set up a meeting to review the items you've come up with.

Just remember what Clint Eastwood said at the end of one of his *Dirty Harry* movies: "A man's gotta know his limitations." Here's to the end of multi-tasking!

CONCENTRATION quiz item #56:

> 56. I make lists and record everything I need to do.

Where Should I Write That Down?

Some people feel as if they are going nuts from all the voices in their heads, constantly reminding them of things they need to do. If you keep everything *on* your mind *in* your mind, you could have brain clutter. At some point, your brain loses the ability to remember everything up there and you drop the ball.

Neuroscientists describe your memory as the "blackboard" or "sketchpad" of the brain. When you're working on one task and remembering to do another, the brain literally switches from one to the other, writing the previous one on the "blackboard." When the new task is completed (or interrupted), the brain returns for a peek at the previous one. If too many of these interrupted tasks stack up, the "blackboard" stops dropping some. That's why, in the middle of the night, you can sit bolt upright and exclaim, "Oh my gosh, I left that load of laundry in the washer!"

How do you help your poor brain and prevent mildewed clothes? *Capture every thought.* Whether you prefer paper or electronic methods, write everything down. Writing things down pulls what you need to do out of your memory and relieves your brain of the burden of repeatedly thinking about it. It gives your brain "resolution": your brain actually thinks you "did" it. Pretty neat, huh?

People who are list makers have already discovered this. The challenge is that the lists can get overwhelming. If you have a to-do list with sixty-seven things on it, you're using it for the right purpose but it's the wrong method. You actually need (at least) two lists: a daily to-do list and a master task (or memory) list. (See Chapter 1 for a description of other lists, like the project and life lists.) Many people keep a daily to-do list, but if you do, you may be missing the master task list.

Your master task list is an ongoing list that you will use for planning. You will keep adding to it and crossing things out. I have a personal master task list and a business master task list. I use blank lined paper the size of my planner and keep the lists behind tab numbers 1 and 2 (the FranklinCovey organizer provides numbered sections you may allot to any projects you choose). To begin one, sit down with blank sheets of paper and do a "brain dump." Write down anything that comes to mind you need to work on, even if it's written on a list somewhere else. If you think it, ink it.

- Phone calls
- Letters
- Errands
- New projects
- Equipment and supplies
- Financial matters
- Feedback to give or get
- Meetings
- Chores
- Furniture to be bought or cleaned
- Vacations or travel
- Car repairs
- Birthdays
- Appliances
- Yard work
- Health/doctor
- Exercise
- Books to read
- Pets

How do I use this list? Each month, I pick the four to six things I want to accomplish that month, pick a day to do each one, and transfer those items to my daily agenda for that day. Or, some people use a monthly or weekly agenda if they have some flexibility about which day a task could be accomplished. I make a monthly list from my master list. For example, one of the items on my master to-do list was "Call agent to inquire about publication process." If I selected that item to complete in January, I would transfer that item to my January monthly goal sheet in my planner and "time activate" that task by picking a day to do it and writing it on the corresponding daily to-do list.

Now that you've created this master task list, when a thought comes up into your memory:

1. Stop.
2. Ask yourself *when* you will do the task.
3. Write it on the appropriate daily to-do list, or
4. if it is a few months from now, write it on your master task list.

Here's an example. If you're working on a proposal and you think, "That couch is really dirty. I really should have that couch steam cleaned," stop. When do you plan to do that? Today? I doubt it. It's probably just something you want to remember to do at some point. I would turn to tab number one and write "Get couch steam cleaned" on my personal master task list.

Keep something with you at *all* times to write on to capture your thoughts. My planner is too large to carry around everywhere, so I keep a simple spiral notebook in my purse to write down things I think of or come across. If you use the Task list on Outlook or an electronic to-do tool, you still need something to write on until you get back to your computer. Write it down, and then enter it later.

If you align with the way your brain works and work *with* your memory, you will not only clear the brain clutter but stay focused as well.

CONCENTRATION **quiz item #57:**

> 57. I read quickly and maintain concentration; I rarely reread sentences.

I've Read This Paragraph Three Times!

Workers have unlimited information available at their fingertips, thanks to the Internet. If you tried to read every Web page, report, magazine article, business book, or email that came across your desk, you could spend your entire career reading. If you simply have too much to read and too little time, you can benefit from new reading techniques to boost your productivity. Getting through your reading tasks more quickly will free up time for other priorities.

Apply this five-step process to help you be a more productive reader:

1. PREPARE YOUR MATERIALS. Batch your reading and put larger documents aside to read during a single sitting. Schedule an appointment with yourself to get through them (I like to use the time on airplanes to get through my reading pile). When you reach the appointed time, gather your documents, along with a pen, a highlighter, and some sticky notes.

2. PREPARE YOUR MIND. If you can, retreat to an empty office or conference room so that you are interrupted as little as possible. Make the mental decision that you are going to attentively read your materials. Don't anticipate how terrible it's going to be or groan inwardly. Think positively and set goals around what you plan to accomplish or learn by the end of your reading session.

3. **SITUATE YOUR BODY.** Sit down with your spine straight and your feet comfortably on the floor. Don't hunch your shoulders, and take a few deep breaths to get oxygen to your brain. Relax your facial muscles, even turning up the corners of your mouth to match your positive attitude. Rest your book and your hands on the table, or prop the book up on a reading stand. Hold your reading square in front of your eyes at a 45- to 60-degree angle.

4. **SCAN.** When you begin, preview the text quickly to get a basic understanding of how the material is laid out and how the main points are organized. For magazine articles, I like to read the title, headings, sidebars, and the first and last paragraphs. By noticing the writing pattern and sections, you'll help your brain quickly organize the material.

5. **READ.** My favorite reading technique is called rhythmic perusal, developed by J. Michael Bennett, a reading expert and professor emeritus at the University of Minnesota. You glide your eyes over the upper half of the letters; read each line in a single, smooth movement. The technique enhances your concentration and, with practice, allows you to increase speed and focus.

If you apply these five simple reading techniques, you will greatly improve your concentration, speed, and retention. You will also have the upper hand for staying on top of important information in today's highly competitive work environment.

CONCENTRATION quiz item #58:

> 58. I recognize signs of brain overload and know how to get my mind focused again.

Can I Shut Down My Brain Now?

As you do, I have some days where I feel I might lose my mind. It starts when the alarm goes off . . . I get the boys dressed for daycare . . . James will want his Bob the Builder shirt again . . . oh yeah, I forgot to put that in the washer . . . the washer had library books all over it . . . oh yeah, forgot to return those . . . I'll do it on the way to Meagan's doctor appointment this evening . . . oh yeah, Meagan needed a sack lunch today because she has a field trip . . . oh yeah, I need to book that ticket for my business trip . . . oh yeah, I got distracted because I have fifty-six emails in my inbox . . . Faced with so many competing, attention-grabbing alternatives, I want to scream.

When your brain is too overloaded, it's nearly impossible to focus on anything. Overtaxed brains, bombarded by so many demands, actually begin to shut down. Have you ever walked into work one morning, looked at all the piles of paper everywhere, notes from your colleagues, emails in your inbox, and just started laughing? Your brain says, "I have no idea what to do first or where to begin, so I'm just going to stop making decisions altogether!"

Here are some ideas to give your mind a break and increase your focus and concentration:

CREATE STRUCTURE AND DEADLINES. Your short-term memory is horrible when you're on overload. Ask your manager and coworkers to put everything in writing. A simple trip to the restroom can be dangerous, as people waylay you en route with assignments. Simply be honest and say, "I don't have anything to write with, and I guarantee you I will forget that. Please send me an email about this." Deadlines help the brain put things into the proper order. Brief weekly meetings with your manager to discuss upcoming priorities may be helpful. Checklists for your regular daily tasks work well.

IGNORE UNINVITED OR UNWELCOME REQUESTS FOR YOUR TIME. If someone speaks to you when you pass in the hall, protocol dictates that you respond. Not so with email and voicemail. The corporate etiquette has changed. You don't have to respond to every message, and you shouldn't feel guilty about it. Some messages simply don't require a response. Doesn't it make you crazy when an FYI email was sent to a group of ten colleagues and *someone* has to "Reply to all" with a smug "I agree"? Arrrgghhh! My mother always taught me, "If you can't say something nice, don't say anything at all." I can extrapolate that to be, "If you don't have *something* to add, don't say anything at all." Even taking the time to say "no" politely can consume a big chunk of your time. Savvy professionals don't take it personally when people don't call back; they just move on to another prospect.

GUARD YOUR ATTENTION. The biggest attention-management culprit I see in the workplace today is instant messaging. You're right in the middle of reviewing those budget figures, and *ping,* a coworker asks you a question. You answer and try again to get focused, and *ping,* someone asks how you're doing with a little smiley face. Ping! Ping! Ping! You can get so many little windows open at once on your screen that it's virtually impossible to work. Like so many others, I have turned off my instant messaging function so I can concentrate. Some people haven't discovered you can "block" messages or take yourself off of buddy lists. If you're busy with something, go offline or "invisible." That way it appears you are offline and unavailable to chat. Unless you work in or interface with customer service or sales, and you need to get or give answers to real-time questions—quick—while you have a customer on the phone, turn it off.

PHONE AND TV AIDS. Consider getting Caller ID. You can tell who's calling and decide whether to accept the interruption. In a similar vein, some people swear by TiVo to record television shows. That way, they can watch them without all the distractions of the commercials, at a time that's convenient for them.

DO SOMETHING "MINDLESS." Some activities have meditative qualities to them: they are repetitive, boring, or don't require a lot of thinking, such as ironing, needlework, or reading. Time just seems to float by, and the mind slows down. For me, exercise is like this. My best ideas come to me on a treadmill or airplane, because I'm focused and my mind is quiet.

TAKE A DEEP BREATH. When your brain is taxed, deep breathing can help restore focus. Sit in a comfortable position, arms at your sides, and shoulders relaxed. Exhale as completely as you can through your mouth, with the chest and abdominal area collapsing and falling inward. Inhale slowly through your nose to the count of five, making your abdomen rise. Your chest, rib cage, and shoulders should not move at all. Exhale slowly through your mouth to the count of ten, sucking in your abdomen. Do ten to fifteen cycles of this breathing for a complete feeling of calm.

CONCENTRATION quiz item #59:

> 59. I get absorbed in a task and achieve a state of "flow" or "momentum," in which time seems to fly.

I'm in the Zone!

Do you ever feel like your mind is a million miles away? You can watch people in a meeting who are "somewhere else," and they have a faraway, glassy look. You *know* they're not hearing a word being said. They may be with you physically, but their minds are somewhere else, thinking about some meeting, worrying about that errand, or figuring out what someone meant by a passing comment.

Contrast that with an occasion when you were so immersed in an activity that time seemingly stood still. Your stomach suddenly growled, and you looked up at the clock to discover you'd worked right through your lunch hour. You didn't notice! You were totally immersed in what you were experiencing or doing.

How do you achieve this wonderful state of flow and become fully present-focused?

MASTER YOUR JOB. Research shows that your ability to experience flow is related to your mastery of the mechanics of your job. The more unfamiliar you are with your work, the harder it is to achieve. Just as learning to drive was at first a conscious behavior, when mastered, it became subconscious. If you're on a learning curve in a new activity, it will be harder to achieve intense focus. The more you learn the job, the better your ability to concentrate and "let go."

PREPARE FOR AND EXPECT TO ACHIEVE FOCUS. Set your mind properly. Consciously, willfully decide that you are going to concentrate. Have a positive attitude going into the task. Prepare your materials before getting started and have what you need at your fingertips.

CLEAR YOUR DESK. Do your piles talk to you? "Do this now!" "Don't forget me!" Clutter can be psychologically distracting. You will focus better on what's in front of you if you don't have ten other things surrounding you. Push other items off to the side or file them away before beginning on a task requiring concentration.

SET ASIDE TIME. Estimate how long the task will take and schedule an appointment with yourself on your calendar. Total absorption is very relaxing. It's splitting your attention—between what you're currently doing and what you have to do next—that's exhausting. When you become focused on the task of the moment, time seems to fly, and you get the job done easier and faster.

ENSURE NO INTERRUPTIONS. The ability to work uninterrupted is critical to an activity. Privacy will help you achieve a state of flow. Tom DeMarco and Timothy Lister, coauthors of *Peopleware: Productive Projects and Teams,* claim reaching a state of flow requires at least fifteen minutes of ramp-up concentration. People are especially sensitive to interruptions during this time. When they are disrupted, they can't go right back in. They require an additional fifteen minutes of time to get started again. This leads to increased frustration and reduced productivity. So close your door if you have one, or leave your office and retreat to an empty office where no one can find you.

BE THERE. Take each step deliberately and with full attention. Strive to be "in the moment." When you read a book to your child, really *read* a book to your child. Don't be focused on all the tasks waiting when you're finished. Be present and available and in the now for those people and tasks you care about.

CONCENTRATION quiz item #60:

> 60. I concentrate on a task that bores me or doesn't really interest me.

Force Yourself to Like It!

I don't like entering credit card receipts into QuickBooks. It would be *really* easy for it to stack up for a month. When it comes time to pay bills and balance the books, I can suddenly discover five or six other urgent things requiring my attention. Unfortunately, not all of our jobs thrill us. Even tedious, boring tasks must be completed. Here are some suggestions to help you concentrate on a task that bores you:

DO A LEADING TASK. Perhaps the task is making you anxious, such as returning a complaint call from a customer. Select a simple, low-effort part of the task to get you started. For example, you could pull the customer's file. Perform another leading task, such as reviewing the file. Pull the phone closer. In other words, complete everything up to the part of the activity you dread. Then the *only* thing left to do is pick up the phone. In order to discharge negative emotions, it might help to write down your thoughts and figure out what you're going to say before you call.

EAT A FROG FIRST. By completing unpleasant tasks early in the day, you won't feel the impending sense of doom hanging over your head all day. I like Mark Twain's quote, "If you eat a frog first thing in the morning, the rest of your day will be wonderful." Identify the "frog" on your list each day and eat it first. You'll feel great all day!

VARY YOUR ACTIVITIES. For mental and physical alertness, be sure to vary sitting activities with standing ones, mental activities with physical ones, and writing tasks with social tasks (such as meetings, phone calls, etc.). It will help prevent fatigue and keep your efficiency high.

CREATE REWARDS. Make a deal with yourself that when you complete the boring activity, you will do something fun afterward. By creating internal enthusiasm, I'm able to sit in front of the computer and enter receipts nonstop for an hour. I know that after I'm done, I get to eat chocolate *and* take a walk!

TURN IT INTO A GAME. Pretend this is the first time you've done this task. Give yourself a "pep talk" and be more enthusiastic. Whistle while you work. Turn on some light background music.

GIVE YOURSELF NEW RESPONSIBILITIES. Tasks that bore you can be changed! Can you find a way to do that task better? Can you make it more interesting? Can you do more research on the project? Can you add another piece to it, to make completing it more exciting? Instead of just paying bills, create a budget and compare items. Learn more about where your money is going.

CHECK FOR JOB FIT. Stress levels that are *too* low can contribute to job burnout. Perhaps you've been doing the same thing for too long. Is it time for a new challenge? Can you ask for new responsibilities? Can you join a committee or start a new task force? Because you know your job so well, you are the perfect person to redesign an inefficient process.

If you try these things and your work never gets more enjoyable or meaningful than before, then you have to look elsewhere. If you are consistently bored, you probably aren't in the right job.

CHAPTER SEVEN

Mastering the "T" in Productive

TIME MASTERY

"TIME MASTERY" REFERS TO how well you manage your activities throughout the day. Some people spend more time planning vacations or finances than they do their lives. Time is like money, because it's a limited commodity and requires thoughtful analysis and planning.

Without good time management, you can experience negative consequences such as missed deadlines, late nights, stress, crisis, and overload. Good time management brings the rewards of results, recognition, free time, clarity, and focus. It gives you a purpose in life, structure to your day, direction, and reduced frustration. Time mastery brings you to the end of the day with a sense of accomplishment. In addition, it reduces stress and illness because it gives you much more control over your day, people, and life. Time mastery allows you to run your life and keeps life from running you.

> 61. I manage my reading pile so it doesn't "mushroom."

Information Does *Not* Equal Power

Does your reading pile look like you poured fertilizer on it? It just grows and grows and grows! You've heard the old adage, "Information equals power." Correction, that's actually *potential* power. If you have the information but don't do anything with it, you have no power.

With the proliferation of information on the Internet, people cannot possibly look at it all. But they still have an almost obsessive-compulsive urge to read everything from aardvarks to zoology. However, when you have more reading material than you have energy to digest, the surplus is converted by stress and overstimulation into an unhealthy state of misplaced guilt for not having read it! You add magazines, articles, and newspapers to the top of your reading pile and feel guilty every time you think of what you should read.

Here are some tips to get you started tackling your reading pile:

LOCATE THEM CONVENIENTLY. Publications often accumulate in a pile because they are physically located at an inconvenient place. Ask yourself where you really *like* to read. Locate your reading pile where you want it versus where you think it should go. Then watch that pile disappear! For example, I had a friend who used to spread out her magazines nicely on her coffee table in her living room. She didn't enjoy reading there because it was a major traffic area and the television was always on. She relocated her stack to the back of the couch in her study. Although her magazines looked pretty in the living room, this location wasn't functional because she never read anything there.

START OVER. Why not throw out most or all of the pile and start fresh? It feels so good! And your career is not going to stall because you missed an article. Every time you get a new edition of *Newsweek* or *Time* or other another weekly magazine, the contents of the old one becomes *old news.* If you haven't read it yet, throw out the previous week's issue when the newer one comes in.

DON'T READ MAGAZINES COVER TO COVER. The task is simply too overwhelming. Besides, most advertising never changes. Go through the table of contents, allow yourself a maximum of three articles per issue, rip them out, and throw the rest of the magazine away. Single articles are much less formidable than a stack of magazines. Put the articles in a folder marked "To be read," stick a few in your purse, or store them in your briefcase. Take your reading with you *everywhere* and read while waiting or during other free times.

SCAN AND MARK. Skim a book when it comes across your desk and mark the sections you want to read later with a sticky note and a key word. Don't read any books or magazines with a low return on investment, unless you're reading for pleasure. There is simply too much to read.

PLAY CATCH-UP. Spend an occasional weekend catching up on the important reading once and for all. Get creative! Try the timer technique. Set an egg timer for fifteen minutes for each periodical. When the timer goes off, that one goes in the trash.

TRY TEAM READING. Team members trade off reading important articles and writing a synopsis of important ideas for the group. They also can read books cooperatively by splitting up chapters and writing a "Cliffs Notes" version of each, consecutively, so one builds upon the other.

DON'T READ AT ALL. Save items in electronic copy, then search for them and read them when required. When I come across an interesting article on the Internet, I click the "Printer Friendly" button, then copy it, and paste the text into a searchable database my IT guy created (or you can scan hardcopy articles and use OCR software to copy and paste the text). My database contains fields for the title, clipping number, publication, date, author, key words, and text. When I need information on a particular topic, I can search for items by key word or do a text search string of the clipping text. The specific articles come up, and I can always print them to take on an airplane to read.

To completely conquer a reading obsession, you have to believe (despite your conditioning) that little of what you insist on saving is of real importance! Remember, 80 percent of what gets filed is never looked for again anyway. Be *ruthless* and *realistic*!

TIME MASTERY quiz item #62:

> 62. I create systems for repetitive tasks.

Never Do the Same Thing Twice

If you perform a task one time and find yourself doing it again, *stop.* Ask yourself, "When have I already done this?" Many people waste time on repetitive tasks instead of putting an automated system or process in place. Figure out how to do a repetitive task efficiently, so you don't waste time each time for the same results. If you're going to do something more than two times, figure out how to automate it. Look through the tasks that you do every day, week, month, over and over again. What can you do to replicate those tasks?

PROGRAM MACROS. For example, to address an envelope or label, I used to look up the contact's name in my ACT contact management software, get out a pen, grab an envelope, and write the information by hand. I knew my printer was capable of printing envelopes and labels, but I was "too busy" to figure out how to use the feature. After I accidentally stumbled across the Print, Envelope feature in my database, I tested it. My printer printed a beautifully typed address on plain paper. After I finally figured out how to manually load an envelope in my printer, I took it a step further and figured out how to create a macro. Now I simply find the name, hit one button, and load the envelope—presto! Everything else is done automatically. By investing a small amount of time in figuring out how to systematize the process, I will save significant amounts of time in the future.

REUSE INFORMATION. My literary agent, Robert Shepard, has always impressed me with his detailed explanations of the publishing process. He takes the time to explain everything to me in terms I can understand. I knew he must spend significant time composing his rather lengthy emails, because they were so jam-packed with great information. Out of curiosity, I asked him if he saved them for future use, which he hadn't. So he copied the most recent messages he'd composed and saved them in word processing documents. Now he will be able to use that information again with the next inquiring author . . . and the next . . . and the next. Why reinvent the wheel?

CREATE DOCUMENT TEMPLATES. A template is a shell document that contains the formatting, text, and graphics you need every time for a specific type of document. When I first started my business, I found myself repeating my words over and over as I composed client letters. I was also switching back and forth between my contact management software and my word processing software to get address information. I manually copied and pasted information from one application to another to create contracts and other agreements. After some trial and error, I learned how to create document templates. Now I execute a few simple keystrokes and the documents write themselves. In MS Word, create templates using the ".dot" format, so they open as an untitled document. When you save it, Word will automatically prompt you to give the document a different name, eliminating the chance you'll accidentally save over a template. In this way, you can create templates for large mailings, letters, newsletters, labels, and reports.

LEARN SHORTCUTS. If you find yourself opening the same computer file over and over from the Start menu, why not create a shortcut on your desktop to that file? Any time you point and click with the mouse for the same feature, speed up the process by using the keyboard shortcut. I often need to change the case of my text from sentence case to capitals, and I find it tedious to use the menu system. Instead, I use a shortcut. With the cursor on the word to capitalize, hold shift and press F3, once to capitalize the first letter, twice to capitalize the entire word, and a third time to go to lower case. If the word is already capitalized, the sequence works anyway: "Capital" becomes "CAPITAL," becomes "capital" in that order (for MS Word). Most shortcuts are a combination of two or three keys that you will need to hold down simultaneously to trigger the command. While they may seem awkward at first, they will become second nature once you use them regularly. Use the Help menu in your word processing program to find a complete list of shortcuts.

CONSOLIDATE CALENDARS. It was simple to schedule my appointments and speaking engagements when I was single, because I only had one calendar. Enter a husband. Enter children. Enter clients who wanted to be able to check my speaking calendar without having to place a call to me. Enter an office assistant.

Suddenly, I had my personal calendar, the family wall calendar, my husband's calendar, the office wall calendar, and a Web-based calendar. Any time a client placed a hold on a date, five calendars would have to be updated. (Don't I teach this stuff?) So I boiled everything down to a single system. All my speaking engagements are now tracked on a single Web-based program. This master calendar links to my website and my speaker bureaus' websites. Clients can check my schedule, and my husband and staff can access my calendar from any Internet location. Anything that affects my time is recorded in my FranklinCovey planner.

PROVIDE INFORMATION. If your coworkers are repeatedly asking the same things, create a "Frequently Asked Questions" (FAQ) document. If people are interrupting you to ask for forms, create a "self-help" center outside your office and load it with the desired information. As much as possible, take yourself out of the middle of the process.

USE THE AUTO-CORRECT FEATURE. If you are constantly typing out the long form of common abbreviations in your company or correcting the same misspelled word, using the auto correction feature of your word processing program will save you much time. Most programs automatically fix commonly mistyped or misspelled words, and you can add your own to the list. For example, you can program it to spell out Table of Contents each time you type "TOC" in quotes, to distinguish it from the actual acronym. In MS Word, select the Insert menu, then "AutoText" to program this feature.

> 63. I know and avoid my biggest time wasters.

That Was a Huge Waste of Time!

If you're interested in a book like this, you're most likely already a fairly good time manager. You know how to make lists; you know how to check things off. So if you're such a hard worker, why don't you get all the work done you'd like to in a day? Lots of things waste time. However, I have *rarely* found circumstances that are 100 percent completely uncontrollable; almost every time waster has a solution.

Reducing time wasters is a three-step process:

1. Discover the time waster.
2. Identify alternatives to address it.
3. Implement your solutions.

DISCOVER THE TIME WASTER. Bob is the manager of the artistic and reproduction services groups. He makes major purchase decisions for his organization on printing, photocopiers, storage solutions, etc. Accordingly, he has vendors stopping by unannounced to demonstrate their products. Since they made the long trip out there, he would feel bad turning them away, but the unscheduled product demonstrations would throw his schedule for a loop.

IDENTIFY ALTERNATIVES TO ADDRESS IT. He will make better use of his administrative support staff that runs the repro shop. Rather than ushering vendors to his office at any time, they will screen vendors. Upon arrival, the staff will pull out Bob's new monthly appointment schedule book, in which Bob has blocked out a half-day twice each month for appointments. Since he wouldn't know the vendor even stopped by, he has agreed to stop feeling guilty for turning them away. Having a policy stating "No walk-in appointments" will keep the turn-away from being personal. Vendors will still have the opportunity to demonstrate their goods, but it will be at Bob's convenience instead of the other way around.

IMPLEMENT SOLUTIONS. Identifying time wasters and brainstorming solutions is the easier side of the equation. Creating the muscle to make it happen is the tougher side. You may have to get your manager involved to give the authority to create new policies that will help you be more productive. One of my clients was the corporate purchasing department for a large beer manufacturer. After I surveyed fifteen people in the department to help design a customized productivity seminar, common complaints emerged about extensive meetings and shortage of support staff. When I talked with the department manager about my findings, she was incredulous that no one had approached her about the severity of these problems or asked her to intervene.

I asked her if they had the authority to set policy in specifying when their attendance was required at meetings. She said they had all the authority they needed. I asked her if the agents could submit their inputs in writing prior to attending the meeting; she said absolutely. Could they ask to be put first on the agenda? Yes. Could they send someone in their place if they thought it was a low-priority meeting? Yes. Could they set fixed office hours, and insist that internal customers schedule appointments before "dropping by"? Yes. Could they institute a policy, requiring certain lead times in different contracting situations? Yes. Everything I asked her was both possible and probable. Because no one had approached this manager about the problems and possible solutions, they were suffering in silence.

Go out on a limb and schedule an appointment with your manager to discuss your findings and brainstorm possible solutions. You don't know what kind of support you'll get until you ask. If you have a good manager, he or she is extremely interested in any solution that will yield greater employee productivity.

TIME MASTERY quiz item #64:

> 64. I eliminate bottlenecks in my work caused by people or processes.

You're Slowing Me Down Here!

You could be so much more efficient if it weren't for other people, right? We waste a lot of time waiting for approvals, return phone calls, opinions, information, or pieces of a project. But if you're waiting on the same people repeatedly, or you routinely use "I'm waiting" as an excuse for not meeting a deadline, you need to take steps to minimize bottlenecks. Here are some techniques to analyze the patterns and minimize common slowdowns:

REORGANIZE THE WORKFLOW. Getting together with all the players in a particular process (sales, engineering, manufacturing, customer service, etc.) may quickly reveal what's broken. Sometimes a simple change in the flow of work will boost productivity. Use sticky notes to plot an entire process, using a wall to diagram the different steps. Ask, "What would work better?" "How can we eliminate this step?" "How can we do this more efficiently?"

ELIMINATE DEPENDENCIES. Do you feel excessively dependent on others to get your work done? Perhaps you need training or additional experience to help you function more effectively in your present job. Perhaps your manager is oversupervising or micromanaging your work to a point where you feel nervous making simple decisions anonymously. Make an appointment with your supervisor and have a candid discussion about ways you can be more efficient.

DON'T BE A BOTTLENECK YOURSELF. If you hear others saying things to you such as "I need you to look at this before I go on" or "When will you have time to review this for me?" these are symptoms of other people trying to control your schedule. On one hand, it's a compliment to your expertise; however, their lack of confidence keeps them from handling things without you. If people truly don't have the skills, that's one thing. But if others are routinely delegating decisions to you, take a stand. State specifically, "I'm confident you'll make the right decision." Or "You are responsible for managing this project." Or "This task is due September 5. This is how I will measure your success. This is your budget. If you run into problems, keep me informed on how you're handling things."

KEEP THE PROCESS MOVING. When coordinating a project with a coworker, get buy-in on the due date. Once promises have been made, repeat and nail down the commitment. Say, "Great, you'll get that to me by close of business Wednesday." Then let that person see you write it down. Say, "Thanks so much for your support. I can always count on you." Appealing to someone's honor in this way may increase the chances of timely completion. When people finish a promised task, no matter how small, thank them. Never take others' work for granted. They will want to help you again the next time.

ACCEPT PARTIAL DELIVERY. Some people are perfectionists, so create the proper expectations from the beginning. Explain what you need at a minimum to get moving. Let people know you'll take incomplete information until the complete information is available. They can provide things in formal or final form at a later date. If necessary, escalate the problem to your supervisor to negotiate the situation at a higher level.

Bottlenecks at work are like traffic jams: they bring things to a standstill. The "traffic jam" in your work will continue to occur until you do something about it. Pinpoint that recurring "thing" that halts your work and put energy into eliminating it. You'll save much time and frustration in the long run.

TIME MASTERY quiz item #65:

> 65. I recognize that different personalities relate to time differently; I understand how to work effectively with each style.

What's Your Sign?

We all seek to be productive and manage our time well, but how we do this will vary from person to person according to individual personalities. You may observe the way someone approaches a project, for example, and think, "That's not the way I would have done it." One person might go around and talk to others, bouncing ideas off them, while you like to work independently at first and collect all the data you will need. You are both productive and get the project accomplished; you just went about it differently.

It's only with this type of understanding of your style that you can self-correct your weaknesses. Though there are variations on all of these, I've observed four major time management styles over the years, each with different characteristics and motivations. It helps you understand your time-effective assets and time-ineffective liabilities.

Here's how to use this section:

1. Read through the "four time styles" and determine which best describes you.
2. Check those time-ineffective liabilities that apply to you.
3. Come up with an action plan on how you can improve your time management by highlighting your strengths and controlling your trouble spots.
4. Go back to the "four time styles" and identify others on your team or department.
5. Go to the section called "How to Work with Others" and read the suggestions there to work more effectively with others.

The four time styles

1. BULLDOZERS

DESCRIPTION: Suzanne is a hard-working, go-go type of person who likes to push hard and accomplish much during the day. She gets great satisfaction in checking things off her list. Time gives her an opportunity to accomplish her many projects, goals, and objectives. Her team views her as a great achiever, but she sometimes rolls over them in her quest to complete her tasks. Suzanne is frequently impatient when someone interrupts her from her current activity.

BEHAVIORAL CUES:
- Makes quick decisions
- Likes to be in charge
- Is task-oriented and doesn't have patience for process
- Is focused on goals

MOTIVATION: Bulldozers are highly motivated by feelings of success.

TIME-EFFECTIVE ASSETS:

- Active and energetic when given a project
- Sees things through to completion, as quickly as possible
- Assertive when deadlines are involved
- Highly productive; gets many things accomplished

TIME-INEFFECTIVE LIABILITIES:

- Can be insensitive and overlook interpersonal factors
- Often perplexed or frustrated by people who need time to think; impatient
- Resentful when others take time for themselves
- Quality sometimes suffers in favor of quantity; result is more important than the means
- Takes on too much work and experiences burnout; may juggle too much

2. ENERGIZER BUNNIES

DESCRIPTION: Chris loves to have a good time at work. He looks forward to his day and is excited about all the things he will accomplish. Time is like a bottomless fount, just waiting for him to fill it. When given a new project, he looks at it like an adventure and enthusiastically jumps in. He loves to think of creative solutions and enjoys the experience of putting new ideas in motion. He's open to others' ideas, and the exchange is fun. When a conclusion is reached, it's almost a downer, because now he'll actually have to do some work to implement it. When he finishes a task, he loves people telling him how wonderful he is.

BEHAVIORAL CUES:

- Chatty and expressive
- Persuasive and motivational

- Fun-loving and adventurous
- Fast-paced and energetic

MOTIVATION: They are highly motivated by the presence of many **options.**

TIME-EFFECTIVE ASSETS:
- Inspires others to get excited about a new task
- Generates options and alternatives
- Spontaneity is engaging and motivating when a team gets bogged down on a project
- Creative; good at brainstorming ideas and options

TIME-INEFFECTIVE LIABILITIES:
- Finds it tedious to complete the work required to finish a project
- Frequently interrupts others "just to chat" about ideas
- Has difficulty focusing and switches spontaneously from task to task
- Doesn't know when to stop talking about work and get down to business; can make others feel impatient to get started
- Can be messy and have a disorganized office

3. HARMONICAS

DESCRIPTION: Sarah has lots of friends at work, and everyone likes her. She operates at a slow but steady pace. She gathers input from the entire team before proceeding and takes the time necessary to make correct decisions that allow everyone to win. Sarah is process-oriented when making decisions: everyone's questions must be answered and everyone's goals must be met. She doesn't make decisions until she considers everyone's needs, so it can take her an hour to make a ten-minute decision (she would feel just *awful* if she hurt anyone's feelings). Sarah will work diligently to implement solutions the team came up with, even if she doesn't necessarily agree with the course of action. If it's for the good of the team, she's on board. Harmonicas are much better at detail than the Energizer Bunnies and much more tolerant than the Bulldozers.

BEHAVIORAL CUES:
- Good listener
- Team player
- Focuses on process
- Takes time to make decisions

MOTIVATION: They are highly motivated by the presence of **consensus.**

TIME-EFFECTIVE ASSETS:
- Ensures buy-in from the entire team and includes everyone's opinions
- Less rework, since everyone's input is considered the first time
- Low conflict: will handle the task your way
- Helps others and pitches in where needed; works hard

TIME-INEFFECTIVE LIABILITIES:
- Takes longer to make a decision
- Completes a task the way someone else wants it done, even if it doesn't make sense
- Might harbor resentment or grudges for picking up slack where others are goofing off; may "tolerate" too long

- Complains inwardly but won't take action; passive-aggressive

4. CEREBRALS

DESCRIPTION: Tom feels dominated by time; there is never enough of it! He is quite the perfectionist and never feels like there's enough time to get things right. Tom pushes for extended deadlines because he knows it will take more time than he's been given. When Tom completes a project, he always has a vague sense of dissatisfaction, knowing it could have been better if he had more time. He gets frustrated in meetings by people who make decisions too quickly, because obviously they haven't considered all the data and facts. He approaches problems logically, coming up with all the pros and cons of every alternative. When he finally makes a recommendation, he's 100 percent sure he's correct. Organized and thorough, he has exacting expectations of himself. Tom is rather quiet and doesn't display much emotion; he's rather private and would prefer to work alone. During team discussions, he holds back his opinions, and gives you the distinct impression he's considering everyone's ideas. When he finally speaks, everyone listens, because he's generally right on target.

BEHAVIORAL CUES:
- Analytical, logical
- Thorough
- Step-by-step
- Rational
- Organized

MOTIVATION: They are motivated by **correctness and principles.**

TIME-EFFECTIVE ASSETS:

- Thorough, applying great attention to detail
- Organized; good sense of order; every item is in its place
- Good at making a team look at all the facts
- Can handle a complex problem requiring extensive investigation of the facts
- When delegating work, provides precise instructions on how to proceed

TIME-INEFFECTIVE LIABILITIES:

- Too much attention to detail; gets bogged down and loses sight of the goal
- Often gets overwhelmed with half-done projects
- Takes too long to make simple decisions; perfectionist
- Can seem aloof and non-caring to people who thrive on relationships
- May require too much data and information; doesn't get off ground zero

Which one describes you? You might have recognized yourself in several different categories; indeed, we are all four-styled people to a certain extent. But one style fits you better than the others. It slips on as smoothly and naturally as a tight-fitting glove.

How to work with others

HOW TO WORK WITH BULLDOZERS: If you give these people a project, you will need to sit them down and establish priorities. They will get it done, but tell them your expectations of the *quality* of the result, especially if the outcome isn't speed. Be direct, brief, and to the point when providing information. Touch on the high points rather than giving a detailed, data-rich history. Bulldozers don't like a lot of chitchat, so focus on the task and get down to business.

HOW TO WORK WITH ENERGIZER BUNNIES: Recognize that they will be excited about new projects, so you must stress the importance of seeing them through to the end. Set milestones and check in with them frequently to ensure they don't procrastinate until the very end. Don't give them too many options; they tend to bite off more than they can chew. Set deadlines and specify exactly what you want the result to look like. Energizer Bunnies will want to talk, so allow time in your schedule to socialize when you delegate. They will enjoy kicking ideas around with you in the beginning, so be forthcoming with all your ideas and possible approaches. Upon successful completion of a task, provide opportunities for recognition and reward.

HOW TO WORK WITH HARMONICAS: Do your homework up front and check with a few people on the team before approaching these people. How do others feel? Who has done this before and experienced success? Give them projects that aren't time-crunched or require more input and consensus. Have them chair cross-functional task forces or committees that stretch across departments. They are good team builders and can rally the support of large groups of people and get them going in the same direction. If you can give them the time, these people will ensure projects get done right the first time. Be patient with them when talking and allow time for discussion. Relax, because you're going to be there a while. Harmonicas will ask you lots of questions, but will rarely offer opinions of their own. So be sure to draw out their opinions and directly ask what they think. When a change is coming down the pipeline, involving them right up front in the planning process will make it less scary for them down the road.

HOW TO WORK WITH CEREBRALS: If you give these people projects, they will take them on and do them perfectly and thoroughly. However, it can take longer than you anticipated. So you need to set a deadline for accomplishment. Spell out the procedure exactly and put limits on the projects. Without specific direction, Cerebrals will give 110 percent to a project only requiring 75 percent effort. Allow time for them to think; don't demand an answer "off the cuff." Use data and facts and examine an argument from all sides. When delegating work or interrupting them for a question, keep on task and don't socialize. Don't take it personally if a Cerebral disagrees with you; it's the facts that are wrong, not the person.

Which is the best style?

The bottom line is that no one style is the "correct" style; no one way is the "right" way to do things (although you probably think so). Optimally, you'd like to have a mix of time styles in a team. If you had all Bulldozers on a team, everyone would want to be in charge, but there would be no one to do the work. If you had all Energizer Bunnies on a team, wow, you'd sure have a great time and come up with fabulous ideas, but nothing would get done. If you had all Harmonicas on a team, you would never leave the meeting because everyone would be so busy being polite to other people and making sure they've been heard. If you had all Cerebrals on a team, it would take forever to consider all the pros and cons of every alternative and the result would never be "good enough" to be finished with the task.

In your next staff meeting, talk with your team members about the four time styles. Have them each self-identify a style, put it up on easel paper, and discuss how you will try harder to understand one another and work more productively as a team.

TIME MASTERY quiz item #66:

> 66. I know how much my time is worth and eliminate those
> things that are a waste of my time.

Take Time to Make Time

Professionals lament, "I just don't have enough hours in the day!"
or "If I just had more time, I could get everything done." Unfortunately, you can't have it. Time is the one thing that *is* consistent—24 hours in every day. Oh, sure, you could get up an hour
earlier every day five days a week, or stay up an hour later. That
would be . . . let's see . . . roughly 240 extra hours a year, divided
by 24 hours in a day, would produce ten extra days a year! However, could you possibly be productive at 4:30 a.m. when you already get up at 5:30 a.m. or at midnight when you already go to
bed at 11 p.m.? You may already be stretched beyond the maximum effort and minimum sleep requirements. Besides, it doesn't
make sense to make that kind of sacrifice for a measly ten extra
days.

So change your thinking. Since you can't create time, you
must realize:

*There's always time to do what's really important. The challenge is determin-
ing what's important.*

Do this simple exercise: Get a blank piece of paper, make two
columns, and label one "Non-negotiables," and the other "Negotiables." The things you *must* do in life are the non-negotiables.
The things you'd *like* to do are the negotiables. Spend ten minutes
brainstorming these areas in your life. Take an introspective look
at how you spend your days and weeks—first a broad view, then
more specific.

Now you should analyze your data. How can you spend

more time in the Negotiables column and less time in the Non-negotiables column?

1. Perform required tasks more efficiently (such as pay bills online or make lists and purchase groceries once a week).
2. Manage your time more effectively (like not socializing too much with your friends at work, so you can leave work on time and be with your family).
3. Get rid of activities in the Non-negotiables column.

I think option number three deserves careful attention. You might be thinking, "How would I get rid of these things? That's not possible." Remember that non-negotiables can keep you from the negotiables. Negotiables can get pushed out of your life altogether as you run from one non-negotiable to the next. Unfortunately, people often put the *really* important things in life in the Negotiables column. I frequently see activities such as hobbies, exercise, sleep, socializing, time with family, reading, and relaxing in the negotiable column. Hmmm . . . shouldn't exercise be non-negotiable? Shouldn't we be spending more time with our families? Do you ever have any time for yourself? How about social activities (do you *have* any friends left)?

Sit back and really brainstorm some ideas for a moment. For every item on your list, challenge yourself, *"Is this item really non-negotiable?"* For example, if you listed doing laundry, cooking, yard work, cleaning, attending PTA meetings, working, and going grocery shopping as your non-negotiables, ask yourself if there's a different way to get those accomplished. Here are some ideas to get you started:

UNDERSTAND THE DOLLAR VALUE OF TIME. Does money buy time? Absolutely! Money buys all kinds of time. How much is yours worth? If a mystical "time fairy" could fly over and "sell" you an hour of free time, to spend on anything in the Negotiables column, how much would you pay for it? Is it worth $5, $10, $20, or more? Your time has an intrinsic value to it. Not what you're paid at work, but how much it's worth. Most professionals I poll informally in my audiences across the country say that at this point in their lives, they would rather have more time than more money.

Do a quantitative analysis of every item in the Non-negotiables column and find out if it's worth hiring it out. I used to say to myself, "I will never hire anyone to clean my house for me; I'm perfectly capable of doing it myself. What a waste of money." But then I starting tracking how much time I spent cleaning and came up with five hours a week on average! That's 20 hours a month and approximately 250 hours a year. At this point in my life, anything worth $15 an hour or below, I pay someone else to do. So I put an ad in the paper, interviewed housekeepers, and selected a woman who has been with me for years. She comes every other week, stays for five hours, and charges me $15 an hour, or $75. Let's see, that's $150 a month or $1,800 a year. Is it worth it? For the 250 hours a year it takes me to clean, if I valued my time at only $10 an hour, I'm saying I'd be willing to pay 250 × $10 = $2,500 a year to get that chore completed for me. So is it worth it? At only $1,800, it's a steal (of course, I'm not going to tell her that). Using this same process to calculate the time value of money, we've hired out our yard work and laundry as well.

PUSH VALUE TO THE LOWEST COMMON DENOMINATOR. In addition to the bigger jobs, I have many little tasks to complete (to the tune of about five hours a week). These don't take more than a few minutes each but are nonetheless time-consuming and offer a low payback. For example: run to the grocery store, return the pants that don't fit, drop off the dry cleaning, take the shoes to the cobbler, pick up the prescriptions, get gas in the car, go to the bank, take the shirt to the tailor, buy stamps at the post office, and get highlighters at the office supply store. Whew!

Like me, you've got so many little things that are necessary to make your life work. But by the time you've completed all these little errands, you've eaten up your precious weekend! Instead, hire a high school or college student to be your personal assistant or gopher for around $8 an hour. Our assistant works twice a month for four hours at a time, $8 × 4 = $32 × 2 = $64 a month, which is an extremely low sum, given all the free time I have! I keep a running list and "save up" all the things my assistant can knock out in several hours. And she'd much rather work for me than flip hamburgers somewhere.

HAVE IT DELIVERED. Anything you normally have to shop for or pick up can be delivered. I first discovered this technique when I observed a van with "Dry Cleaning Express" written on the side driving around my neighborhood. Think about all the time you spend running back and forth to the dry cleaner—it's a no-brainer to use a delivery service for things like this!

Many grocery stores will do your shopping for you and deliver food. You can have diapers and dog food and birthday presents delivered. Take advantage of Internet and catalogue shopping as well. In many cases, the delivery is free as a value-added service to get you to buy. And do I ever! Even if they do charge a nominal shipping or delivery fee, it's cheaper than doing it yourself, if you factor in the value of your time. And it frees up your personal assistant to do other tasks.

RUN ERRANDS WHEN OTHERS ARE NOT. Finally, if you *must* do the non-negotiables, don't do things when everyone else is doing them. Determine when most people traditionally perform that particular activity and do it at a non-traditional time. For example, John and I like to go grocery shopping with our kids on Friday night. Exciting, huh? But hey, no one else is there, the experience is much more pleasant, and we get through the activity much more quickly.

Get creative! How about commuting? Why drive when everyone else is driving and waste time on the road? When vacationing, go at off-peak times to find higher service levels and less crowding. How about getting to work early, packing your lunch, and having an earlier dinner at a restaurant, when there's no wait? When John and I want to see a new movie, we wait a couple weeks until the lines die down. If you want to start an exercise routine, work your schedule so you take your long break at an odd time, like ten or two, so you can actually get on a fitness machine. If you go before or after normal work hours, you will have to wait. Don't go to the library on weekends, the post office at lunch, or the bank on Fridays. It just makes sense! You have to plan a bit and schedule errands differently, but you'll soon find out how much time you can save each week by not following the same schedule as everyone else.

In summary, having fewer non-negotiables will let you experience more of what's really important in your life and free up valuable negotiable time. Practice these strategies, and you will find more time to do what you want to do, rather than what you feel you have to do.

TIME MASTERY quiz item #67:

> 67. I save time in bits and pieces; I know that little things add up.

A Stitch in Time

If you're like many people, an extra ten minutes before a break, lunch, or the end of the day isn't productive time, because there's not enough time to start anything. Do you ever wait for a "block of time" to begin a task? How often do blocks of time suddenly appear in your day? All your big stretches of time may be accounted for, but what about in between? The truth is there's plenty of time to do many things in ten minutes, five minutes, or three minutes. Those fragments of time, when saved, collected, and weighed, add up to the same big chunk of time. Set a big bucket under a little drip, and the bucket will be full in a few hours. Granted, you can't achieve the high level of concentration in ten minutes that you can in twenty. However, those bits and pieces of time are opportunities to either chip away at larger projects or finish off smaller activities.

Think about the bits and pieces of time you waste:

- Riding as a passenger in a car
- Watching commercials
- Daydreaming
- Socializing
- Waiting for appointments
- Standing around
- Gossiping
- Taking breaks

Always ask yourself, "What is the very best use of my time at this exact moment?" The key is preparation. Some bits of time, like waiting, are inevitable. You must plan for them so that you're prepared when one strikes. Carry low-priority work or reading around with you, because you never know when or where dead time will occur. I keep stamped postcards with me in my briefcase so that I can whip out a thank-you note when I have a spare minute. Have running lists of fifteen-, ten-, and five-minute tasks ready:

FIFTEEN-MINUTE LIST

- Read a newspaper
- Sketch a proposal
- Plan a project
- Complete one small piece of a larger project
- Enter business cards into your contact file

TEN-MINUTE LIST

- Plan for tomorrow
- Pay some bills
- Write a thank-you note
- Read an article
- Water the plants

FIVE-MINUTE LIST

- Write a grocery list
- Make a phone call
- Dust a shelf
- Clean out one file
- Do some sit-ups
- Stretch

You won't have a three-minute list, because if you can complete something in three minutes or less, you should do it immediately, regardless of the seeming importance. Small things, such as an initial, approval signature, and surveys add up quickly. You wind up with thirty-three things to do, in which the cumulative time spent shuffling and rereading the items amounts to far more than it would have taken to just complete the task in the first place! Get into the habit of asking, "Would this take me three minutes or fewer to complete?" If the answer is "fewer," *don't put it down.* Make yourself do it right then.

Thoreau said it best: "What good is immortality, if we cannot use half an hour well here?" Glean instead of dream, and meditate instead of vegetate. Seize the moment and do something with all those bits and pieces of time.

TIME MASTERY quiz item #68:

> 68. I make effective use of downtime.

Take Time to Take a Breather

The only thing worse than wasting time is having someone else waste it for you! I *plan* for people like my doctor to be late, and I've been known to be disappointed when I don't get my half-hour in her lobby. If I'm meeting a client or friend for lunch, there's the inevitable traffic jam that could leave me at Applebee's for twenty minutes with nothing to read but the menu.

Here are some ideas on making your downtime productive time:

READ. I keep a large wicker basket in my living room. When I receive catalogues, magazines, or trade journals, I just toss the "keepers" in there (many get thrown in the trash). When I go on a plane trip, I simply gather up all I've saved and pack it in my briefcase. Or I save my information-only mail to read over lunch and decompress a bit.

LISTEN TO TAPES. When driving around town or on long trips, I make the best use of commute time by listening to a bimonthly audio series for professional speakers called SpeakerNet News (www.speakernetnews.com). The time passes quickly, and I'm able to keep up with the latest in my profession. If you have a big reading pile, try ordering the books on tape from the bookstore or your library. The average person drives between twelve thousand and twenty thousand miles each year—that's an incredible opportunity to learn instead of listening to the radio, even if you can only listen for ten minutes on the way to the store. Also purchase a portable tape player or CD player to use with earphones when you fly, when you're waiting in line at the supermarket, or just puttering in the garden. A tape recorder is also handy for dictating ideas while driving, since you can't always stop to write something down.

SET TIME LIMITS. Don't sit on hold or wait for an appointment for too long. Abandon the "I've waited this long, it would be a waste to hang up!" mentality. Be productive while you're waiting. Use the speakerphone so you can work while you wait. Get a headset, preferably wireless, so you can still use your hands and move around your office, filing, reading mail, answering email, or doing other computer work. If you've waited long enough, don't waste any more time. Ask the assistant to have your client call you back, or ask the receptionist to call your party's extension and leave a message that you'll call to reschedule.

SORT MAIL. When I'm waiting to pick Meagan up from Girl Scouts or soccer practice, I keep a pile of low-priority mail to read and sort through while waiting. However, sometimes I just want to relax. Listening to the radio may sometimes be soothing. Or I might just sit there, on purpose, as a way of emptying my mind and decompressing.

TIME MASTERY quiz item #69:

> 69. I avoid time wasters within my department or organization.

Overcoming Organizational and Departmental Speed Bumps

COMMUNICATION. How can you say, "Professional growth is important," if you don't spend time talking with your employees to help them determine how to be successful? In employee focus groups across the land, one of the main reasons identified for employees leaving one company to work for another was leadership's failure to provide a clear picture of the company's direction and how the employees figured into this journey. Employees need to be kept current on the big picture—where the company wants to go, how it plans to get there, and how employees can fit into this goal. In fact, the mission statement hanging on the wall often says one thing, you tell them another, and their compensation rewards them for something else.

FEEDBACK. Employees want to know how you think they're doing—and not just during annual reviews. Consistent feedback is essential for employees to do the job you expect. They want to know that you care. Motivate your team by showing them appreciation *immediately after* they achieve a significant goal. Keep employees informed how the team is doing and where they fit into the bigger picture. Sometimes they don't know if they're winning or losing because they don't know what you think or how the score is being calculated.

STRATEGIC PLANNING. If unclear priorities plague your team, you must take action to resolve the confusion. Employees often complain, "I cannot get anything done during the day because my manager is constantly interrupting me, having me chase the next fire or reshuffling my priorities." To reduce time spent by your staff on crisis management, spend time doing long-term, proactive, important activities, rather than always responding to the urgent. Don't facilitate crises at work by procrastinating on tasks until they become urgent. Leadership in time management requires you to: (1) figure out what matters most, (2) empower yourself and others to develop the abilities needed to accomplish those important objectives, (3) remove obstacles to their accomplishment, and (4) eliminate procrastination. Ask yourself, "What ideas, projects, and programs—if implemented now or in the near future—would significantly impact the profitability or productivity of my staff or your organization?"

MISTAKE CORRECTION. Almost anyone in business is familiar with the work of Edward S. Deming and his impact on Japanese business practices during the seventies. Deming told a reporter one of the chief differences between Japanese and U.S. business practices was in problem solving. When a problem occurred, U.S. leadership wasted valuable time seeking the person(s) responsible for the glitch. The Japanese, on the other hand, made correcting the problem a first priority. Finding the culprit took a backseat to fixing the problem and redeeming corporate credibility. Speed in making corrections obviously enhances valuable customer satisfaction but also facilitates creating more effective strategic plans in the future. Not addressing a problem as soon as it erupts ultimately sabotages the forward progress of any corporation. Putting off a problem makes implementing a solution more expensive and more difficult. When managers minimize finger pointing, employees will be less intimidated about making decisions.

UNDEFINED ROLES AND RESPONSIBILITIES. Were job descriptions written four years ago—in another time, for another purpose? When performance reviews come around, do you tell employees they should have been doing something completely different? If you want to achieve better results and improve morale, clearly communicate where you're going and why. Employees want to know your vision on a timely basis and what you want them to accomplish.

TIME MASTERY quiz item #70:

> 70. I make decisions quickly once I have the appropriate information.

Just Make a Decision, Already!

You've gathered all the information, you've researched alternatives, you've priced it, and now you can't decide. The project sits in its manila folder and gathers dust. Another half-done project bites the dust.

Indecision is one of the worst time bandits around. Look around your desk. Many of the piles represent decisions you haven't made yet. At some point, you stopped asking yourself, "What's next?" Eventually, the only thing left to do is *decide*.

Let's say you're deciding whether to attend a conference. You've got the conference schedule. You know the pricing information. You have the hotel information and flight schedules. You just can't decide whether to go. Or you've passed those travel lounges many times and thought how nice it would be to have a membership. You've compared different programs and researched cost differentials. Not knowing exactly how many times you'd be traveling in the coming year, and not wanting to pay for visits you wouldn't use, the file just sat. And you continued to look wistfully at the lounges as you head to the boarding area. Examples abound of professionals who don't demonstrate forward progress in their careers or daily activities because they stopped making decisions.

Star performers know when and how to make a decision. In the old days, risk-averse workers knew they'd never get in trouble for avoiding a tough decision. In fact, it might even have been the fastest ticket to a promotion, because it was one sure way to keep the dirt off their feet. But these days, if you can't make a decision, you're out of the action. *Any* decision that is likely to serve you and your company is better than *no* decision. There are almost no decisions that won't turn out for the best if you work positively on the results of your action.

People avoid making decisions by saying things like "I'm waiting to get more information." Or "I need more input on this." The truth is, more likely, that you're not willing to look the situation in the eye and make a decision, right or wrong. So you put off acting on what you already know. The project stalls. You wait until your boss or coworker asks you about it, then you're literally forced to make a decision. Delay in making decisions official can mean staying up all night, making more mistakes, or spending more money. Then you fall back on the old "I work better under pressure" comment.

Before you put *anything* down, ask yourself, "What is the very next step required to see forward motion on this task?" Finally, the answer is going to be, "Make a decision." At that point, take a deep breath, face the music, and choose. Only then are you free. Productive. No leftovers, nothing half-done.

Ending bad decisions

Sometimes you want to make a decision, but a previous decision prevents you from making a new one. For example, when I first began my career as a professional speaker, I signed on with a public seminar company to present public seminars around the country. After a couple years of doing that, I felt I had learned all I could from the experience. I made a decision to stop working for them and market my own services, but I couldn't move forward with that decision, because I hadn't ended the first decision. Realizing your current situation is never going to get you where you want to go is the key to getting to where you belong. What decisions have you made in the past that, if eliminated, would make room for better decisions now?

To learn how to be more decisive, flip a coin. For insignificant decisions like "Should I eat turkey or tuna for lunch?" flip a coin. You'll learn to be quick and definitive when the end result doesn't matter all that much. Some people just need practice in getting unstuck and moving on.

CHAPTER EIGHT

Mastering the "I" in Productive

INFORMATION MANAGEMENT

I HEARD A JOKE ABOUT A BUSINESSMAN who dragged himself home and dropped into a chair, exhausted. His sympathetic wife was right there with a tall, cool drink and comforting words. "My, you look tired," she said. "You must have had a hard day today. What happened?" "It was terrible," the husband said. "The computer broke down and all of us had to do our own thinking."

I know that's how many of us feel today, after having become so dependent on our computer, email, voicemail, the Internet, Blackberries, PDAs, cell phones, pagers . . . the list goes on and on. Who would have thought, even five years ago, that we would be so connected to and reliant upon these electronic devices today? But the new reality dictates that you learn to be technologically savvy, want to or not; indeed, you may have gone kicking and screaming into the Information Age. Technology can undoubtedly improve your productivity, but it can make you *less* productive if you're not careful. This chapter discusses how to use the latest technologies to your advantage, without letting technology take advantage of you.

INFORMATION MANAGEMENT quiz item #71:

> 71. I understand I can have too much information and try to reduce "information overload."

Too Much Information!

Statistics, communications, advertisements, and data—ever feel information is out to get you? Information overload can make you feel overwhelmed and hurt your performance on the job. The amount of information available today is incredible. Every second, the Web grows by seventeen pages. According to some sources, the world has generated more data in the past thirty years than it did in the preceding five thousand years. What good is all that data, though, if you don't have any time to analyze it? Fortunately, there are ways to deal with information overload.

KEEP DOCUMENTS TO ONE PAGE. The leaders at Proctor & Gamble once decided that paper or electronic documents could not exceed one page. Even their multimillion dollar proposals are summarized on one page. Support materials are available and provided if requested, but this practice ensures the tedium of reading and reviewing the document is gone (and it saves lots of trees, too).

GET OFF MAILING LISTS. Here are some great references to remove your name from junk mailing lists:

Junk mail:

Direct Marketing Association

Mail Preference Service

P.O. Box 9008

Farmingdale, NY 11735–9008

Give all addresses and former names

Write "Please remove me from your members' mailing lists."

www.the-dma.org

Credit cards offers:

Associated Credit Bureaus, Inc.

Opt Out Program

1090 Vermont Avenue N.W., Suite 200

Washington D.C. 20005–4905

Include social security number.

1-888-5-OPT-OUT

Phone calls:

The federal government has launched its national "Do Not Call" registry, designed to curb residential telemarketing calls. Telemarketers who call people on the list could be fined as much as $11,000 per call. The registry can be found at www.donotcall.gov. You may also register by phone at (888) 382–1222.

Junk faxes:

If you're repeatedly bothered by the same junk fax company, especially after attempting to remove yourself from the list, complain to the Federal Communications Commission (FCC) at http://www.fcc.gov. Find "Form 475," and check "Unsolicited advertisement sent to a facsimile machine" on question 6A. The form takes about three minutes to complete and should end the problem!

USE "RULES" OR "FILTERS." Check your email program's Help file, search for "rules" or "filters," and learn how to set up this automated feature. The filters "watch" for specific email—from a specific sender, from a specific domain name, or all those with a specific word in the "Subject" field, for example—then perform a variety of operations, including filing in a special folder, turning it a certain color, tossing it into the trash, or marking it as "urgent." For example, you can automatically send weekly electronic newsletters to a folder and read them when you have time. If you find them stacking up unread, you'll know it's time to unsubscribe.

NARROW YOUR WEB SEARCHES. If you frequently use the Internet to search for material, it's worth your while to spend time learning to do effective searches. When you use Google or another search engine and type in a couple of words, it can return thousands of website "hits," linking to outdated or unrelated information. If you're looking for a keynote speaker for your conference, don't simply type "motivational speaker." Rather, give a topic and several words to narrow your search. Using quotation marks to keep phrases together helps target your searches. Most search engines have a help document with easy-to-understand instructions on conducting effective, specific searches.

LEARN TO USE YOUR SOFTWARE CORRECTLY. Take the time to figure it out rather than struggling each time you use your Web browser, contact management program, word processor, or accounting software. Local computer superstores and community colleges offer inexpensive courses on many common packages.

ELIMINATE HARDCOPY FAXES. Use fax software such as WinFax Pro 10.0 from Symantec to receive faxes directly into your computer. You can fax any document on your computer directly from the application to any fax number *or* email address. Instead of using a phone line, you can sign up for an Internet-based fax service.

Faxes are sent to your own fax number, converted into an attachment, and routed as an attachment to your email address.

LEARN SHORTCUTS. If you use the Windows version of Microsoft's Internet Explorer browser, it's not necessary to type the whole domain name (e.g., www.yahoo.com) to get to a website. Just type the middle part ("yahoo"), hold down the CTRL key and press Enter. Internet Explorer will add the "http://www." and the ".com" and go right to the site, rather than doing a search on "yahoo" as it does if you don't hold town CTRL.

CANCEL SUBSCRIPTIONS. Many magazines and periodicals are available on a related website without charge or through your local library. Instead of subscribing to different magazines and trying to keep up, subscribe only to the most important. When you require specific information, conduct "real time" searches on the Internet.

INFORMATION MANAGEMENT quiz item #72:

72. I use proper email protocol and don't waste the time of others with its use.

Use Proper Netiquette

I remember opening my first email account and thinking how much fun it was to send a message to a friend. If you're like many people, you no longer find email simple or fun. Email messaging now exceeds telephone traffic and is the dominant form of business communication. Some workers tell me handling their emails can consume half their day. A recent *Wall Street Journal* report indicates that soon employees will spend three to four hours a day on email.

Don't you wish every person who received a new email

account had to agree to follow certain "rules of engagement"? I'd love to see a master protocol list to govern what you can and cannot do. Here's what I'd include on the netiquette list:

UNDERSTAND THAT INFORMAL DOESN'T MEAN SLOPPY. If your coworkers use Blackberries or text pagers to communicate internally, use the commonly accepted abbreviated language. When communicating with external customers, however, always follow standard writing protocol. Your email message sends a message about you and your company, so normal spelling, grammar, and punctuation rules apply.

KEEP MESSAGES BRIEF AND TO THE POINT. Just because your writing is *correct* doesn't mean it has to be *long.* Make your writing as concise as possible. Nothing is more frustrating than wading through an email twice as long as needed. Get right to the point; concentrate on one subject per message as much as possible.

USE SENTENCE CASE. USING ALL CAPITAL LETTERS LOOKS LIKE YOU'RE SHOUTING. Using all lowercase letters looks lazy. For emphasis, use the asterisk to make words * really * stand out. Also, don't use a lot of colors or graphics embedded in your message, since not everyone uses an email program that reads HTML. Without HTML capabilities, colors and graphics show up as garbled code.

USE THE BLIND COPY AND COURTESY COPY APPROPRIATELY. Don't use the BCC feature to keep others from seeing who you copied; it shows confidence when you directly CC anyone receiving a copy. *Do* use BCC, however, when sending to a large distribution list, so recipients won't have to scroll through a huge list of names. Be cautious on your use of CC; overuse simply clutters the in-boxes of your supervisors. Only copy people if they are directly involved, not to grandstand or "CYA."

DON'T USE EMAIL AS AN EXCUSE *NOT* TO COMMUNICATE. Don't forget the value of face-to-face or even voice-to-voice communication. Email communication isn't appropriate when sending confusing or emotional messages. Think of the times you've heard someone in the office indignantly say, "Well, I sent you email." If you have a problem with someone, get up and walk three doors down to find that person and have a conversation. Don't use email to avoid an uncomfortable situation or to cover up a mistake.

REMEMBER YOUR EMAIL ISN'T PRIVATE. I've seen people fired for using email inappropriately (like forwarding items with sexual or off-color content) or for personal use. Email is considered company property and can be retrieved, examined, and used in a court of law. Unless you are using an encryption device (hardware or software), you should assume that email over the Internet is not secure. Never put in an email mail message anything you wouldn't put on a postcard. Remember that an email can be forwarded, so unintended audiences may see what you've written. Or you might inadvertently send something to the wrong party, so always keep the content professional to avoid embarrassment.

BE SPARING WITH GROUP EMAIL. Send group mail only when it's useful to *all* recipients. Use the "Reply-to-All" button only when compiling results requiring collective input.

USE THE "SUBJECT" FIELD TO INDICATE CONTENTS AND PRIORITY. Use the "Subject" field to give a quick summary of the contents and the priority. Don't just say, "Hi!" or "From Laura." Agree on acronyms to use that quickly identify actions. For example, your team could use <AR> to mean "Action Required" or <MSR> for "Monthly Status Report." It's also a good practice to include the word "Long" in the subject header so the recipient knows the message will take time to read. A message over one hundred lines is generally considered long. Instead of sending a one-line text message to a Blackberry, send the message in the subject line, using <EOM> to signal "End of Message." The recipient doesn't have to even open the email to get the message.

DON'T SEND CHAIN LETTERS, VIRUS WARNINGS, OR JUNK MAIL. Always check a reputable anti-virus website before sending out an alarm. If a constant stream of jokes from a friend annoys you, be honest and ask to be removed from the list. Remind them it's nothing personal, but you have more email than you can handle. Alternatively, you can set up a personal account at home and direct non-work email to it.

REMEMBER THAT YOUR TONE CAN'T BE HEARD IN AN EMAIL. Have you ever attempted sarcasm in an email, and the recipient took it the wrong way? Email communication is missing facial expressions, vocal tone, volume, and body language, and it can't convey the nuances of verbal communication. In an attempt to infer tone of voice, some people use "smileys" such as ":-)," but use them sparingly so you don't appear unprofessional. Also, don't assume that using a smiley will make the recipient happy with what you say or wipe out an otherwise insulting comment.

USE A SIGNATURE WITH A WEBSITE LINK. Make things easy for the recipient. To ensure that people know who you are, include a line or two at the end of your message with your contact information. Always include your complete mailing address, website, and phone numbers. Don't make it obnoxiously long with a page of information for people to wade through; put most of that on your website. You can create this file ahead of time and add it to the end of your messages as a signature line (some programs do this automatically).

INCLUDE PORTIONS OF THE ORIGINAL EMAIL IN YOUR RESPONSE. Scrolling through ten pages of correspondence to understand the point of a message or question can be annoying. Instead of continuing to forward a forwarded message, take a minute to write a quick summary for your reader. You could even highlight or quote the relevant and specific passage, then include your response. One word of caution: if you are forwarding or reposting a message you've received, do not change the wording, which is lying. If the message was a personal message to you and you want to repost it to a group, you should ask permission first. You may shorten the message and quote only relevant parts, but be sure you give proper attribution.

Use the suggestions above as points of discussion with those in your department or team and create your own list of email protocol.

INFORMATION MANAGEMENT quiz item #73:

> 73. I leave effective voicemail messages.

It's Me Calling!

Handling phone calls and voicemail is a constant productivity challenge. Rambling, three-minute voicemail messages with no organization make me crazy. Sometimes the caller uses "stream of consciousness" hoping to remember one of the reasons for the call. Here are some things you can do to leave effective messages and avoid wasting the time of the recipient:

PLAN YOUR MESSAGE. Consider the points you want to make and jot down a few notes. If a planned phone call takes you seven minutes, and an unplanned call takes twelve minutes, the five-minute difference, multiplied by twelve calls a day, could represent an hour of wasted time each day.

BE BRIEF. Voicemail messages should be one minute long or less. Anything else might be better voice-to-voice or in an email. Take more than sixty seconds and you risk having your message deleted. Remember, the purpose is to leave a message, not give a speech. Stream-of-consciousness communication doesn't work.

Think about your message and begin with your purpose. "The reason I'm calling is . . ."

LEAVE A MESSAGE, NOT JUST YOUR NAME AND NUMBER. It makes me crazy when I receive a voicemail message that only says, "Hi, it's so-and-so, call me back." How do I know whether it's a telemarketer or a prospective client? Never leave a generic message. You're much more likely to get a return call if the recipient knows what's up. Specifically ask for the information you require. The recipient will be able to look up the answer prior to calling you back. Without the proper information, you may have to respond, "I'll have to get back to you on that," thus creating another volley of phone tag.

LEARN THE SHORT-CUT KEYS AND FEATURES OF YOUR VOICEMAIL. Track down a manual for your phone system and learn how to speed up and slow down messages. You can skip right to the end, automatically delete, forward with a comment, or reply automatically without ringing the caller's phone. For the great amount of time you will spend processing voicemail, the time you invest in learning these shortcuts will pay you back many times over.

WATCH YOUR TONE. Without any other nonverbal cues such as face and body language, your tone is all you have to communicate with. A monotone lacks enthusiasm, so put vitality in your voice. Stand up and smile as you leave your message. Standing increases your energy, and people can hear a smile over the phone. Avoid sarcasm and irritation if you want your call returned. I have a client who says that if she detects even the slightest amount of irritation in a prospective vendor's voice, she won't do business with that person. She also waits until she receives three messages before calling back, to see if the vendor is kind and persistent.

WATCH YOUR VOLUME AND ENUNCIATION. The telephone distorts high-frequency sounds such as "ef" and "ess." Pronounce word endings and do not swallow syllables. This is especially important when giving your name: "My name is Laura Stack, 'S' as in Sam, 'T' as in Thomas, 'A' as in Adam, 'C' as in Charlie, 'K' as in Katie." A voice that is too loud is irritating. A soft voice will not always be heard, and the listener may miss important information, like your phone number.

BEGIN AND END WITH YOUR PHONE NUMBER. Speak slowly and say it twice. The listener needs time to process the information and write it down. Pause as you say it: "Hi, Mary, this is Laura Stack at 303 (pause), 471 (pause), 7401." Your name and number should also be the last thing people hear, so they don't have to rewind if they missed it at the beginning.

GIVE YOUR MESSAGE A HEADLINE. To help the recipient distinguish urgent from non-urgent calls, flag your message as "urgent" if your phone system allows. Your message will move to the top of the call list and be the first one heard. If your system doesn't support this feature, start out by saying, "Hi Joe, please call me back as soon as you get this . . ." or, conversely, "No need to return my call until you return Monday."

GIVE OPTIONS TO SKIP THE GREETING. If your greeting is rather long, tell callers how to bypass it at the beginning of the message. "Hi, you've reached Laura Stack. To bypass this greeting and leave a message right now, please hit pound." If you must have a long greeting that you want callers to hear at least once, explain how to skip it in the future.

AVOID TELEPHONE TAG. Tell listeners when you can best be reached to prevent the frustration of telephone tag. If you continually get someone's voicemail, give options for a phone appointment. Tell the person what time you'll be calling and the purpose of the call, so important information can be gathered ahead of time.

> 74. I use my phone as an effective productivity tool.

Rrrrring! Rrrrring!

Do you find yourself groaning inwardly (or outwardly) when the phone rings? The phone can be a huge time waster or a potential time saver. Here are some tips to help you use your phone more productively:

PICK UP THE PHONE. Pick up the phone? What a concept! By the time someone leaves a message, you listen to it, write down the details, and call back, you could have saved much time by simply answering.

STAY FOCUSED. If a conversation is off-target, use your agenda to bring it back on track. Bridge back to your point. Keep the conversation focused. Pick out a word from the other's comments, mention it, "Speaking of XYZ, that reminds me about . . ." then come back to your point.

GET CALLERS TO COME TO THE POINT QUICKLY. Ask, "What can I do for you?" or "How may I assist you?" When asking these questions, don't be too abrupt. Practice by physically smiling and lifting your voice at the end of the question. It's important to watch your voice tone. A warm, crisp tone will make the caller trust your competence and shorten the length of your call.

USE NATURAL START AND STOP TIMES. If you must call a known chatterbox, phone right before lunch or at the end of the day. If you call at 11:30 a.m. or 4:45 p.m., people tend to keep the conversation brief so they can leave.

SET ASIDE TIME. Return *all* phone calls at once if possible. Get out your list and start cranking them out. If you do one after the other, you will naturally eliminate much of the social niceties and get right to the point.

USE VOICEMAIL STRATEGICALLY. Let your voicemail pick up when you have a pressing deadline. Or screen your calls via the digital display on your phone and allow the call to go to voicemail if you think it won't be important.

USE A WIRELESS HEADSET. I love being able to pick up my phone, even if I'm not sitting right next to the base. I don't miss an important call and walk around my office and use gestures to keep my energy and professionalism at its peak.

CALL IN THE EVENING. If you know you are calling someone who talks a lot, leave a message on the person's voicemail in the evening.

SCHEDULE A CONFERENCE CALL. When you're going out of town and need to connect with your staff during your absence, schedule a conference call. Handle all matters once a day. It's much more effective to pause and discuss ten things than to be interrupted ten different times for one thing. Before leaving, distribute a tentative discussion agenda. Participants in the call can then be prepared and keep the call short.

PRIORITIZE THE ORDER IN WHICH YOU RETURN CALLS. You've returned from a long business meeting to find twelve phone messages waiting for you. If they each take an average of ten minutes, you have two hours of calls to make. Not everyone has that kind of time! So how do you decide which to return first? Many people sort through them and call a person they like, regardless of the priority. To keep those calls from overwhelming you, return them in order of perceived priority.

WRAP UP A PHONE CALL BY TALKING IN PAST TENSE. Begin by summarizing your follow-up action and promises. Then say, "It was nice to have talked with you! Thank you!"

> 75. I find electronic files quickly; my computer files are well
>   organized.

Where Did I Save That Document?

What happened to the paperless office? We generate more paper now than we ever did before the advent of the computer! What's more, a computer's hard drive can get just as cluttered as any other part of the office. With seemingly limitless storage capacity, it's easy to create piles of files on your computer. This section will help you file your documents more logically and find them more easily.

USE DIRECTORIES AND SUBDIRECTORIES. The first step in creating your electronic filing system is to create the structure. Let's say you had a filing cabinet in which you stored your paper files. If every folder were labeled "My Documents," you wouldn't find anything. Microsoft automatically sets up a folder titled "My Documents," in which you can save your documents. If you save *everything* under this directory, you will never be able to find what you need. Just like your paper files, you should save your computer documents into folders, sometimes called directories and subdirectories.

SET UP YOUR FILING SYSTEM. The most important thing is to point all your saved files into *one* main directory. By doing so, you make it incredibly easy to do backups: you simply burn one directory to a CD. I don't use the "My Documents" directory (although you can, with subfolders). In Windows Explorer, I created a directory called "c://a_laura" under my c: drive. If you put the letter "a" in front of your name with an underscore, it will always be the first directory in the folder list, making saves faster. Under your main directory, create subfolders with the main categories of documents you save. Don't worry about the *type* of document (word processing, spreadsheet, database, etc.). Just think about the category. For example, I use the following subdirectories:

a_laura/business
a_laura/personal
a_laura/school

Then within each subdirectory, I create additional folders. Under my business directory, I use:

C://a_laura/business/Articles . . . Associations, Backups, Book, Clipart, Contracts, Courses, Keynotes, Marketing, Media, Newsletters, Policies, Postcards, Products, Promotional, Templates, Websites

Many of the above have additional subdirectories. Some folders go eight subfolders deep.

SAVE DOCUMENTS IN THE CORRECT LOCATION. Each time I create a document, *regardless of the program it was created in,* I save it in the appropriate directory. You will have Word documents, Excel spreadsheets, and PowerPoint presentations all in the same directory, which doesn't matter because the correct files display when you open a file from the correct software program. Select "File," "Save As," and use the "up" arrow until you locate the correct directory. Change your saving preferences in Word under "Tools," "Options," "File Locations." When you save a new document, it will automatically go to the correct directory location.

CREATE NAMING CONVENTIONS FOR YOUR FILES. Now that you've located the correct directory, you have to give it a name that will make it easy to find later. I save contracts in the format YYMMDD CLIENT PROGRAM. I would save a contract under "c://a_laura/

business/contracts/2003." All the contracts within that directory would be listed in chronological order. When I first started using computers, they were all DOS-based (now I'm feeling my age). I used to have to name files with eight letters. Thank heavens for Windows! Now we have a 255-character capability for file names, so go ahead and make the name as long as you want. The longer the name, the more likely you will be able to find it again using a key-word search. Ask yourself, "If I want this file again, what words or phrases would I think of first?"

If your directory system hits a snag, don't despair. You can still find that file you created using the Search feature of your operating system. If I'm out of town and John needs to quickly locate a file to send to a client, he can go to the Start menu, Search, files or folders, select a_laura, and type in any words he thinks would describe the document, and it's there.

It's easy to create documents and save them. The big trick is *retrieving* them. The above tips will allow you to find the files you want—when you want them—in thirty seconds or less.

INFORMATION MANAGEMENT quiz item #76:

> 76. I know the available productivity features of my email
>   program.

Look Out for Outlook

One of the biggest productivity frustrations people report is the constant battle with email. Not only is it difficult to concentrate when you have 367 emails in your in-box, but you also have a sneaking suspicion you're missing something. Instead of "cleaning it up" once every two weeks, or getting a message that your mailbox is over the size limit, keep up with it each time you read a new email. Most people weren't given formal training in their email program, so you may be unaware of some really neat features of MS Outlook (and other email software such as Lotus Notes, GroupWise, AOL, Eudora Pro, etc.).

The best response is to read an email, reply, and delete. If you can't do that, move the email based on the purpose and next steps of the email. For specific steps on how to follow the tips below, look under the Help menu of your email software.

MOVE REFERENCE-ONLY EMAIL TO A PERSONAL FOLDER. If an email is a project update or status report and requires *no* response, move it to a custom email folder just for that item or project. Create new personal folders to describe the different types of email you receive, such as people, projects, clients, personal, jokes, travel, bulletins, etc.

MOVE EMAIL REQUIRING FUTURE ACTION TO TASKS OR THE TO-DO LIST. The Tasks feature is used to track your to-do list and action items. If you need to reply to an email or complete a particular task but can't do it immediately, don't leave it in your in-box. You can either drag the email to Tasks or use the Move to Folder feature to move it. Email will be removed from your in-box and attached to the task. When you double-click the task on the task list, the email will be attached and can be viewed. Use these electronic to-do lists to work from, rather than keeping messages in your email in-box.

MOVE MEETING AND APPOINTMENT-RELATED EMAILS TO YOUR CALENDAR. The Calendar feature schedules meetings and appointments for a specific day and time. Do not put action items in a specific day on the calendar, because they don't roll over if you don't complete them *and* they aren't tracked in history. You can drag email to Calendar, and a new appointment window will automatically open. No more copying and pasting! Your email will be inserted in the text field, along with any attachments. When you double-click the Calendar item, the original email can be viewed.

MOVE THE EMAIL TO CONTACTS. Performing the same steps as described above with the Contacts icon automatically saves the sender's address as a new contact. Outlook will automatically fill in the information and keep a history of all emails from the contact.

CREATE RULES TO AUTOMATICALLY MOVE EMAIL. Once you create personal folders, you can create rules to automatically move certain types of email, such as weekly reports and newsletters. Any time you can avoid moving an email manually, you save time. However, only use this feature for "reference" items, not emails requiring a response. You don't want to be checking multiple folders to see if anything new came in. Check under Help for "filters" or "organize."

CONVERT EMAILS CONTAINING REMINDERS TO NOTES. The Notes feature is great for lists such as grocery lists, gift lists, chores, errands, shopping lists, repair lists, and birthday lists. You can then print a note and take it with you when you run errands.

INFORMATION MANAGEMENT quiz item #77:

> 77. I run regular maintenance routines on my computer to ensure high performance and protect my data.

Preventing Crash and Burn

To free up space on your computer and make it run more quickly, perform standard maintenance functions each week. Because I use a Hewlett-Packard (HP) computer, these scenarios assume a Windows environment. Mac users, you can still follow the same principles.

RUN A FULL SYSTEM SCAN USING YOUR ANTI-VIRUS SOFTWARE. To detect and eliminate files that can damage your computer or render it useless, invest in anti-virus software from Norton, McAfee, or other popular programs. Make sure your definitions are up-to-date and run a full scan Friday night when you leave work. If you work on an office network, this is probably done automatically.

RUN A COMPLETE BACKUP. It never ceases to amaze me how many people lose critical data because their computers crash. *There has never been a more important instruction ignored: backup your data regularly.* If you don't have time, make it. If you forget, post a reminder. If you don't know how, learn. Conducting a regular backup is critical, because *every* computer will fail at some point due to wear and tear, heat, dust, viruses, or power surges. I use Roxio CD Creator every Friday to back up my important business files. Even if your company performs a backup for you, back up every file that would be devastating to lose or a pain to retrieve or re-create. I keep my important documents and backups for my accounting and contact management files in a single directory. I simply select the directory, hit "Record," and burn a single CD. If your files are *really* large, use a Zip drive or tape backup with WinZip to save space. I keep backup CDs for several months, then toss them as I replace them with newer versions.

PURGE FREQUENTLY. Just as you clean out your paper files (you *do*, don't you?), you should purge your computer of duplicate copies, outdated material, and old versions or unused software. Try storing old files that are simply long-term records on CDs instead of your hard drive. The only alternative to *not* purging is buying a computer with more memory, which is the equivalent of buying more filing cabinets. Ask yourself if you really need to spend that money or if you can just clean out your current files and directories and "find" some space.

DELETE TEMPORARY INTERNET FILES AND RARELY USED FILES. If your computer is starting to seem sluggish, you may need to free up your cache and file space. Uninstall programs, files, and games you no longer need or use. Also uninstall older versions of upgraded software programs. Most software programs include an "uninstall" option. Don't delete this uninstall function, because simply deleting the file, rather than uninstalling the program usually doesn't cleanly remove it from your computer.

Instead of remembering to perform these tasks on a regular basis, you can create a recurring activity in the to-do feature of your email program and set a reminder on a regular basis.

INFORMATION MANAGEMENT quiz item #78:

78. I understand the features and purposes of electronic and paper systems and when to use each.

Paper People Versus Electronic People

Many, many different options exist for tracking your appointments and to-do items. To determine whether to use a paper or electronic system (or a combination of both), you must decide two fundamental things:

1. Which methods you prefer; your predisposition; your personality
2. How you work; where you work; what you need

Personality and preferences

Are you a *paper* or an *electronic* person? Your decisions will largely be dictated by this choice. Paper people, forced to use PDAs and electronic gadgets, get extremely frustrated. Electronic people will pass out at the mere suggestion that you print out an email.

It doesn't have to be all or none; it's possible to use a combination approach. PDAs are great if you need to retrieve client phone numbers on the road, access large documents (without the bulk), or send yourself reminders. Paper systems are better for reviewing a monthly calendar, taking notes at meetings, or planning projects. Bottom line, if you are a paper person and your organization forces you to use Outlook to allow others to schedule meetings with you, comply, but reenter the information on your planner pages, rather than forcing yourself to be a grumpy electronic person who fights with their a machine each day. Go ahead and note your commitments in Outlook if you have to, but copy them or print out the pages to store in your planner if you prefer to carry that with you. If forcing yourself to use something you hate makes you not use it at all, I would absolutely recommend double entry back to your paper system. I do it. I can beat you hands-down finding something using my paper system versus an electronic tool. Not that I'm against them; I just don't prefer it for myself. I like a written to-do list and a visual view of my monthly appointments, so I stick with the planner.

Work location and need

Do you work primarily at a fixed-office desk? You can probably conduct most of your work "real-time," without the need to sync to a PDA.

Are you constantly on the go? Portability is the key. Use organizing software to manage your schedule and contacts, then sync to your PDA or print pages for your organizer.

Find out which way works best for you and stick with it, no guilt and no excuses. Here are some advantages and disadvantages of paper versus electronic tools.

Paper Organizer/Planner

Advantages

- You take notes right into your planner. No double entry.
- It can't break or run out of batteries.
- You can quickly flip to a month-at-a-glance calendar and view your schedule.
- Planner pages and page finders are pretty.
- It provides more room to write at meetings.
- You can write and look up info quickly versus using the stylus with a PDA.
- Customizable. You can add or subtract features and forms that meet your needs.
- Yearly planner inserts run about $40, therefore it's inexpensive to maintain.

Disadvantages

- You can lose your planner and have no backup.
- You can run out of room in A–Z tabs to write names, addresses, and phone numbers.
- You must rewrite information when people move.
- It gets messy with frequent updates.
- No security or password required, so others can flip open your planner and view your information.
- It can be large and bulky. Smaller versions often don't have enough writing surface and calendar space.
- It's often overflowing with assorted papers and sticky notes.

Electronic organizer/PDA/Palm Pilot

Advantages

- It's lightweight, small, and portable.
- A PDA can hold thousands of contact names and numbers.
- It has a search capability to find tasks and contact names.
- It's always current when "synced" with desktop computer.
- It's perfect for frequent travelers.
- A PDA integrates with Outlook and popular contact management databases.
- You can access your email if your PDA has wireless capability.
- You don't run out of room to list today's to-do items.
- You don't have to rewrite to-do lists when you don't complete items; they roll forward automatically.

Disadvantages

- There is no month-at-a-glance view. You must click on individual days on a monthly calendar to see appointments for that day.
- Note taking is tedious and time-consuming with cryptic shorthand, or you must carry a separate keyboard.
- It requires the use of a pad of paper to take notes, which must be typed into computer a second time at home base. Double entry.
- You can't carry papers and notes in it for a meeting.
- It's an expensive machine with add-ons.
- You risk crashes, data wipeouts, and being on the road without your calendar.

Feel free to create your own customized system that best meets your needs *and* fits your personality. Just as you are unique, so too are your organizing needs. Experiment with different techniques and tools. Don't purchase the latest gadget just to "keep up." Stick with what works for *you.*

INFORMATION MANAGEMENT quiz item #79:

> 79. I eliminate email "spam."

Spam for Dinner, Anyone?

Email was supposed to reduce the amount of time spent communicating. However, email may actually be making workers less productive: In a recent survey, mid- and senior-level executives from U.S. companies who use email regularly reported that more than 30 percent of emails they receive aren't directly related to their jobs. Welcome to the land of spam, ruled by porn, drugs, and obscure royalty offering free money. Time is money, and spam has a direct impact on bottom-line business revenues. In addition to decreased profitability, spam can be annoying and time consuming. So what can you do to help reduce it?

USE A POP-UP BLOCKER. Do you hate those annoying pop-up ads that slow down your Internet work? Not all spam comes via email! I recently downloaded a free pop-up blocking software program. It blocked 109 pop-ups in the first twelve days. It's been a lifesaver! Anyone wanting to increase productivity while working on the Internet should consider getting such a tool.

DON'T READ OR REPLY TO SPAM. Automatically delete obvious spam without opening it. Remember, big companies do *not* do business via chain letter, so be suspicious of every message about

Bill Gates giving you money. No matter how tempting it may be, never respond directly to spam you receive, even to unsubscribe (unless the message comes from a recognized and trusted company). In most cases, a reply of any kind will never be read by a real person, and will most likely only confirm that your address is good—leading to an onslaught of even more junk email. Never, ever buy anything from a spam message. If you do, you're opening yourself up to credit card fraud and ensuring your addition to every spam list known.

GET AN ANTI-SPAM UTILITY OR SET UP FILTERS. My spam-filtering software has truly helped me reclaim my in-box. You'll want to purchase a comprehensive program that blocks specific addresses of known spammers, has preset and programmable filters, can check subject lines, and filter text within messages. My program can filter on the sender's address, subject line, body text, message header and can even block spam based on its country of origin. I used to get about 125 emails a day; now I get about 20 legitimate ones.

CREATE A FAKE ACCOUNT. If a website asks for personal information to enter the site, and you do not want to provide it, what do you do? Create an email account with one of the free email sites such as Hotmail or Yahoo. When signing up for this email account, enter false information. When a website asks you to sign in, use the fake email account. That way you will not be bombarded with spam and no personal information will have been given out.

LIE. Anytime a website asks your age, answer that you are under thirteen years of age. This will discourage its operators from pestering you with targeted spam emails, because most advertisers don't want to market to under-thirteen-year-olds.

PROTECT YOUR ADDRESS. The most effective way to avoid spam is to keep your email address to yourself. Spammers can't get your address if you don't make it public. Only give your address to clients, friends, family, and coworkers, and ask them not to circulate it. If your email address is published on a website, be aware that special "email harvesting" software programs will find you.

REPORT SPAM. The "Received" field of the full header will show the path the email has traveled in order to reach you. In practice, the final address listed in parentheses will be the originating ISP. You can then go to the ISP's website and look up its policies for reporting spam. Alternatively, you can forward the full message and header to www.SpamCop.net, a service that will automatically compose a complaint for you. If the ISP is legitimate, it most likely will take steps to prevent that user from sending further junk email.

Our government is creating spam laws to regulate the sending of unsolicited mail. Until the time comes when we are protected from junk mail, keep your inbox clean the best you can.

INFORMATION MANAGEMENT quiz item #80:

> 80. I control my technology; it doesn't control me.

Who's the Boss Here?

High-tech devices mean speed and availability. They should save time, increase efficiency, and make life easier. Many times, however, we feel like technology is the master and we are the servants. Technology can waste time and decrease productivity if not used correctly. This section gives ideas on realizing the advantages of technology and avoiding counterproductive behaviors.

I got my first (real) corporate job with TRW Defense Systems in Colorado Springs, Colorado. I remember my coworkers "oooohhhing" and "ahhhhhing" over a new fax machine in the department. (Remember the grease-paper rolls?) Even at my young age, I can recall thinking, "This cannot be a good idea." We used to put documents in the regular mail, and the turnaround time was at least a week. Then the fax machine came along . . . and when did customers want it? Now! "You can *fax* it to me." Instant gratification. Our customers got spoiled and wanted more. You tell me: Has email made this time compression better or worse? It's as if people think we're checking emails as they come in. Are you?

DON'T BE CONTROLLED BY YOUR EMAIL. Email obsession and real-time response is a huge productivity drain. It prevents you from concentrating on one task or getting any work of reasonable length accomplished. Don't read each message as it arrives; instead, turn off the function on your email program that indicates you've got mail. Set aside a specific number of times a day to check and handle your email. Enforce the same schedule on yourself each day, so that you aren't distracted by constant email and can concentrate on the task at hand.

TURN OFF YOUR CELL PHONE. It's not much fun to leave the office earlier if you'll just be on the phone. While it's productive to use your cell phone to return calls while commuting, it invades your personal time if you don't shut it off. If possible, use it only during regular business hours and insist on privacy at home. I don't give out my cell phone number to anyone; only my husband knows the number. People leave messages for me on my office voicemail box, and I'll retrieve the messages in good time. I don't want to check multiple mailboxes to get all my messages.

GET HELP FOR A WEB ADDICTION. Do you become restless or irritable when you don't have access to the Internet? You could be addicted to the Web. In a recent survey of seventeen thousand Internet users, ABCNews.com and psychologist David Greenfield found that 6 percent of Web users—11 million people—are in some way addicted to the Internet. Greenfield found that people who access the Internet excessively (often up to forty hours a week) spend a third or more of the workday surfing or chatting, which could be a huge productivity problem for employers.

USE THE AUTO RESPONDER WHEN YOU'RE UNABLE TO RESPOND WITHIN TWENTY-FOUR HOURS. It is customary to expect people to check their email at least once a day and respond to messages. If you think the importance of a message justifies it, immediately reply briefly to an email message to let the sender know you got it, even if you will send a longer reply later. If you will be gone, set your out-of-office message to specify when you'll return and who is covering for you in your absence.

BATCH YOUR TASKS. Block out certain times of the day for writing, administrative work, and researching. Enter all your business cards into the computer once a day. Make all your copies at one time. Save receipts and log them into your accounting software weekly. By batching, you eliminate interruption time between activities. Stay focused; don't dart around from task to task.

UPGRADE YOUR TELEPHONE MODEM TO DSL OR CABLE. When you have a slow Internet connection, too much time is required to upload/download files and load Web pages. By installing cable and paying an extra $50 or so each month, you will eliminate your frustration and increase your efficiency. Call your local cable company to find out about options in your area.

These tips will help you be in control of technology, instead of being controlled by it.

CHAPTER NINE

Mastering the "V" in Productive

VITALITY

HOW HEALTHY ARE YOU? How good do you feel? How much energy do you have throughout the day to accomplish the things you want to?

Social and behavioral research scientists today have more information than ever on the factors associated with productivity. Recent studies have revealed that we have the potential to dramatically affect our productivity by paying closer attention to our health. We eat too much, drink too much, don't exercise enough, work too much, and don't sleep enough. So it's not surprising you're less than fully productive when tired or ill.

The choices you make today will affect how you feel tomorrow. When you feel good, you can accomplish more. This chapter will guide you in making the choices that give you vitality and productivity every day.

> 81. I get adequate sleep each night; I'm not sleepy during
> the day.

Zzzzz-zzzz, hmmmm?

Sometimes I wish I were a bear, so I could hibernate for six months. Alas, I'm only human. How much sleep do you think the average adult gets per night? A March 2001 National Sleep Foundation (NSF) poll of one thousand adults found that a third of Americans get less than seven hours per night and only a third are getting the recommended eight hours per night. John Shepard, medical director of the Mayo Clinic Sleep Disorders Center, says that most adults need between 7½ and 8½ hours of sleep per night, teens need 9¼ hours, and small children need even more than that.

In 1910 the average adult got nine hours of sleep per night, because without electricity, people generally went to sleep when darkness fell. Now we just flip on the lights and keep working. Americans tend to undersleep by choice, burning the candle at both ends due to hectic work and family schedules. The average workweek in 2003 was forty-six hours, and 40 percent of adults are working fifty hours or more a week. We believe we can have more time for work and family by allowing ourselves less time for sleep. However, many of us do snooze—at work, driving to and from work—in a state of stupefied sleepiness.

The NSF poll actually showed that 85 percent of people would sleep more if they were convinced it would contribute to a healthier life. The bottom line is this: sleeping well is not a luxury—it's a necessity. Sacrificing sleep is actually counterproductive. How do you know if you're getting enough sleep? Answer the following questions "yes" or "no":

1. Do you get sleepy while at your desk during the day?
2. Do you consistently get grumpy or "low"?
3. Do you need an alarm clock to wake you up in the morning?
4. Do you hit an afternoon "slump" after you eat?
5. If you were a passenger in a car for an hour during the day without a break, would you nod off?
6. Would you fall asleep if you sat and read during the day?
7. Are you likely to doze off while watching TV during the day?
8. Do you get less than six hours of sleep per night?

If you responded "yes" to four or more of these questions, it is likely that you're sleep deprived. With very high numbers (six or more), it's important to see a doctor to rule out possible medical or emotional causes for your sleeping problems. Get a complete checkup, and tell the doctor you're having trouble sleeping; explain your exact patterns. Many things, from sleep apnea to depression to anxiety, can cause insomnia or non-restorative sleep. You may need to deal with your sleep problems through medication or other means.

When I take an informal poll during a seminar and ask participants if they think daytime sleepiness is normal, about 75 percent say yes. Most people also believe that feeling very sleepy in the afternoon is normal. However, sleep experts tell us that daytime sleepiness is *not* normal *if* you are getting the correct amount of sleep for your needs. When people start nodding off, they blame the heavy meal they just ate, the stuffy air in the room, or the boring movie they were just watching. These things don't cause sleepiness; they unmask it. Many people don't make the connection between the amount of sleep they get at night and how drowsy they feel during the day.

The One-Week Sleep Challenge

If you find no medical cause, your sleep deprivation may be self-induced. Perhaps you don't know how to get adequate sleep. Try this program for one week for restful, predictable sleep:

1. Awaken at the same time every day, including weekends. If you sleep late on Saturday and Sunday morning, you'll get Sunday night insomnia and you'll be a wreck on Monday. Instead, go to bed and get up at the same time every day.

2. Get as much bright light as possible (preferably out of doors) during your desired wake time to reset your body's clock. If you're getting sleepy too early, force yourself to go out in bright light.

3. Take a twenty- to thirty-minute walk *every day* out of doors, even if it's cold. Try to walk in the morning before work to get a jump-start on your day. Physical activity enhances the deep, refreshing stage of sleep.

4. Avoid or limit caffeine (coffee, tea, soft drinks), nicotine, and alcohol. Herbal tea in the afternoon is okay. Caffeine and nicotine can keep you from falling asleep. Alcohol causes fitful sleep and frequent awakenings.

5. Don't nap in the daytime, which steals from nighttime slumber. If you *have* to nap, limit your sleep to twenty minutes.

6. Use your bedroom only for sleeping and intimate relationships. Do not use your bedroom as an office, a place to read, to eat, or to watch TV.

7. Start bedtime preparation *nine* hours before your desired wake time. You are going to sleep for a total of *eight* hours each night this week.

- One hour before bedtime, end your day (nine hours prior to your waking time). Spend the time before bed in relaxing, non-alerting activities such as light reading, listening to classical music, taking a warm bubble bath, meditating, writing in a journal, and drinking a small glass of warm milk and honey.
- Don't eat or drink a lot before bedtime. Make sure you finish your dinner at least two hours before sleeping.
- Keep your room slightly cool and quiet.
- Complete your bedtime rituals, then lie down, close your eyes and enjoy sleep onset.
- If you find you have trouble sleeping, get up and go to a different room and relax until you are sleepy. Don't engage in any work or stimulating activity. Then go back to bed. Repeat this procedure until you fall asleep.
- Do not agonize about not falling asleep; the stress only makes it worse and prevents sleep. No matter how little you slept, make sure you wake up at the same time every day.

Hang in there! By the third day, you'll be on your way to a new level of energy during the day, and you'll see what a proper amount of sleep will do for your productivity.

> 82. I get sufficient exercise.

Does a Trip to the Bathroom Count?

If your doctor told you she had a new drug that would prolong your life, reduce your chance of death from all causes by 50 to 70 percent, enhance your quality of sleep, and improve your ability to manage stress, would you take it? The only catch is it takes fifteen to thirty minutes a day to "swallow."

You may be tired of hearing how important exercise is for your energy level, but most people need to hear it again, because over 60 percent of the population doesn't exercise regularly. No other factors influence your productivity at work and the quality of your life at home more than your mental and physical health.

If you're consistently low on energy, an ironic paradox is the *less* active you are, the *less* energy you will have. We all know this, yet we still don't exercise. It's no wonder. Americans watch an equivalent of fifty-seven days of television a year, in addition to passive activities like surfing the Internet and playing video games. The labor-saving devices in our homes have also eliminated much of the work involved in doing household chores. Today's knowledge workers invest countless hours in front of a computer with no physical activity during the day.

Indeed, many people work so hard, they feel "too tired" to exercise. However, if you are facing an evening of paperwork and feeling exhausted, getting some exercise before going home will give you the energy you need. Running, walking, biking, lifting weights, sports, or any kind of aerobic activity are good for getting rid of stress and frustration. (No, kicking the dog and punching the wall do not count.) The benefits of exercise are tremendous: a healthier heart, more energy, weight loss, etc. The real boost I get from exercise is a sense of well-being. I see it more as a mental health exercise. I'm much more happy and alert and apt to be productive.

Being healthy is a win for employer and employee alike. Many organizations offer health incentives, such as gym membership reimbursement, aerobics and yoga classes offered at lunchtime, an on-site gym, a walking program, or free cholesterol screenings. If these programs aren't available, you can lobby your company to provide them by showing their benefits.

How to increase your activity

Even if your organization doesn't offer a formal program, you can create one on your own. A 2001 study from the University of Minnesota shows that once women have kids (we don't know about the guys), they cut back on exercise by an average of 20 percent. Add on a full-time career and it's easy to see why you use your stepping machine as a clothes rack. So step one: stop feeling guilty about not working out. Step two: stop feeling guilty when you do.

If you have to make an appointment with yourself three days a week and write on your calendar to go to the gym, so be it. It's easy to cross "Work out" off an already packed to-do list. Resist that temptation. That appointment is as important as any other. Don't cancel it; simply work other appointments around it.

What's the key to sticking with exercise? Find something that you enjoy doing and you will readily adjust your workweek schedule. Do you like water activity? Walking (my activity of choice)? Yoga? Shooting hoops? Toning? As few as fifteen minutes of exercise a day can greatly improve your health and quality of life, according to the Harvard School of Public Health. I believe you can find fifteen minutes a day.

You can even exercise at your desk. I have two eight-pound dumbbells on the floor of my office. Whenever I feel my shoulders getting fatigued or my back needs a good stretch, I'll do a quick set of fifteen overhead presses for instant relief.

Desk stretches are also great for releasing tension. Sit up straight, grasp the side of your chair with one hand, lean away while keeping your elbow straight, and tilt your head slowly until you feel a nice pull in your neck muscles. Hold for ten seconds and stretch the other side. Do three sets per side for a quick pick-me-up.

Please realize that you don't have to run a marathon to get into better physical condition. Moderate exertion will almost certainly be enough to keep you from joining the two-thirds of the American population who are either overweight or obese. It's fairly easy to increase your activity, once you make a conscious effort to get moving.

VITALITY quiz item #83:

> 83. I use all my allotted vacation time each year.

Recreation Means to Re-Create

If you feel like you're stuck behind your desk on a beautiful day while the rest of the world is on vacation, it's because you *are* and it *is.* The World Tourism Organization lists Americans as having the least vacation time in the industrialized world. Workers in the United Kingdom are guaranteed twenty days by law (and average twenty-five); Japan grants ten days per year and averages eighteen days per year. U.S. workers aren't guaranteed any vacation time by law. According to the Bureau of Labor Statistics, U.S. workers average 10.2 days of vacation per year *after* three years on the job.

Yet, despite the small number of vacation days a year, one in six employees (roughly 18 percent) is so overworked that she or he is unable to use up annual vacation time, according to a 2001 Oxford Health Plans survey. The Europeans and South Americans make fun of Americans about this, you know. Not taking vacation time does *not* make the United States more productive. For example, countries like Italy, France, and the United Kingdom, whose workers routinely take four to five weeks off a year, saw increases in productivity in 2001. According to the latest figures from the Labor Department, the United States experienced a slight decline in manufacturing output per hour in 2001.

The curse of the overworked American

Gen-Xers really need a vacation, according to the 2001 Hilton Hotels Corporation's Generational Time Survey, a random telephone study of 1,220 Americans by Yankelovich Partners research firm. The survey found that 77 percent of Generation Xers (born 1965–1975), more than any other generation, say they need a long vacation because of the pressure and stress of their daily lives. Overall, two-thirds of Americans say they could use a long break. Why don't we take it?

With many companies possibly looking to further cut head count, many workers are hesitant to leave the office for vacation, lest they be perceived as expendable. Feeling pressured and pushed, not respected, tension at work, or that your work isn't of real value also lead to overwork. People who feel these things are more likely to neglect themselves and less likely to feel successful in their personal and family relationships. I know people who lost their families because of overwork, only later to have their jobs eliminated. One of my colleagues sent her family ahead of her to the beach while she stayed behind to work. Yes, she genuinely loves her work, and she gets recognition for it. But when a sudden change in leadership throws her for a loop, will she find her neglected family life and friendships in tatters? It's just not worth it.

Overworked employees can lead to drastic on-the-job consequences. They are more likely to look for a new job, feel angry with their employers, and make mistakes. In the Oxford study, 17 percent of respondents who said they felt overworked said they often made mistakes at work, compared with only 1 percent of those who said they did not feel overworked. So when I hear people brag that they haven't had a vacation in five years, I'm seriously unimpressed.

How to go on vacation

Once you're convinced that you'd better do yourself, your coworkers, and your family a favor by going on vacation, the next question is how to do it. That might seem like a silly question, but seriously, some people tell me they take a vacation just to accomplish all the things they can't do while they're at work. That's not a vacation! You don't get recharged, refreshed, and rebooted unless you actually get away from the office and into an environment that's conducive to relaxation. Here are some tips:

LEAVE FOR TWO WEEKS. If you are only off for one week, your coworkers and staff will hold things for you "until you get back." If you're off for two weeks, it's more likely others will do it themselves since it can't wait that long. It takes three days just to unwind and another three days just to ramp back up before returning. So challenge yourself to get bored on your vacation. Be off long enough to ask, "What is today, anyway, Monday or Tuesday?"

LIMIT OR ELIMINATE YOUR CONTACT. The objective of a vacation is to get a psychological break from work to recharge your batteries. Don't think you are oh-so-important that you have to contact the office every day when you're gone. You're not really as indispensable as you think you are. If a bus hit you tomorrow, the work would still get done. If you are that irreplaceable, I would point out you're not developing your replacement properly, so you can be promoted. Get the right people to cover for you and forward your calls. Put an auto responder on your email saying you'll be gone until (x) time and so-and-so is available to respond to immediate needs. If you *must* be in touch, limit your time to set hours such as 8 to 10 a.m., and then enjoy the rest of the day. If you spend your vacation worrying about clients, prospects, and computers, you aren't really taking a vacation.

PRETEND YOU'RE A TOURIST. Leisure time doesn't have to be fancy, just away from the office. Even if you don't have the funds to take an expensive vacation, you can relax in your own backyard. Go to museums, local attractions, and historical sites in your state. Make plans with friends or plan a camping trip. Take the time to remodel your bathroom, organize your photo albums, or complete your child's baby book.

ENJOY YOURSELF. Go ahead and eat those desserts you would typically avoid. Spend money on things you wouldn't normally buy. Stay out and sleep in later than you normally would. Take the dinner boat cruise and the water-skiing lessons. Buy souvenirs and clothing and treasures of the area. Consider expenditures as investments in your emotional health.

ALWAYS HAVE THE NEXT TRIP PLANNED. Coming back from vacation is depressing. Allow for it with an extra day before you go back to work, because you might have the blues. When John and I return from our annual Hawaiian excursions, I'm always commenting, "This time last week I was on the beach." To combat this, plan another trip. Put a date on the calendar, because if you don't, it won't happen. Buy plane tickets and schedule around it. Start planning and getting excited.

When my four-year-old Johnny is fussy, I tell him, "You're grouchy. It's time for you to take a nap!" Similarly, you might need to lovingly tell a colleague or a friend it's time to take a break. If your significant other tells you to take a vacation, take it seriously and don't shoot the messenger. Your friends and family may have a point, and your productivity and happiness depend on your listening to that advice.

VITALITY quiz item #84:

> 84. I pamper myself on a regular basis.

Just Give Me One Minute!

When our family only consisted of three people, John, myself, and my then-four-year-old daughter, Meagan, we took a trip to visit my brother Paul and his wife, Susan, in Boulder, Colorado (okay, I was really going to see my niece Sophie and nephew Simon). We all have different tastes in music, so we figured with three people during an hour car ride, we would each get twenty minutes to listen to our personal music selection. We grabbed our tapes and headed out. Meagan went first, and she chose kids songs from the Disney movie collection. John was next with his favorite Christian album. When my turn came, I handed John my tape: a twenty-minute blank tape. Ahhhhhhh! The silence and peace of doing and hearing nothing was glorious. There is something about our condition that no longer allows us to just sit still, to relax, and to do nothing—to just BE. When I hear myself say, *"I just need you people to give me five minutes to myself!"* then I know I'm not tak-ing good care of myself. Being a wife, mother, daughter, volun-teer, business owner, friend, etc., I've been conditioned to take care of everyone else before I take care of myself. The irony is when I don't take some time and space for myself, my ability to take care of others diminishes. When I do things for myself, my mood, energy, and productivity instantly increase.

If you're like me, it's difficult to break out of the mindset that taking care of yourself is selfish. I used to get the garbage emotion of guilt if I took a five-minute bath! After paying with headaches, back trouble, and burnout, I now know better. The secret, I've discovered, is to find little ways to cherish myself every day. Tak-ing time out for myself in some way on a regular basis gives me a chance to unwind and get ready for life's next challenge. I take a half-hour bath every night, with candles, bubbles, and soft music.

What do you like to do? How do you affirm yourself and show that you hold yourself in high regard? The key is to learn to pamper yourself. Learn what relaxes you—whether it's dancing, movies, deep breathing, or reading trashy novels—and make time for it when you're feeling particularly stressed. Make an ap-pointment with yourself on your calendar if you have to. You make time for everyone else in your life—aren't you just as, if not more, important?

Don't know what you would do even if you did have some free time? Here are some suggestions:

WHAT THINGS HAVE YOU GIVEN UP SINCE YOU BECAME AN ADULT? You started a career, maybe got married and had kids; you just got busy. What did you like doing when you were younger that you don't do anymore? Did you enjoy playing the piano, working with clay, doing puzzles? Commit to doing one thing every day that makes you happy. It will be easier to take life more lightly. If you're too busy to play, you're just too busy.

OBSERVE WHAT YOU DO WHEN YOU ARE HAPPY. How are you playful? Do you whistle? Hum? Work out? Sing? Dance? Listen to music? Help your brain make the transition from being stressed to being happy. If you fool it into thinking you are happy, you will become more so.

TRY SOMETHING NEW.
- Give yourself mini-breaks every hour to relieve stress.
- Stretch or take yoga.
- Enjoy a gourmet cup of coffee.
- Listen to your favorite music with your eyes closed.
- Write a positive affirmation to yourself at the end of the day and put it on the mirror to see in the morning.
- Walk around the neighborhood.
- Read a novel.

SEEK QUIET. You deserve quality alone time. You need to nourish, to replenish, and to renew. Take care of the most important relationship in your life—the one you have with yourself. Nothing will help you have greater daily composure as much as protecting at least ten minutes of quiet time each and every day. Turn off all the noise in your life—the TV, the VCR, the radio, the computer, the telephone, the CD player, the kids, and your mind. You may never be able to get quiet time at home. Go to your church, find a quiet place at lunch hour, go to the park; don't answer the phone at dinner; drive to work without the radio on.

"DO NOTHING." The art of "doing nothing" is a strange concept for some people. It doesn't mean you have to literally do nothing, however. John knows I'm happy when I'm humming a little tune and wandering around the house. When he asks, "What are you doing?" I reply, "Nothing." Then John will smile and wink, because he knows I'm in a happy little state I call "puttering." Not feeling driven to do anything important, I amuse myself for an hour by wandering from room to room and doing whatever I notice needs to be done there: put a stray glass in the sink, water the plant, clean out the coffee pot, etc. This mindless activity is near Nirvana for me.

Determine what "doing nothing" looks like for you. Watching airplanes go by might be your idea of Nirvana. Whatever your "do nothing" activity is, do it. Done on purpose, "doing nothing" makes perfect sense.

VITALITY quiz item #85:

> 85. I maintain a noise level in my office that is conducive to productivity.

I Can't Hear Myself Think!

Here's one more reason to be jealous of coworkers who have their own offices. According to a 2001 study by Cornell University, an open environment with low-level noise—like keyboards, chatter, and the hum of a photocopier—leads to increased levels of the stress hormone cortisol. What's worse, participants in the study didn't think they were as stressed as medical testing showed them to be.

Gary Evans, the study's lead researcher, said that while the open office has become a way to increase community and facilitate teamwork, it causes other problems. The study found that workers in noisier settings run out of steam more quickly. Also, they're less likely to adjust their desks, keyboards, and chairs for better fit because they're so busy trying to concentrate. Their bodies hurt and their productivity declines even further.

One newsletter subscriber said, "My physical work location comes with a great deal of noise and activity. I find it difficult to concentrate and can't get deep into a project when there's a lot of residual noise. I'm not one who visits others, so I don't waste time with 'water cooler' chatter, but if I had a quieter work location, I could reduce the time I spend at the office." How true!

A recent survey of office workers, cosponsored by the American Society of Interior Designers, Steelcase, and other workplace industry manufacturers, found that:

- 71 percent of respondents found noise the most significant workplace distraction
- 81 percent believe a quieter work environment would help them be more productive

Try some of these noise busters for increased productivity:

RELOCATE YOUR OFFICE. One seminar participant told me she worked in the cubicle right next to both the coffee machine and the copy machine. She was constantly distracted by conversations, loud laughter, and the hum of the machines. In addition, she was next to the entranceway when guests got off the elevator. Since the company didn't have an official "receptionist," she ended up getting the lion's share of the requests for direction. Not wanting to be rude to customers, she tried to perform that role as well. She felt so frustrated and burned out by her inability to get work done that she called a meeting with her boss and HR, presented her evidence, and requested that she be allowed to relocate. To her delight, they complied. Her new office was out of the way, in a back corner, free from loud noise and traffic. To walk by her office, people actually had to be coming to see her. Delighted by her new digs, she was finally able to concentrate and gained greater productivity.

COMBAT NOISE WITH NOISE. Some people swear by white noise or nature noise machines to help them create their own background noise. When my son James was an infant, he wouldn't sleep at daycare unless he had the "Birds of Paradise" playing in his ear. His caretakers soon learned to place the little machine right in the crib with him, and he slept like they wanted him to: like a baby. (Personally I'm driven to distraction by these types of machines, but I do well with a soft country music radio station in the background. I've also heard from seminar participants that their organization bought a Sonet Acoustic Privacy System for each of them. It's a little desk speaker that sends out low, natural sounds to muffle noises [617-499-8077]).

USE NOISE-ELIMINATING EQUIPMENT. Noise-canceling headsets are wonderful for flying. They effectively cut out the drone of the engines, while still allowing you to hear the flight attendant. Similarly, worn at work, they reduce the background noise, while allowing you to hear a colleague who drops by. If your workplace is particularly noisy, more drastic measures may be needed: some organizations pipe white or "pink" noise (which our ears interpret as natural, even noise) into every office.

SEEK OUT QUIET. A few times a day, find a retreat to work and give your ears a rest. Do you have an empty conference room? When people go out of town on travel, ask them if you can borrow their offices occasionally. Coworkers can't find you as easily, and you might actually find some valuable time to get some focused work accomplished.

BUCK THE TREND. If you're a morning person, come in early and take advantage of the "quiet time" to tap into your energy level when it's at its peak. This also allows you to get a jump on the day if you need to leave early, so you don't feel like you've neglected your responsibilities.

> 86. I ensure my workspace is comfortable and ergonomically correct.

Oh, My Aching Back!

Workers moved from the farm to the manufacturing plant to the computer cubicle. We've gone from moving our bodies in large, gross movements to holding our bodies in static, prolonged postures. Employee sick leave, medical claims, and litigation have all increased as the office environment affects today's worker. In addition, static posture and high repetition in typing can lead to one of the most prevalent problems in working America today: cumulative trauma disorder (CTD), an injury to the soft tissues of the body, including tendons, joints, blood vessels, and nerves.

If you don't want your job to add to your emotional stress and decrease your productivity, make sure your workspace is ergonomically correct. Spending hours in front of a computer can literally be a real pain and workplace injuries can be severe. OSHA and the National Academy of Sciences estimate that every year, nearly a million Americans are injured by common workplace activities like typing, surfing the Net, or sitting at their desks.

Here are some things to do to ensure that your workspace isn't physically hurting you

PREVENT BLURRY VISION. The computer monitor has become a real sight for sore eyes for millions of American workers. Long hours at the screen can spell aching eyes, blurred vision, and headaches. In fact, eyestrain surpasses even wrist pain as the top physical complaint among heavy computer users. The American Optometric Association (AOA) says that more than 70 percent of computer workers suffer from a vision condition dubbed "computer vision syndrome" (CVS). Burning eyes, blurred vision, and headaches are among the most common symptoms of CVS, which is also characterized by eyestrain, dry eyes, slowness in changing focus, contact-lens discomfort, neck aches, and back pain. What can you do to alleviate or avoid CVS?

- Keep your eyes aligned with the *top* of your screen. It's much better on your neck to look slightly down, rather than slightly up.
- Refocus occasionally by staring at a spot at least twenty feet away. It's unnatural to stare at a box for hours at close distance.
- Get special "computer glasses" from your optometrist. Single-prescription bifocals, trifocals, and progressive lenses (which incorporate bifocals or trifocals but without the visible lines) can be designed for focusing on the specific distance and height between the eye and the computer monitor. Patients should provide an eye doctor with workstation measurements, including the height, angle, and distance of the computer monitor, relative to their eyes.
- Blink! Make a conscious effort to blink more often to prevent eyes from drying out.
- If possible, use a large monitor.
- Make the display sharp and clear, with a light background and dark letters.
- Locate your document holder as close to the screen as possible.
- Position your screen at arm's length from your body.
- Most important, experts recommend having regular eye examinations. If you experience eyestrain, dryness, blurriness, or frequent headaches, consult an eye doctor to rule out eye disease as a cause of your symptoms.

COMBAT CARPAL TUNNEL SYNDROME. Use a wrist guard or a desk with an adjustable keyboard tray. When typing, keep your wrists and hands straight, and your fingers loose and relaxed. When using your mouse, keep your forearms close to your side and face straight ahead. Don't twist your body. Limit extended periods of typing and take breaks.

WIPE OUT LOWER BACK PAIN. Choose a correct chair that allows you good back support and lets your legs relax at a 90-degree angle with your feet flat on the floor. Don't cross your legs at the knees, which leads to varicose veins. Get up to walk around at least every hour. The American National Standards Institute has developed standards for office chairs:

- Seat height should allow feet to be placed firmly on a surface to provide stability. Adjustment should range from 16 inches to 20 inches. A footrest should be provided if the user's feet are not placed appropriately on the floor.
- Seat depth should be a minimum of 18.2 inches.
- The seat pan angle should be adjustable between 0 and 10 degrees forward.
- Seat back angle should be adjustable between 90 and 105 degrees.
- The backrest should provide lumbar support and the width should be a minimum of 12 inches.
- Armrests should possess a minimum inside distance of 18.2 inches.

BUY PLANTS. Office air can be as polluted as the air on the highway. Plants suck toxic chemicals out of the air and have a calming effect on the eyes.

GET GOOD LIGHT. Office fluorescent lights that constantly flicker can act as a stimulant that saps energy. Switch to full-spectrum lighting or sit by a window. One worker told me she disconnected one of the two fluorescent tubes above her workstation, which made it easier to see the computer monitor.

Ask for what you need, and keep asking when you're turned down!

VITALITY quiz item #87:

> 87. I practice healthy eating habits.

Work-Related Food Stressors

Poor eating habits can make you fuzzy-headed and less productive. The American Dietetic Association in Chicago says that people perform less efficiently on an empty stomach. Fatigue from low blood sugar levels leads to poor concentration. So your brain needs to get away from work to function optimally. You can't expect your car to start if you don't put gasoline in it, and your body is the same way. It's also easier to catch colds and other viruses when your body is weak from a lack of nutrients.

If I'm the morning speaker at a conference, I always ask my client if breakfast will be served prior to my presentation. If the reply is, "Yes, we'll have a continental breakfast," it means sugary pastries and muffins: no eggs, fruit, yogurt, or granola. So I make my own breakfast arrangements before arriving because the last thing the client wants is a sleepy speaker.

Similarly, when I conduct on-site training in a large organization, I'm always *amazed* at the array of available food. Someone made cookies and someone is having a birthday. There are left-over doughnuts from the board meeting, vending machines full of fat and sugar products, and the bottomless pot of coffee....

No wonder it's so hard to eat right with all these food temptations and few healthy alternatives in your workplace. It all begins with *you* making changes to your eating habits. Here are some tips to get started:

HAVE HEALTHY ALTERNATIVES ON HAND. One of my clients in Denver, VISA DPS, offers one of the best little employee perks I've seen: fresh fruit in every break room. Oranges, apples, and bananas are available for the taking. Steer clear of "sleepy foods" that have refined flour and sugar like bagels, muffins, cookies, pasta, doughnuts, and bread items, which are common items on the catered breakfast meeting menu. Sleepy foods will "drop" you an hour later. Keep food on hand that contains healthy ingredients. Purchase the following items to keep in your desk drawer: snack boxes of raisins, dried fruit, low-fat granola bars, power bars, cans of juice, snack cans of fruit, nuts, and bite-sized whole wheat cereal.

DON'T GO MORE THAN SIX HOURS WITHOUT EATING. Personally, I never have to worry about this one. How can you forget to eat? Go longer than six hours and your blood sugar level will drop, leading to headache and fatigue.

BE CONSISTENT. When I'm traveling out of state for a speaking engagement, it's tempting to order a big, fattening dessert from room service. "After all, I am working hard, I deserve it," I might justify to myself. But when I feel sluggish and bloated the next day, it's never worth it. Paying attention to the foods you eat will help you today—and tomorrow.

> 88. I take a lunch break every day.

I'm Working Through Lunch Today

I had a lunch date with one of my clients and you would have thought she was on vacation—it had been almost three months since she had enjoyed a leisurely lunch at a restaurant. A 1999 National Restaurant Association survey concluded that a third of Americans forgo lunch at least once a week. A 2001 study by Oxford Health Plans showed that a typical lunch for 32 percent of American workers consists of microwaved food at their desks.

Things to remember:

DROP THE GUILT. Many people say, "I never have time to take lunch," and wear it like a badge of honor. If you're so pressured that you can't break for lunch, get some perspective. Are those deadlines really life-or-death issues? If they are, so be it. Most aren't, and if you're panicking about some future event, ask yourself if you can't focus on one half-hour at a time. Taking time out to feed your body is not an indulgence you can't afford—it's a necessity you can't afford *not* to take.

BE REALISTIC. The traditional "sit down and relax with your coworkers for an hour" lunch may indeed be the exception, but an hour for lunch may actually be more time than necessary. The lunch "hour" was started in the 1960s when workers drove home for noon meals. Try starting with thirty minutes. Go to a break room, sit down, turn off your cell phone, eat, and read a nonwork-related magazine.

GET SOME EXERCISE. A brisk walk around the building may be just what you need.

TRY TO EAT *SOMETHING*. Experts agree on the need for food at midday. According to the American Dietetic Association, missing meals affects productivity by decreasing problem-solving abilities and increasing fatigue, making concentration in the afternoon a struggle.

EAT AND RUN. Some people skip lunch completely in favor of running errands. That's okay, as long as you get away from your work environment for a while. You really need a psychological break and a change of scenery to get a second wind. Try to eat at least a power bar and some fruit.

Consistently working through your lunch hour is not only bad for the employee, it's bad for the employer. The employee has low energy levels and doesn't give the highest return on investment.

VITALITY quiz item #89:

89. I drink the proper amount of water each day.

I Feel Like a Fish Out of Water

I went into my doctor about a year ago with a fairly consistent "caffeine" headache during the day. After asking some questions, he concluded that I was just slightly dehydrated . . . all the time. I'm not alone. According to some experts, nearly half of all Americans are mildly dehydrated, and 10 percent don't drink *any* water.

If you were like me, you thought drinking water would make you gain weight and feel bloated. Not so! Now that I'm more educated about it, I know that excess salt actually causes bloating, and water helps the body maintain correct fluid balance, "flush out" toxins, and aids digestion. Since I started drinking eight glasses of water a day, I've never felt better!

Here are some benefits you'll realize when you begin a committed water regimen. Water:

- Eliminates headaches, increases energy, and decreases blood pressure. A hydrated body more easily transports oxygen and nutrients to the muscles.
- Flushes toxins out of the body. Studies show that drinking water may cut your risk for colon, breast, and bladder cancer.
- Makes you feel better overall and boosts mental performance. Mild dehydration can give you a headache and impair your ability to concentrate.
- Assists in elimination and prevents urinary tract infections and kidney stones.
- Decreases the risk of strains, pulls, and muscle injuries. Water keeps muscles supple and joints lubricated.
- Aids digestion and helps the body absorb nutrients. Water causes blood to move nutrients into the kidneys rapidly.
- Helps with weight loss. Need I say more?

Convinced? The challenge for me was making water a regular part of my daily routine. Here are some ideas:

BUILD SLOWLY. I remember thinking, "Yeah, right," when my doctor handed me my prescription of eight 8-ounce glasses of water a day. Great, now I'll waste tons of time in the restroom. So the trick was to add one glass at a time over a period of several weeks. By then, my body was used to the additional fluid.

BE PREPARED. Each day, I have my two liters of water sitting on my desk in a big container. I have to finish them by the end of the day. I pour water into my smaller bottle and take it with me everywhere, refilling as I go. Or bring 64 ounces in several water bottles each day and keep drinking until they're gone.

BE DONE BY DAY'S END. I finish my water by five o'clock to avoid midnight trips to the bathroom.

COFFEE DOESN'T COUNT. I love Hawaiian coffee. I love Einstein Brothers' Holiday Brew. I really love coffee, period. But caffeine and alcohol act as diuretics and increase water loss, so they don't count toward your daily total. Decaf soda, juice, and milk hydrate you, too, but water is the easiest for your body to process. Fruits and other water-rich foods are a bonus, not a subtraction.

VITALITY quiz item #90:

> 90. I control my environment and rid myself of things that bring me down.

Surround Yourself with Happiness

Does your environment affect how you feel? Absolutely! It affects your attitudes, emotions, and moods. It can drag you down, lower your productivity, and sap your energy. Why, then, would you choose to surround yourself with things that don't make you happy? Surround yourself with joy instead of misery; positive people instead of negative people; peace instead of chaos. Watch your self-esteem and energy level skyrocket!

What about your "stuff"? Do you keep things that conjure up bad memories or make you unhappy? What about the "thin" section of your closet? Why would you keep clothes that don't fit you? ("I'm going to lose the weight some day.") If you're going to lose the weight in the next three months, or you just had a baby, fine. After a point, there's no point. You are not a number on a piece of fabric.

Ask yourself some tough questions about each item in your home and office space:

- Am I using it?
- Can someone else use this more than I can?
- Does it make me happy?

A seminar participant once told me he kept a little bench in his home that was from his childhood home. The bench had little bears painted on it and was a reminder of his youth. He said every time he looked at it, he felt sad, because it had been the "time out" place he had to sit when he misbehaved. He kept it because he thought he should. He resolved to give it away to a friend who didn't have the same negative emotions tied to it. Great! One less thing to bring you down and sap your energy.

Another woman told me she had a box for all her old love letters, corsages, and keepsakes. Looking at it reminded her of past failed relationships. Memorabilia is fine to keep *if* it gives you joy. If you have your grandmother's journal and old letters from your grandfather, and you love to read them and smile, then obviously keep that sort of thing. Memorabilia that brings you down, however, ditch. Get rid of gifts you hate, items that remind you of failed relationships, or anything that makes you unhappy.

Instead, surround yourself with things that make you feel happy: cartoons that make you chuckle, screen savers that make you happy, photos of your loved ones, or fresh flowers for a bit of the outdoors.

CHAPTER TEN

Mastering the "E" in Productive

EQUILIBRIUM

WORK AND FAMILY BALANCE is a hot topic in organizations to-day. Balance is tough to achieve, because employees have a real commitment to their jobs *and* to their families. They love their work lives and their personal lives, often with equal vigor, and don't want to give up either. But many professionals find it diffi-cult to participate fully in one area without sacrificing the other.

Since I often give speeches on life balance, people expect more out of me or expect that it's easier for me than anyone else. Not so. Being a professional speaker and author places extra demands on our family, since I am out of town several times a month. It's never easy, for me, or anyone else.

One of the ways John and I balance our lives is working to-gether in our company. When we met, John was a letter carrier with the U.S. Postal Service (yes, I really *did* marry the mailman). It was a challenge just trying to get vacation days approved, and he had to work on Saturdays, which made it tough when I traveled. Basically, he found the job miserable, stressful, and physically demanding. In the summer of 2000, I was looking for a marketing director. The lightbulb went on and in a blinding flash of the obvious, I pointed at him and said, *"You!"* To my delight, John quit the Postal Service and joined my company as the chief operating officer.

One particular morning, we were in a rush (as is usually the case with three children) to get ourselves ready, get the kids up and dressed, and get them to school and daycare. John was dressed in a business suit for a meeting with a potential client and was responsible for getting our then two-year-old son, Johnny, ready for school. Johnny was hopelessly addicted to his binkie (pacifier); without a binkie at school Johnny would not take a nap. So not knowing whether there was another binkie downstairs to take to school with us, John stuck one from Johnny's crib in his pocket. We dropped the kids off and headed to our meeting.

When we arrived at the facility, we stepped out into its lobby with marble floors and mirrored walls. The receptionist apologetically told us our prospective client was caught on a call and would be a bit tardy for our meeting. She ushered us into a conference room to wait, where we sat and read and chatted a bit. John got up to take a look at the view out of the tenth-story, and strolled around a bit, hands in his pockets. Just at that moment, our client came walking into the room and loudly said, "Sorry I'm late!" Since John's back was turned to the door, the man took John by surprise. When John whirled around to greet him, he took his hand out of his pocket and out flew the binkie! Somehow, unbelievably, the binkie struck the man in the head . . . creating what amounts to the ultimate first impression.

John stared, horrified, mouth open; I started laughing loudly; the client looked stunned. We all looked at the binkie, which had safely landed on the conference table, and John said, deadpan, "I always carry mine with me." The client burst out laughing, and thus began the start of a beautiful relationship. Thankfully, he has kids too.

EQUILIBRIUM quiz item #91:

> 91. I allocate my time according to my values and the top priorities in my life.

Time Flies When You're Having Fun

Once you've created a personal mission statement, you need to assess if you're spending your time in ways consistent with what's important to you. Other people should be able to look at your life, observe what you do, and tell you what you value. If you say your health is important, one would expect to see physical activity. If you say your family is important, one would expect to see you spending quality time together. Are you spending your time in ways that reflect your priorities? The more congruent you are with what you say and what you do, the more balance you have.

A client from Time Warner Cable told me, "I am the last of the baby boomers. It gets very difficult to make time for myself because I was brought up to be, and have been, a person who works extremely hard for the 'company.' Many times, I feel guilty for leaving a large workload to spend time with the family. And I also feel guilty for not being there all the time for the family. It's a difficult balancing act. Why do I feel guilty at all?"

Perhaps you're struggling with how much time you should devote to your personal and professional lives. Psychologists use the term "cognitive dissonance" to describe this state of conflict within us. In terms of balance, dissonance means that what you believe and what you do are different. The more out of alignment you are with what you value and how you spend your time, the more stress you will have.

Let me illustrate with a personal example. When Meagan was born in 1995, I was traveling extensively with CareerTrack, a public seminar company. My speaking business was going nicely, and I was gaining recognition in the marketplace. Not wanting to slow my momentum, I started traveling again when Meagan was three months old. I arranged for one of my girlfriends, Angie, to care for Meagan during the day while I was gone.

As was my custom, I would call Angie from the hotel prior to departing to the next city (I was usually gone four days in a row). When Meagan was fourteen months old, I vividly remember calling home from a pay phone in the lobby of a Holiday Inn Motel in Mansfield, Ohio: "Angie, hi! How are you? How's Meagan?" "Oh Laura," she replied, "we had a wonderful day today. Meagan walked today!"

Thud. I felt like I had been punched in the stomach. I dropped the phone and crumpled to a heap on the floor. Tears streamed down my face as the words echoed in my ears, "Meagan walked today!" I had missed it. I could never get that experience back.

"What am I doing?" I shouted at myself. How could this be happening to me? It was my own fault. I had put my career, my fame, and my success ahead of my child. I had invested my time in things that, fundamentally, weren't even part of my value system. I wasn't following my personal mission statement, and my own choices had put me in that predicament. That's when I realized I was out of balance and needed to make some changes.

Have you ever had something bad happen to you before you realized you needed to make a change? I've heard of people having heart attacks and saying afterward, "I guess I should take care of my health." What I hope for you is that you can make needed changes now, before anything happens you'll regret later. If you continue to live your life the way you are right now, what regrets are you going to have? At the end of your life, will you say, "If I had it to do all over again, I would have done this differently," or "I wish I had . . ."? Make the commitment now to turn those into "I'm glad I did this . . ." Different choices today will produce different results tomorrow.

Identifying imbalance in your life

You may know you're out of balance, but you can't pinpoint exactly where you should make changes. Here's a good exercise:

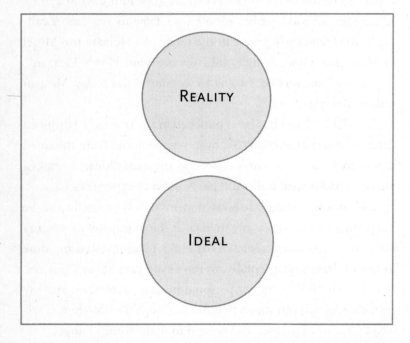

- Divide up the pie marked "Reality" into segments according to how you are *now* spending time on the categories (use the legend below).
- Divide up the pie marked "Ideal" into segments according

to how it would look if you could design the ideal life for yourself. How would you divide your time if your life was balanced and aligned with your values? (Be realistic—you're not going to win the lottery and quit working, so don't take work out if it's not a financial reality for you.)

Legend:

1. Social/Friends
2. Family/Kids
3. Household
4. Community/Volunteer
5. Health
6. Self/Leisure
7. Education
8. Career/Wealth
9. Spirituality
10. Other

Compare your two pies. Are they the same? Usually not, because that would mean you are already living your ideal balanced life. Most people have differences in their two pie charts. What are they? What changes would you need to make in order to get your "Reality" to mirror your "Ideal"? Very simply, these changes are your life balance goals.

> 92. I achieve my ideal life balance; I don't accept "close
>   enough."

Time Flies When You're Having Fun

Do you really have a lot of time to fritter away? Do this simple exercise:

0_____100

1. The line above represents your life. The "0" is when you were born, and "100" is the age you will be when you die.

2. Assuming that were true, draw a vertical line to intersect where you are on your lifeline—your current age.

3. Cross everything to the left of the vertical line out and write "History" above it.

4. Everything to the right of your current age represents the time you have to live.

5. How much of that will you sleep? Roughly one-third. So mark off one-third of the remaining line segment and write "Sleep" above it.

6. The line segment remaining represents the time you are both alive and awake.

7. How much of that will you spend working? Half? What's the phenomenon with retirement? People are still working. So mark out roughly half of what's left and write "Work" above it.

8. Circle what's left and write "Me" above it. That's all the time you have left to accomplish your goals and fulfill your dreams.

What's your reaction to the exercise? Surprise? Depression? This illustration is intended to point out how little time is truly left to accomplish the important things in life. We didn't even mark out time spent in the bathroom, waiting in line, cleaning house, shopping for groceries, etc.—not really life-changing activities, for sure. If tomorrow were D day, what would you regret not having done?

Implementation of goals

Once you know what changes you'd like to make to achieve a better balance, you have to figure out how to make it happen. This is where most people get stuck. They recognized a problem, identified specific problem areas, and made a decision to change. But, they don't take action.

Here's a good analogy. Have you ever had a Krispy Kreme doughnut? When I mention that name, doughnut devotees go "Oooohhhhh." Krispy Kreme isn't really a doughnut—it's more like a religion. People who have tried them speak of them in quasi-mystical terms, like manna from heaven. Even the name "Krispy Kreme" sounds magical, like "Abracadabra."

If you have no idea what I'm talking about, Krispy Kreme is a legendary Southern doughnut maker known for its secret, fresh, yeast-raised, cholesterol-filled, glazed doughnuts. One of my Southern buddies says it's a tradition to pick up a dozen when you head to the beach, the mountains, or just to the store. When the doughnuts are hot, right out of the oven, stores put up the unique glowing red "Hot Doughnuts Now" sign, which draws people like moths to a flame. People see that red glow and start to salivate—like a Pavlovian response.

Recently, Krispy Kreme decided to open its first Colorado store in Lone Tree, Colorado (a couple of miles away from my house). I was able to observe the ensuing cultlike frenzy. Coloradoans went nuts. People literally drove *hundreds* of miles just to get a taste. The drive-through line stretched for blocks. The lines were three hours long; it was completely insane. They hired off-duty police officers to monitor and control the traffic. We had Krispy Kreme gridlock!

I could not believe it. People who get impatient waiting on a microwave were waiting up to three hours for a doughnut! I'd like to also point out that these are the same people who say they don't have time to exercise, and believe me, after a few Krispy Kremes, you need to. Yes, they are delicious but deadly. But what a way to go. (I will point out that the company says that the *fudge* iced glazed has 8 percent of your calcium needs for the day so for you health nuts, that's a bonus! Hey, you have to have balance.) After waiting all that time, you're not going to buy just one doughnut. You're not leaving without a box . . . or two.

Until this time, I had never experienced a Krispy Kreme doughnut. I couldn't appreciate what the ruckus was about, but I was completely fascinated by this lack of logic. What could possibly motivate busy Coloradoans to sit in a three-hour line for a doughnut? I decided I'd better investigate. I had no other motivations, of course. I didn't really want to *taste* one; I just needed to do some . . . field research.

So I waited for one month until the lines died down to two hours, then drove five minutes to the Krispy Kreme store. I ordered a dozen so my family could check them out too. My family is still wondering what they taste like! Those babies never made it home!

Then it occurred to me. Through my little experiment, I discovered that people go to Krispy Kreme for health reasons. Not physical health, but emotional health reasons. A Krispy Kreme doughnut is comfort food. It reminds people of happy times; it brings back memories. People are emotionally hungry, and Krispy Kreme fills that empty place inside, causing them to loosen their belts. What motivated people was that feeling of connection, of memory, of happy times.

Here's what's important about balance: if the *why* is strong enough, the *how* becomes easy. No matter how busy people were, they found time to wait in line, just to feel those good feelings. And such it is with life. People never have enough time because they've lost the joy in doing what they're doing. It's like the carrot before the horse or the doughnut in front of your face. When something is really important to you, when it motivates you—like your values—no matter how busy you are, you will find the time to do it.

To find your *why*, listen to the yearning in your heart. What fulfills you? What is your passion? What makes you put your feet on the ground every morning and say, "Yes, it's another day. I'm excited to . . ." what? When you are deeply connected to what you're doing, time is abstract. You can't tell the difference between when you're working and playing because you enjoy the heck out of it. When you act in contradiction to what you truly believe is right, you'll be in a constant struggle with yourself. The trick is rediscovering your core values, the *why*, and focusing on *how* to make your time congruent.

> 93. I set appropriate boundaries and stick to my guns.

Don't Cross This Line

Learning to set boundaries is critical if you want to increase your personal productivity. Setting limits is a way of defining who you are and what you're all about; what you will do and what you won't; what's acceptable to you and what's not.

Creating boundaries is a crucial step in regaining control of your time. One reader said, "I will either have to stop talking to people at work or learn to draw and maintain some boundaries, so that I don't get caught up in the office moaning and groaning sessions. This is not always easy since there is really no one else to chat with at lunch or when I need to get away from my computer." The hard part of setting boundaries is telling other people what's important to you in a way that *doesn't* compromise the relationship.

First of all, schedule everything in your calendar. Crazy as it sounds, I write everything in my planner: exercising, going to church, taking the kids to the zoo, having a date with my husband, or spending time with friends. That way, when a coworker says, "Will you come help me raise money at this event?" I can open my calendar and honestly say, "Gee, I'm really sorry. I have something planned." Without having it written down, you might accidentally say, "Uh, no, I'm not doing anything on Saturday. I guess I can help you out." Then you spend two hours on Saturday with a coworker when you had planned to be connecting with your kids.

A second way to help set boundaries is to think about what's important to you, and then write "rule" statements. Here are mine:

- I question all client requests for a face-to-face visit. After defining the purpose of the meeting, I determine whether a conference call would be sufficient. If so, I explain that a personal visit isn't required.
- We do not answer the phone during dinner. Even an emergency can wait for thirty minutes while we spend undisturbed, quality time together.
- I will speak at a maximum of one National Speakers Association chapter meeting per month.
- John and I have a standing date every Saturday night. Period. Unless I'm out of town giving a speech, we assume the appointment is on our calendars.
- When people are interested in having me mentor them and "want to take me to lunch," I explain that I provide free coaching via phone but I charge for in-person appointments. Most people are content with phone calls.
- Even though I'm self-employed, I have regular office hours and treat my position as a job. I wake up at the same time, follow an established lunch hour, and leave work at the same time every day.

Once you've determined what your boundaries are, you can actually get creative in figuring out how to meet them.

> 94. I stop thinking about work at the end of the day and enjoy my personal time.

Coming Off the Work High

Have you ever left work and, all of a sudden, arrived in your garage? You were completely on autopilot and don't even remember making that turn. You're still having leftover conversations in your head from your day at the office. Many people want to know how to ease into family life after experiencing a crazy day because it's so hard to turn work off. Here are some ideas:

PLAN FOR TOMORROW BEFORE YOU LEAVE WORK. When you "download" the day's activities before you leave work, you will be fully present to your family. Planning helps you leave work *at* work. I know I haven't done a good job planning when I've been reading a book to one of my children and realize I haven't heard a word I've read. I'm only thinking about what I need to do when I'm done reading the book. That's when I confess to my family that I need ten minutes in the office to download my day, and then I'll emerge again, fully ready to be mommy and wife.

MAKE ANY LAST-MINUTE ESSENTIAL CALLS ON THE WAY HOME. Make it your goal to complete your work by the time you arrive home. I like to call John on the way home from a speaking engagement to catch up before arriving home. If we can get "business" out of the way before I return home, we can focus on more meaningful interaction in our discussions. Make sure you turn off the cell phone before you greet your family.

GET A BABYSITTER. If I need to run a few errands in the evening and don't think I can handle the chaos of dragging three kids along, I call Grandma and ask her to come over. I can enjoy the alone time, get my errands done in record time, and provide a quality experience for my children and their grandma. John and I also take one night a week to go on a "date," sans children, to spend some quality time together. Every couple of weeks, I also plan a Girls Night Out with my girlfriends.

FIND SOMETHING THAT RELAXES YOU. I like to take a bubble bath after the kids are in bed. You might like to curl up with a good book for a few moments of solitude. Do whatever nurtures your soul.

DRAW A LINE IN THE SAND. Don't apologize for making a clear distinction between work and personal time. If you work Monday through Friday, devote every minute of your weekend to your family. Try to do whatever they want to do on the weekends. Rarely does work encroach on my weekend time with my family. Yes, for people who always ask, even "The Productivity Pro" does what normal people do: sit down to dinner, go grocery shopping, take a trip to the park, watch soccer games, and go out with my spouse.

EQUILIBRIUM quiz item #95:

> 95. I ask for help when I need it.

Grounding Superperson

My father used to wistfully describe the full-service gas station days when someone would check your oil, clean your windshield, and fill your gas tank. Many people act like these full-service gas stations of days gone by. "What can I do for you? Just pull on up into my life, and I will take care of all your needs. I'm a quart low myself, but no problem, I will fill up your tank and check under your hood (but don't look under mine, because I'm in serious need of some repairs)." We are so quick to take care of others, but so slow to ask that our needs be met.

Today you maintain your own car; you fill it with gas; you put air in the tires. But if you need your sparkplugs changed, you probably don't do it yourself. You ask someone else for help. This is the power of a team. You draw upon the resources of your pit crew when you encounter trouble.

Don't "should" on yourself

It's perfectly fine to ask for other people to help you. You don't have to do everything yourself, as hard as you may try.

I once made up a little stage comedy to mock my feeble attempt to do everything myself: "I deftly juggle anything that comes my way with skill and ease and grace. I jump out of bed in the morning at 5 a.m. to exercise, I spend an hour making myself look ravishing, and then I make homemade soup for the kids' lunchboxes and get them off to school. I spend a rewarding day at work *and* stay an hour late, pick up the dry cleaning, go to the store to get fresh vegetables for dinner, and whip up a wonderful spread. I lovingly greet John as the children, clean and shiny, give him hugs. We have a stimulating conversation over dinner, the children never saying a word, and I do the dishes and a couple of loads of laundry, humming the whole time. I help Meagan with her homework, get the children to bed, and then I run off to chair the PTA meeting. After returning, I talk to my mother on the phone for twenty minutes, work on that report for tomorrow, and spend intimate time with my husband. I faithfully perform my Clinique three-step face cleaning ritual and go to bed at the early hour of 1 a.m. and wake up at 5 a.m. again, fired up and ready to do it all again."

This is the myth of the superman or superwoman: I "should"

and can handle anything that comes my way. I can have it all. I can do everything perfectly. I can be everything to all people. Women often become caught in the trap of trying to do it all—trying to be everything to everybody—working harder and longer, but enjoying it less and less. There always seems to be more to do than time to do it. You have to get some help.

Here are some of the typical excuses why people don't ask for help:

I'M AFRAID. If I give it to so-and-so, he is going to mess it up. Stop this! Resist the tendency to continue performing tasks in your department when positions and responsibilities are shuffled around. If there is another person who can handle the task, stop doing it. If someone else can do the job 80 percent as well as you can, let that person do it!

PEOPLE WILL THINK I'M WEAK. Really! Has anyone ever asked for your help? Did you think that person was a failure? We have such a hard time asking for help because we're afraid of what others will think. Do you find yourself saying things like, "I should be able to accomplish more in a day." "I should be able to do everything without feeling stressed or tired." "I have to please others by doing what they ask me to." "I can't relax until I finish what I have to do." If these are typical messages you send to yourself, listen carefully because I have great news for you—there *is* a limit to what you can do. You *cannot* do it all.

I'M NEEDED. If you started this week being honest with people by saying "no" to the things you don't really want to do, how much time would you save next week? Some people have a jam-packed calendar because they can't say "no." Your friend is not going to hate you if you can't go shopping. The world will not stop revolving if you don't chair the PR committee.

Don't exaggerate your responsibilities and make unrealistic demands on yourself by taking on more than you can comfortably do. You are not in charge of everyone's happiness or responsible for making sure everything goes well in every life yours touches. Don't do what belongs under someone else's hood.

EQUILIBRIUM quiz item #96:

> 96. I create rituals with my family to reconnect during stressful times and to create fond memories.

Do You Remember When . . .

In this rush-rush, hurry-hurry society, I think most people worry a bit that they're not spending enough time with the people they love. As a parent, I'm often anxious that my kids are going to grow up without enough contact time. But strangely enough, even the parents who devote large amounts of time to their children tell me they feel it's not enough. I wonder: No matter how much time you spend with your loved ones, family, or children, will you ever feel like it's enough?

What about from a kid's or spouse's point of view? What would the ideal balance be? Do you know? When I think about my childhood, I wonder if I'm putting too much pressure on myself. When I think back on my childhood, I don't remember the toys I had or the day-to-day, twenty-minute here-and-there routine activities with my folks. I can, though, easily recall the larger, more significant events.

Experts on child memory and child psychology agree that we tend to remember things that stir our emotions and forget about things that don't. Painful or traumatic experiences are the exception to this—they are sometimes repressed and pushed below a child's level of awareness as a defense against their frightening qualities. So the question becomes: How can you create positive experiences for your children that stir their emotions and will therefore impact them, so they will remember?

Create pictures

Can you picture a magical event or trip or feeling experienced with your family? I bet you can, because you can connect with that feeling years later. The lesson is to create experiences with your loved ones that will help them connect you to their emotions—something powerful and memorable. Perhaps it's the memory of sharing dinner with your family at night or an annual trip you took to the shore.

When I was a young girl, we once went on a family camping trip. The entire trip has pictures. I remember helping Daddykins set up the tent (okay, he pretended to let me). I can see Mom, bent over our Bunsen burner stove cooking the day's catch, no matter how small. I remember how my face burned hot in the roar of the fire when we roasted marshamallows on twigs (you have to burn them just right, you know). I vividly recall the bumpy ground and the down sleeping bags that carried the scent from previous potty accidents. I remember waking up in the morning, watching my parents move around in the bulky down coats that made them look like the Michelin people.

Do you have times like this that are so embedded in your mind you'll never forget? Events that you can relive so vividly, it's almost like yesterday? Those pictures are forever etched into your memory.

Today, as a parent myself, looking at my own three children, I'm amazed and grateful for all that my parents did to create those experiences. I know those trips took a lot of planning, energy, and preparation. But remember this: life was really busy during the week, just like it is today. We only went on a couple of trips each year, but that was all I needed to remember having a happy childhood.

The question becomes, how do we create these memories for our children? By shifting your perspective on balance with your kids, away from the number of hours and concentrating on the quality of your activities. Provide anchors, rituals, and experiences for your children.

EQUILIBRIUM quiz item #97:

97. I spend appropriate amounts of time watching television, playing video games, or surfing the Internet.

I Live for "Friends"

Today's children spend an average of fifteen hours a week watching television, playing video games, and surfing the Internet. Is there any wonder why childhood obesity has risen at alarming rates? My daughter Meagan is now eight years old and still doesn't watch TV. We allow an occasional Disney video and *Arthur* and *Clifford* on Saturday mornings. My three children spend hours playing outside, jumping on the trampoline, climbing in the playground, and digging in the sandbox. Meagan gets her homework done effortlessly and spends a lot of time reading. She enjoys playing soccer and the piano and participating in Girl Scouts. It's amazing what children and adults can accomplish without television.

LIMIT YOUR TELEVISION WATCHING. When I was a child, I was allowed to watch two hours of television each week. When the Sunday TV listings came in the newspaper, I would plan my shows for the week. My two brothers and I couldn't flip channels, because we might chance upon a "forbidden" show. So I watched *Little House on the Prairie* and *The Wonderful World of Disney*.

I didn't grow up watching television, and I don't watch it as an adult. When I married John, I thought he watched an inordinate amount of television. It soon became as issue, and I asked him to go on a "TV diet." He turned off the cable for one month. Today he will tell you it was the best thing he ever did. He broke his addiction to TV and created time to dedicate to his hobbies. Did I say addiction? How many hours would someone have to devote to gambling or drinking before you'd label it an addiction?

I'm not suggesting you rid yourself of *all* television. If you feel particularly rested, motivated, educated, or inspired after watching a particular show, fine. Otherwise, find something else to do! Think of all the times you complain about having so much to do. TV has a way of robbing you of quality time to accomplish the things that really matter to you.

LIMIT YOUR WEB SURFING. Ever sit down to look something up on the Web and later look up at the clock, only to discover that you just spent three hours surfing in cyberspace? Mindlessly surfing the Web not only wastes time, but also brings you lots of information that is of little use to you. Go to the Web with a specific purpose in mind, focus on the task, and skip the rest.

LIMIT YOUR USE OF THE COMPUTER FOR ENTERTAINMENT PURPOSES. Instead of playing a game that returns no measurable result, think of something "fun" but useful to do. I used to have a card box full of stained and mismatched recipes and magazine clippings. So I decided to type them up and save them as a "cookbook" to give to my family for the holidays. I created a numbered table of contents with different categories, just like a cookbook: appetizers, casseroles, main dishes, etc. I created a file folder named "Recipes" and created a separate document for each type of food. I put the printouts in plastic page protectors and filed them in a three-ring binder behind the appropriate tabbed section. It was a hit with my family, because I'd gathered all the old family favorites. Now any time a recipe is stained or I want to send a copy to a friend, I print it out. Or you can learn new software applications, put your budget on the computer, start a family website, or create digital photo albums.

EQUILIBRIUM quiz item #98:

> 98. I turn off the technology when I'm with my family or on personal time.

Turned "On" 24/7?

Laptops, PDAs, pagers, cell phones . . . The technological devices that were supposed to make our lives simpler are taking away our lives. We're working harder to keep up with our own inventions. The "always available" nature of technology wreaks havoc in some people's personal lives. The price of being available 24/7 is the loss of time for loved ones, reflection, relaxation, and spiritual growth. It's time we asserted control over technology and used it to enhance our lives, rather than robbing ourselves of sacred time.

Take control of your cell phone

When traveling, some people work on projects that require thought and creativity. Others like to listen to audio books or learning resources during their commute. If you carry a cell phone, you may not have any "unavailable" time. This is intrusive and leads to premature fatigue, resulting in more mistakes and re-work. Cell phones can violate your privacy. Pleasurable activities such as lunch with a friend or a brisk walk quickly lose their pleasure if you're required to be "on-call" at all times. The resulting feeling is that you have no control of your time, which increases your stress and lowers your effectiveness on and off the job.

Set limits on your cell phone usage so that it works for you. Negotiate appropriate boundaries and deadlines with others. If you find that you cannot live without your cell phone, know that you're in trouble and take steps to be less reliant on it.

Don't let the Web interfere

It's easy to spend incredible amounts of time on the Web and let it interfere with your personal relationships. Are your Internet relationships threatening your personal relationships? Ask yourself these questions:

- Do you spend more time on the computer emailing pals than you do with your significant other?
- How would you feel if your spouse could read your email? Would any of it be considered flirtatious?
- Are you visiting websites or chat rooms you wouldn't want your spouse to know about?
- Can you spend an evening with your partner without thinking about whether there's email in your in-box?
- Does your heart beat faster when you see a message waiting for you in your in-box from a certain email friend?

Set limits and stop communicating in affectionate ways with people who may interfere with your ability to remain committed to your partner. Tell your partner you're sorry you've been so unavailable, and make steps to change. Don't let the anonymity of technology let you cross boundaries you wouldn't in person. If you're single, get out and about and meet real people in real situations.

Be present

Avoid the tendency to multi-task at home. Some people don't feel productive when they're not doing four things at once (such as driving, talking on the phone, drinking coffee, and putting on makeup). If this describes you, shift your focus. You must be especially attentive to children. On weekends, turn off the technology, slow down, and reinvest in yourself. Don't go to bed physically and mentally exhausted on Sunday night and expect to be alert and efficient on Monday morning. Draw the line somewhere.

EQUILIBRIUM quiz item #99:

> 99. I take advantage of the wellness and family balance programs offered by my company to the fullest extent.

Can I Compress My Workweek and Share My Job?

In previous decades, employers maintained a hands-off approach when it came to employees' families. Today, more organizations are looking to work/life programs to help employees balance the multiple demands of their work and family lives. Each year, *Fortune* magazine publishes the "100 Best Companies to Work for in America." Many of the listed organizations cite work/life programs as one of their top tools to attract and retain the best employees.

That's not surprising. Profitability in business is inevitably dependent on the productivity of the workforce. Productive citizens are essential to a stable society, and a stable society of productive workers is essential to prosperous business. My clients cite many benefits resulting from their work/life programs:

- Decreased health care costs and stress-related illnesses
- Reduced absenteeism
- Increased output due to increased focus and motivation
- Increased employee retention
- Increased profitability
- Improved employee morale and loyalty
- Enhanced employee recruitment
- Enhanced public and community relations

If your organization doesn't offer work/life programs, make it your goal to request them and convince management of the high cost of doing business without them. Actively pursue arrangements that will help you strike a healthy balance in life, such as these:

COMPRESSED WORKWEEKS are great for parents with small children at home. Could you both work four ten-hour days? If you worked Tuesday through Friday, and your partner worked Monday through Thursday, a small child would only require daycare Tuesday through Thursday (three days versus five days).

FLEXIBLE SCHEDULING is helpful for parents with school-aged children. If you work from 9 a.m. to 6 p.m. and your partner works from 6 a.m. to 3 p.m., one of you would be available to see the kids off to the bus and the other would be home when they return.

JOB SHARING is good for people who only want to work part-time. One employee works Monday through half of Wednesday, and the other takes over Wednesday through Friday.

TELECOMMUTING is excellent for people whose jobs are largely technology based. You could work Mondays and Fridays from your home office, for example, and go to the office Tuesdays through Thursday, to attend meetings.

PATERNITY LEAVE is great for parents of newborns. Rather than both parents taking leave at the same time, one parent can take leave the first two months after baby's birth, and the second parent can take months three and four. This extends the amount of time before the baby goes to daycare.

If your company offers these benefits, you are entitled to take them! Don't feel bad about taking advantage of programs you know will be good for you.

EQUILIBRIUM quiz item #100:

> 100. I consistently leave work on time.

I'm Out of Here!

This is the perfect topic for the last section of the last chapter of this book: leaving the office earlier. Staying late started innocently enough: "If I just stay a little later today, I can 'catch up' on this work I haven't been able to get to." Eight hours went to nine. It became a habit. Then: "If I just take this reading home with me, I can 'catch up' after the kids go to bed." Nine hours went to ten. You did this on a regular basis; sixty-hour weeks became the norm. Sure, if you're starting a new business or have an important short-term project, you'll have to put in some extra hours. But if years later you're still working those hours, it's now a habit. You have forgotten what it's like to have a free weeknight or weekend.

Where do we draw the line when it comes to life balance? Is the worker the one who draws it? Does that task belong to our companies or to society? It's difficult to define where personal responsibility ends and companies' responsibility begins. I think both share it. In the final analysis, responsibility for your life is yours alone. You must draw the line and insist on leaving work on time to create the balance for yourself. If you don't, you will perpetually chase the clock.

I've studied many successful people and discovered they place a high priority on *not* working extreme hours and striking a healthy balance between work and home. Here are some strategies to help you draw the line and leave work on time:

STOP PARTICIPATING IN THE CULTURAL RULES. Commit to getting out the door on time. Who decided that you should work until 7 p.m.? Are you getting paid for forty hours or sixty hours? How much is the time "I'm devoting because I'm a salaried employee and obligated to do what it takes to get the job done" worth?

START MEETINGS BEFORE 4 P.M. If you have some say or control regarding meeting times, schedule them to end by 4:30. Preferably, start meetings right after lunch. Block out your calendar beginning at 4 p.m. every day, so people can't schedule with you. Set a good example and encourage others to do the same. If you have an assistant or a team that reports to you, don't ask people to begin projects at 4:45 p.m. Respect their right to a life, too.

BE ASSERTIVE. Don't be afraid to tell others, "I leave work at 5 p.m., on time, every day. I have a 5:30 commitment I must adhere to." It's none of their business that your commitment is with yourself or your family. People tend to support others when their goals are made public.

SCHEDULE FIXED OFFICE HOURS. If you have an assistant, block off certain hours a few days a week to accept appointments. Perhaps Monday, Wednesday, and Friday you take appointments from 9 to 10:30 and 2 to 3:30. This way, you don't have interruptions overlapping the time you're trying to leave the office.

MAKE PREPARATIONS TO LEAVE. Gather up your coat and put it in a visible spot so others can see you're closing shop. Close your door a few minutes before quitting time so people will think you're busy or already gone. Whatever they want, it can wait until tomorrow.

CHALLENGE YOUR ASSUMPTIONS. Long hours aren't "the way it is." To reduce the time pressure you feel, decide to reclaim your day . . . not by working longer, but to finish your work within the workday. Don't focus on "catching up." You will *never* catch up. There will always be more things to do than there is time to do them. People have a tendency to create work to fill up any amount of time they have. They'll accomplish the same amount of work in a forty-five-minute meeting as a ninety-minute meeting. When working late is a habit, you tend to slack off a little. By being more productive during the day, you'll get the same amount of work done . . . and leave earlier.

START SMALL. Think about how productive you are right before you go on vacation. Everything inside of you supports your desire to leave! The unimportant things magically disappear, and you focus on higher-value activities. Similarly, you can pick a single day, perhaps Thursdays, to be "the" day you leave work on time. To support this decision, you will automatically begin to be more productive on Thursdays and work your day more carefully. Even though you work a normal workday on Thursday, you don't get any less work done. After you sense what it's like to have Thursday nights to yourself, you benefit from a system of self-reinforcement, because you enjoy the rewards you created. Then add another day, like Monday, and do the same thing. Keep working on productivity skills and adding more days, until you're working your forty-hour workweek again and accomplishing even better results.

The problem is *not* a shortage of time. The problem is your *habits,* which collectively create decreased productivity. Don't unwittingly fall into the trap of throwing more time at problems.

REMEMBER THAT WORK ISN'T LIFE. You are working to live, not living to work. Yes, you want to be productive. You want to enjoy your work and get raises and promotions. But you need a worthwhile life in the process. Become a role model for others to seek equilibrium and find a life of their own—something worth leaving the office earlier for.

My hope for you is that this book will help you avoid that trap. No, actually, my hope is that this book will help you take a different path. The easiest way to not fall into the trap is to stay far away from it.

Make it a productive day!

ABOUT THE AUTHOR

Laura Stack, MBA, CSP, is "The Productivity PRO!"® She is the president of a Denver-based international consulting firm specializing in productivity improvement in high-stress industries. As a speaker, author, and consultant, Laura specializes in improving output, lowering stress, and saving time in today's workplaces.

© Gary Phillips

Since 1992, Laura has presented keynotes addresses and training seminars to associations and Fortune 500 corporations on reducing information overload, managing multiple priorities, balancing work and family, getting organized, and reducing stress. Laura is a high-energy, high-content speaker, who educates, entertains, and motivates employees to improve their productivity.

Laura received a bachelor of science degree in business administration and an MBA from the University of Colorado. She holds the Certified Speaking Professional (CSP) designation, the National Speakers Association's highest earned designation (held by less than 10 percent of professional speakers worldwide). Laura is on the board of directors for the National Speakers Association (NSA).

Her clients include IBM, Coors Brewing Company, Qwest, MCI, Lockheed Martin, Lucent Technologies, McDonald's, First Data, Xcel Energy, Coastal Companies, Coca-Cola, Wells Fargo, Time Warner, the Denver Broncos, Visa USA, Enterprise Companies, Dairy Queen, Mobil Chemical Company, plus a multitude of trade associations. Government agencies she's helped include the U.S. Department of Agriculture, U.S. Postal Service, Small Business Administration, Department of Corrections, Environmental Protection Agency, Department of Revenue, along with numerous city governments and utilities.

You can contact her at **www.TheProductivityPro.com.**